BEYOND CIVILITY

RHETORIC AND **DEMOCRATIC** DELIBERATION
VOLUME 23

EDITED BY CHERYL GLENN AND STEPHEN BROWNE
THE PENNSYLVANIA STATE UNIVERSITY

Cofounding Editor: J. Michael Hogan

Rhetoric and Democratic Deliberation focuses on the
interplay of public discourse, politics, and democratic action.
Engaging with diverse theoretical, cultural, and critical
perspectives, books published in this series offer fresh
perspectives on rhetoric as it relates to education, social
movements, and governments throughout the world.

A complete list of books in this series is located at the back
of this volume.

BEYOND CIVILITY

THE COMPETING OBLIGATIONS OF CITIZENSHIP

WILLIAM KEITH AND ROBERT DANISCH

The Pennsylvania State University Press | University Park, Pennsylvania

Library of Congress Cataloging-in-Publication Data
Names: Keith, William M., 1959– author. | Danisch,
Robert, 1976– author.
Title: Beyond civility : the competing obligations of
    citizenship / William Keith and Robert Danisch.
Other titles: Rhetoric and democratic deliberation.
Description: University Park, Pennsylvania : The
    Pennsylvania State University Press, [2020] | Series:
    Rhetoric and democratic deliberation | Includes
    bibliographical references and index.
Summary: "Examines the problem of social change
    in a modern, mediated democracy. Argues that
    civility is not simply a virtue but a functional set of
    tools that must be adapted to specific situations"—
    Provided by publisher.
Identifiers: LCCN 2020017344 | ISBN 9780271088044
    (cloth)
Subjects: LCSH: Civil society. | Courtesy—Political
    aspects. | Democracy. | Social change.
Classification: LCC JC337.K45 2020 | DDC 323.6/5—
    dc23
LC record available at https://lccn.loc.gov/2020017344

Published by The Pennsylvania State University Press,
University Park, PA 16802-1003

The Pennsylvania State University Press is a member
of the Association of University Presses.

It is the policy of The Pennsylvania State University
Press to use acid-free paper. Publications on uncoated
stock satisfy the minimum requirements of American
National Standard for Information Sciences—
Permanence of Paper for Printed Library Material,
ANSI Z39.48-1992.

For Kari, who taught me the how and the why

—William Keith

For Eliot and Julien, who inspire me every day

—Robert Danisch

Thinking about the civility in civil society, then, suggests that civility is more than simply good manners, or more than an agreement not to hurt each other's feelings. It suggests that any healthy society should set civility as a goal, even while it debates what civility means for us today. Perhaps we can survive as a society even while agreeing to shrug off a certain amount of rude language or blunt assertion of our goals.

But setting civility as a goal requires that we deliberate, that we have, at a minimum, a shared agreement that we are in this together—that we are a society. It suggests, as well, that we should not use calls for civility as a means of silencing others. Perhaps paradoxically, having a civil society may well mean that we must tolerate a certain amount of incivility, or that we not respond to incivility in a tit for tat fashion.

—ROBERT BOATRIGHT ET AL., *A CRISIS OF CIVILITY?*

"I might, perhaps, wish to be informed why, with so little endeavor at civility, I am thus rejected. But it is of small importance."

"I might as well inquire," replied she, "why with so evident a desire of offending and insulting me, you chose to tell me that you liked me against your will, against your reason, and even against your character? Was not this some excuse for incivility, if I was uncivil?"

—JANE AUSTEN, *PRIDE AND PREJUDICE*

CONTENTS

ACKNOWLEDGMENTS

William Keith: Thanks to everyone who endured my enthusiasm for this project, which was probably too long in the making. I am grateful for the sabbatical support of the University of Wisconsin–Milwaukee and the UWM Department of English. Ryan Peterson did a terrific job of shepherding us through the review and publication process; his thoughtful responses to the content have been impressive and inspiring. Thanks also to Craig Froehle for the use of one of his deservedly famous cartoons; Tara Mleynek did excellent work on the illustration in chapter 2. My gratitude goes to the University of Illinois and Cara Finnegan and to the University of Copenhagen, Lisa Storm Villadsen, and Christian Kock for inviting me to present my work there and giving me the chance to work through my ideas with smart audiences.

Andrew Cole contributed his knowledge about online communication, and Warren Scherer showed me how learning theory helps us understand social change. I tested many of these ideas in dialogue with Michael Pollak, and even though he will still find them wanting, I am grateful for what I learned in our exchanges. Scott Graham, Jansen Werner, and Geoff Gimse were invaluable sounding boards and cheerleaders, while Jim Vining helped me explain my ideas to myself. Roxanne Mountford, as always, is a model for academic integrity and the virtue of cutting to the chase; Rob Smith listened patiently, and his nudges made a bigger difference than he knew. Chris Lundberg not only gives outstanding pep talks but also knows where your argument is going before you do. A special thanks goes to the brilliant and indispensable Ersula Ore, who cared enough to tell me when I lost my way and pointed me down a better path. Brian Hyland and Janet O'Mahony helped me stay centered and healthy.

I cannot thank Rob Danisch enough. Finding a kindred intellectual spirit who is a great thinker and writer is hard enough, but finding a friend who can challenge you is a gift. He has been the ideal coauthor: smart and incisive, focused and supportive, possessing strengths that balance my weaknesses; this is a far better project for his participation.

Finally, the greatest thanks are due to my better half, Kari Whittenberger-Keith, who had the courage to write a dissertation on etiquette manuals more than thirty years ago, when virtually no one was willing to hear what she had to say. But I did, and the reading and thinking that started then led me to think I just might have something to say about civility in the twenty-first century.

Robert Danisch: Thanks to the University of Waterloo and my colleagues in the Department of Communication Arts. I am very fortunate to work with so many excellent people who embody the spirit of collaboration, democratic citizenship, and thoughtful caring necessary for making such a wonderful place to work. Thanks especially to Jennifer Simpson, from whom I continue to learn so much; Imre Szeman, whose endless intellectual curiosity has been an inspiration; and my many excellent students, whose ability and promise make me hopeful for our collective futures. The research and publication of this book were supported by a generous grant from the Social Sciences and Humanities Research Council of Canada; a special thanks to that organization for its continued support of high-quality work.

Thanks to Ryan Peterson for warmly and competently guiding this project to completion, and thanks to Penn State University Press for hosting such a thoughtful, important, and excellent book series on rhetoric and deliberation. I continue to learn so much from so many excellent colleagues in rhetorical studies. My friends at the American Society for the History of Rhetoric continue to set the bar high for the kind of scholarship that is constantly informing my views. And thanks to the many pragmatists out there working across a variety of academic fields; I am always learning from pragmatism in all its many forms.

My deepest thanks to my coauthor, Bill Keith, who has been a supportive mentor since I was a newly minted Ph.D. I have been very fortunate to enjoy his friendship, conversation, and intellectual acumen for years now. The best of this book is really his; he brought me the ideas, and I happily went along for the ride. I admire his enthusiasm, curiosity, and commitment to good-natured citizenship and productive conversation. Bill models the best of what is in here, and I have learned a great deal from that over the years.

My greatest thanks are to my two budding young citizens: Eliot and Julien. In all my work, I think about what kind of world I would want to leave them, and in their lives, they are always teaching me how to be a better father, friend, professor, teacher, and person. The intensity, wonder, and joy they bring to my world matter more than anything.

INTRODUCTION: WHY CIVILITY MATTERS

Civility isn't just being nice, it isn't just showing manners. Civility is coming together as a civil society, and making people uncomfortable, and doing the right thing, and yelling at people who are not doing the right thing when you have to.

—LARRY WILMORE, *BLACK ON THE AIR*

Civility holds a paradoxical place in our culture and, at this moment, in our public discourse. For some, civility is an unquestioned good whose lack is to be mourned; the loss of civility makes them wonder if we are politically in crisis and how we can continue without improved civility. For others, civility is the source of our problems, responsible for the failure of calcified systems of oppression to change; if only, they think, we were not constrained to be so nice, then maybe real change would be possible. Both sides can point to cases for evidence of their claims, and we would be foolish to think that a strong element of truth does not reside in both characterizations. Yet the friends of civility, we will argue, often provide weak defenses of it, just as the attacks by its opponents do not always hold up well. So what should we make of a talismanic object that all agree is important and surely holds the key to *something*, even though we cannot seem to agree what exactly that is or why we should care? Is civility good or bad? Yes. Is civility a choice with consequences? Yes. Our answers, unsurprisingly, point to a set of partly true and partly false oppositions; we need a better way of analyzing and talking about civility. The argument of this book is that civility is paradoxical in that it is a framework for social and political life and yet has limits and must be set aside in some cases. We come neither to praise nor to bury civility but to understand its place in our discourse and our lives.

Approaching Civility

Before attempting any analysis of civility, we would like to acknowledge its complexity and multidimensionality by exploring some of the places where it contains important tensions and contradictions. First, we can identify synchronic (in a particular historical moment) and diachronic (through time) versions of civility. Diachronic or genealogical accounts of civility describe how sets of norms for behavior appear, evolve, and disappear over time. Sometimes the timescale is brief; specific words about race and sexuality have disappeared from civil discourse in remarkably short order. Sometimes the timescale is much longer; we have been trying (at least in the United States) to figure out how to simultaneously enable and constrain lively political argument since the founding. We want to emphasize the evolutionary quality of civility in this context, and our explanation is unabashedly functionalist in spirit. No group of elders or authorities sit around a table and decide what is and is not civil; as much as language or other elements of culture respond to (and also create) problematics that require resolution by changing norms of behavior, civility (untheorized) arises organically out of perceptions about what works in human relations over the long haul (keeping in mind the cultural plasticity of *works*), and this functionality is historically conditioned by hierarchies and exclusions at a particular time and place. Synchronic accounts of civility focus on "what we (should) do" with one another as we see things now and where we see social arrangements going. While they can be useful, synchronic accounts often have a brittle, artificial quality, arising from the attempt to freeze a moment in a living tradition, often for the purpose of cementing a particular set of (sometimes unequal) social relations. Synchronic civility represents time- and place-bound attempts to catch lightning in a bottle, whether in a posted code of conduct, in some ground rules for discussion, or in a book. The books, often called behavior manuals (usually having some combination of the words *etiquette, manners,* or *politeness* in their titles), themselves come in a variety of genres, from Castiglione's 1588 *Book of the Courtier,* through nineteenth-century works that combined cooking, housekeeping, and etiquette (Walden 2018), and then to a profusion of twentieth-century books, from the very general to more specific registers (a whole subgenre of military etiquette books, for service people and their families, exists). The patterns of behavior recommended in these books change strikingly over time, though in the contemporary era, one element still predominates: they are highly gendered, mostly written by women and apparently for women; for example, a number of books for "Army wives and spouses" still exist, but later editions of them (Conetsco and Hart 2013) at least cover wedding situations where the service member is a woman.

Behavior manuals deserve a whole separate study, but for our purposes, their most important quality is a kind of reductionism implicit in the genre, its innate tendency to suppress the evolutionary, nonessentialist character of civility itself. Not only are they highly perspectival, but their attempts at codification reduce the subtle complexity of civility (which is vast and contains multitudes) to a set of rules, whether "ground rules" or "codes of conduct." As much as these might be a useful starting point for someone, especially in specific contexts ("Oh, that's how you address people in the military"), such rules not only underdetermine what one is supposed to do but artificially constrain behavior in ways that may not be fully functional. Many objections to civility flow from objections to a particular version of the messages in these manuals, presenting seemingly arbitrary rules imposed "from above." Sometimes these rules are quite mundane ("Forks on the left"); in other cases, the rule may try to point to a complex and thick interactional norm ("Don't insult people for no reason"). Or take the case of the rule "Try to get the person's name right." This used to seem like a harmless bit of common courtesy, often in a professional context, but the respect it implies for the other person's identity has taken on new meaning and urgency in the case of transmen and transwomen. Or take the case of "rules" about the taboo quality of the N-word in the mouths of those who are not African American. This is a rule, and yet it is not *just* a rule but a recognition of the long history of failures in civility that came before and results from the attempt to find a way to both acknowledge that history and move forward. We approach civility with the long history of commitments to these rules in mind.

Civility and Oppression

Any codification of civility/politeness also brings with it the possibility that the rules, once written, might be weaponized. Many objections to civility point to the trauma inflicted by the misuse or gaming of rules of civility/ politeness (we will call this *pseudocivility*), and rightly so. The sting of a contemptuous or condescending put-down can last for decades, curdling the very possibility of functional—let alone pleasurable—social relations between the victim and the insulter, and perhaps a whole group of people. Mustering rules of civility/politeness to put others "in their place," shutting people out or silencing them, is of course contrary to what we will call the central egalitarian and inclusive obligations of civility. But we should be clear: Other obligations (to justice, equity, etc.) exist, and situations do arise where civility must momentarily be suspended. The hard cases are ones where the injustice is systemic—must then an uncivil response be systemic? We will argue no, realizing it is a legitimate subject for disagreement. Consider, for example, not just the scholarship of Ibram X. Kendi (including *Stamped from the Beginning* [2017]) but also his rousing editorial "What to an American Is the Fourth of July?" from July 4, 2019. Kendi riffs on Frederick Douglass's famous 1852 oration "What to the Slave Is the Fourth of July?," which highlighted the gulf between America's values and its practice of slavery and made the case that abolition was the only consistent position for anyone who believes in the principles of the Declaration of Independence. Kendi, however, sees this project applicable not just to the institution of slavery but to virtually every other facet of American life, rendering civility, a dialogue between equals or near equals, moot: "Pundits talk of American disunity as if the divide is brothers and sisters fighting. This is a power divide. Let's not ask why the master and the slave are divided. Let's not ask why the tyrant and the egalitarian are divided. Let's not ask why the sexist and the feminist are divided. Let's not ask why the racist and the anti-racist are divided. The reasons should be self-evident. There's no healing these divides or bringing these powers together." Unsurprisingly, he wants to expand the practice of civil disobedience from explicitly racist laws or institutions to structural oppression generally. And that practice will be an uncivil resistance: "On this Fourth of July, the rest of us—and our wealthy white male allies—should be celebrating our ongoing struggles for freedom and not celebrating as if we are free. We should be celebrating our disobedience, turbulence, insolence, and discontent about inequities and injustices in all forms. We should be celebrating our form of patriotism that they call unpatriotic, our historic struggle to extend power and freedom to every single American. This is our American project" (Kendi 2019). For us, this is the central problem of civility in the twenty-first century: How do we account for the justice of Kendi's position while recognizing the value and force of civility in many contexts? How do we valorize incivility while realizing we have also valorized President Trump's rhetoric? Part of our answer will be the weighing of competing obligations; part of our answer will be to note the ways in which strong civil resistance is entirely possible (to an extent, this was the project, under a different vocabulary, of Martin Luther King Jr.'s Christian ethic of disobedience).

Given our acknowledgment of the perspectival character of any account of civility, we must ask, Whose civility? Whose experiences inform it? Civility has evolved, but not perfectly, and its past is sometimes very dark, though civility-as-ground-rules does not always want to acknowledge this ugliness. Keith Thomas confronts this history directly:

> In the later eighteenth-century "civility" fell back to its more restricted meaning of good manners and good citizenship, whereas "civilization" came into general English usage, both as the word for the civilizing process and also as a description of the cultural, moral and material condition of those who had been civilized. The word was widely employed with unembarrassed ethnocentricity to suggest that the "civilized" nations exemplified the most perfected state of human society, in comparison with which other modes of living were more or less inferior, the products of poverty, ignorance, misgovernment, or sheer incapacity. . . . The Eurocentric idea of a single standard of civilization reflected contempt for the norms of conduct in other cultures; and the notion of Western superiority was invoked to justify the forcible colonization or commercial exploitation of supposedly barbarous peoples, in the name of a "civilizing mission." (2018, 5–6)

John A. Hall notes, "The behavior of European states in the rest of the world was anything but civil. Remember the slave trade. Additionally, European 'liberalism' within empires overseas was characteristically dogmatic and vicious" (2013, 35). While voices still exist that speak to these assumptions, they no longer have presumption; "unembarrassed ethnocentricity" does not appear defensible. The last fifty years have seen the civil rights movement evolve into a revolutionary appreciation of the struggles for recognition, respect, and equal rights by women, LGBTQ people, Latinx people, Native Americans, those from disparate socioeconomic and educational backgrounds, immigrants, those from non-Christian or nondeistic religions, and many more. This revolution has necessarily created a tectonic shift for civility, displacing old assumptions and problems and introducing new ones.

Let us consider a trenchant current critique that identifies this problem: the phrase "walking in white" has gained currency as a way to critique the tendency for straight, white male authors to take their experience as universal, as everyone's experience (Báez and Ore 2018). It is certainly the case that with respect to both civility and pseudocivility, people have very different experiences based on their social location. Kristiana Báez and Ersula Ore take civility to task in a deep way; in their experience, civility in academic settings is primarily a tool for shaming and silencing: "Our interest in the rhetorical construction of civility is driven by our shared and individual experiences with the civilizing strategies of the academy. Civilizing discourse is understood here as a call to insulate white fragility through appeals to language and scholarship that protects whites from racial discomfort. This includes calls for more gracious and less 'angry' speech around race as well as calls for more 'civil' and 'courteous' exchanges that don't offend white sensibilities" (332). With some justification, Báez and Ore do not see this orientation as a deviation but as the dominant version of civility, entirely predictable from its history: "Civility as a democratic good and social ideal cannot be divorced from its historical usage and meaning. Its etymological and ideological ties to 'civilization' and 'civil society,' its demarcation of the white 'civil citizen' from the nonwhite 'savage' and 'slave,' and its tie to citizenship and belonging render civility and civilizing discourses racialized technologies of the flesh" (334). Has civility transcended its admittedly racist history, either practically or in principle? This is a complex question (one Kendi and many others ask as well) to which we will be returning. A related question for Báez and Ore follows from Kendi's notion of resistance: "For us, coping with the expectation to be 'civil' means flipping the script in ways that highlight the cognitive dissonance of whiteness. It means managing racial battle fatigue by shouting 'Look, A White!' in ways that redirect the burden of whiteness—i.e., the guilt, discomfort, and shame of walking-in-white—back to those who consciously and unconsciously leverage it to dehumanize us and others. Coping means declining invitations to white racial communion while simultaneously agonizing over instances of 'white-splainin' and repelling white tears" (335).

Báez and Ore also call upon the notion of "white fragility" (DiAngelo 2018), the defensiveness that marks the reaction of dominant racial groups (and by extension men, heterosexuals, and cisgender individuals) to the recognition of their privilege; without question, that defensiveness can manifest itself as some version of "Well, it's really uncivil/rude of you to critique me for something I didn't choose." If we take the next step of adopting an intersectional stance, recognizing that people have multiple intersecting identities and can be simultaneously privileged and oppressed, we see that the problem of discomfort can have layers and is not simple. We will return to the question of whether making people uncomfortable is the mark of the uncivil or impolite (spoiler alert: mostly not). Báez and Ore's incisive analysis follows a pattern that requires our engagement: identifying the (mis)uses of civility and finding their cause and then seeking the kind of agency that redresses them. We cannot find fault (nor have we been asked to) in the

"Look, a White!" strategy in the context as they describe it. We want to argue that civility can (often) be the means to inclusive and just social relations, knowing full well that our confidence in our argument rests in part on not finding ourselves endlessly the targets of injustice and exclusion.

We would like our work to be seen as the work of allies. One of the questions motivating this book is "How do we save civility from racists?" In the past few years, Americans witnessed neo-Nazis marching through the campus of the University of Virginia; saw their president mocking, defaming, and insulting a variety of public figures on Twitter; and beheld the return of raucous and violent debates over free speech across university campuses. The ability of racists and neo-Nazis to claim civility is literally amazing, and that anyone takes them seriously is mystifying. But we know—as Báez and Ore have pointed out—that it is actually not all that mysterious, since any progress we have made toward justice and inclusiveness sits alongside a history of civility used as a cover for power and, in a nineteenth-century twist, turning the tables through the conversion of power into victimhood, as some in the antebellum American South pioneered the use of a pseudocivility to refuse engagement with arguments about abolition (roughly "the mere idea of abolition offends my cultural norms and is therefore uncivil and you must stop talking about it"). As indefensible as this move is, no one can be surprised to see it resurface when racist or nationalist factions feel they can show their faces in civil society once more.

On what basis can we judge such behavior as "indefensible"? Sometimes civility is posed (especially synchronically) as a framework in which it is a set of rules that referee interactions among equals. We think this is mistaken. Instead, we will distinguish civil behavior from uncivil based on a commitment to realizing a kind of democratic equality between people. While imperfect, the framework we seek to describe has directionality (stemming from its history, as we will explain in chapter 2) toward relationships that are more equal; less conditioned by economic, political, or social power; and more respectful of mutual humanity. We want to avoid bromides and easy answers. We seek to enrich, or make more complex, our understanding of the role that civility plays in democratic societies—its uses, its limitations, and its possibilities. Such an analysis of civility also requires an analysis of incivility, since both can serve as strategies for making different kinds of connections among citizens. Furthermore, this analysis also demands that we pay attention to the context within which civil or uncivil communicative acts unfold. In other words, civility or incivility is understood and practiced within what we call (to use Charles Taylor's term) the *social imaginary*. A specific social imaginary may make agonistic techniques of mutual engagement more or less likely and more or less productive, just as it may make courteous, other-centered practices of mutual engagement more or less likely. Our aim is to show that the meaning, richness, and complexity of civility are greater and more pressing now than at perhaps any other moment. The fragility of both the systems of government to which we are bound and the social relationships that we inhabit are the impetus for this kind of analysis; the hope that democracy might be rehabilitated drives our commitment to understanding the communication practices we use to engage one another. Our social imaginary allows both forms of civility and incivility, both the use of strategy and the search for connection. Our aim is not to endorse one form of engagement universally over another form but to show when, where, and why specific kinds of communication practices may be more desirable or impactful.

Why Civility?

This book concerns how we think about how we should treat one another; how we choose to engage others with different beliefs, attitudes, or goals; and how we establish relationships with diverse citizens who hold opposing views. Therefore, it is a book about communication and how communicative practices create our shared political and social world. It is also a book about sociopolitical change and what set of communication practices are more or less likely to produce change. By communication, we do not mean the transmission of information; rather, we mean the complex and shared practices that constitute the process of making meaning. Many of these practices go unnoticed because they constitute our daily social interactions. Sometimes this process may require aggressive forms of protest, while other situations might require polite and respectful forms of engagement. Either might engender momentary and evanescent change or generate sustained or enduring change—depending on circumstance, occasion, or context. In the study and practice of communication, there are no universal rules, and this is not a handbook or how-to manual about how to preserve the fragile social stability that marks our moment. Instead, we intend to make a series of arguments about the complexity and value of civility and a descriptive account of how forms of civility or incivility are practiced in an effort to drive social or political change. Such arguments and descriptions seem especially pressing when we read the apocalyptic predictions about an impending civil war and witness the public displays of acrimony that are now so commonplace on the nightly news, but they also point to enduring and time-less questions about democracy as both a system of government and a way of life. In the *Atlantic*, Adam J. White looks at a book by Supreme Court justice Neil Gorsuch, to make an argument about why institutions by themselves cannot "keep" democracy:

> For Gorsuch, civic virtue requires civility. His book highlights the example of his own court. The justices are able to argue and disagree so vigorously in their judicial opinions only because they work so hard to foster a spirit of community with one another: "We eat lunch together regularly and share experiences and laughs along the way," he wrote, "and whenever we gather for work, no matter how stressful the moment, every justice shakes the hand of every other justice." . . . "My worry," Gorsuch warned, "is that in our country today we some-times overlook the importance of these kinds of bonds and traditions, and of the appreciation for civility and civics they instill." In a time when many "people are actually calling for an *end* to civility," when people believe that "more anger is needed [because] the stakes are too high and the ends justify the means," Gorsuch urged that for "a gov-ernment of and by the people" to work, the people themselves need "to talk to one another respectfully; debate and compromise; and strive to live together tolerantly."

How we treat one another ought to always be a consideration when attempt-ing to cooperate or collaborate with others in social or political spaces; this is not a vain hope but an acknowledgment that we live in an intensely inter-dependent world, not a state of "all against all" or "winner takes all," and we have many institutions and practices that have, over time, formed (how-ever imperfectly) around making economic, social, and political relations possible.

From the perspective of this book, civility is a form of communicative agency in which power lies within a person's ability to use language (and other symbol systems) to form relationships. We hope to build a model of communicative agency that begins with the assumption that the power to form relationships is an essential communication practice and that our forms of communicative agency are implicated within social imaginaries that make some practices and relationships easy and possible and others dif-ficult or impossible. In chapter 1, we explain the moral quandaries associated with civility as a form of communicative agency, and we show how civility and incivility both try to drive social and political change. In chapter 2, we outline the modern deliberative imaginary and its critical counterpart in an attempt to understand how and why our forms of communicative agency are limited by the ecologies we inhabit. In chapter 3, we describe civility as a set of communicative practices in interpersonal and public settings. In chapter 4, we articulate a set of uncivil communicative practices that serve as forms of resistance and rebellion. And in chapter 5, we argue that we ought to find a balance between uncivil and civil forms of communicative agency and that our obligations to others might draw us toward different ways of enacting our communicative agency. We will argue that we ought to hold on to our tradition of civility because it gives us the best chance to both preserve the systems of democratic decision-making and to make durable social and political change happen.

We suspect that some who read this might find the idea of treating morally offensive others with civility to be a form of capitulation or quietism. We prefer to see our approach as promoting reform rather than revolution. We do not fear a few examples of people on one side of a debate screaming at and denigrating those on the other side with such vituperative language that both sides remain entrenched with no sign of change possible and a growing sense of the inevitability of violent conflict as an outcome of an encounter. But we fear scaling those moments up so that they become normal. Democracy is a fragile and difficult possibility because the social fabric that underpins it is always threatened by plural opinions and beliefs that could tear it apart at any moment. We are living one such moment, and we have no doubt that others, at some point in the future, will also live such a moment. We know that democracies collapse for many complex reasons. But at the root of those reasons lies our obligations to others within our democratic systems. When those obligations weaken and cease to drive our interactions or when they get replaced by more calculating or instrumental values and forms of communication, then we might lose more than we realized. As inheritors of the pragmatist tradition, we are inclined to ask about the consequences of the ways we choose to enact our communicative agency. We think the potential consequences of civility are the maintenance and cultivation of relationships between strangers, durable social and political change, good and effective cooperation and decision-making, and the material realization of the democratic values of equality and freedom. In other words, there is much at stake in all this talk about good and bad manners.

We will also argue throughout that civility is more than forms of courtesy, good manners, or graciousness. When we engage one another in civil communication, we are doing more than just offering polite remarks that seek not to offend. By looking beyond courtesy, we consider civility to be a way of foregrounding, assessing, and analyzing how relationality functions politically at the heart of democratic culture and how communication enables specific kinds of relationships. In other words, we argue that relationships sustain the fabric of democratic culture by the ways in which they constitute meaning and guide decision and judgment. But broken relationships may be the greatest challenge to both democracy and civility. Steven Salaita, a professor at the University of Illinois, was fired in 2014 for his "uncivil" behavior on Twitter, allegedly, and recently gave urgent clarity to this problem: "When I make a public comment, I don't care if it conforms to the etiquette of a speech manual. I'm instead concerned with the needs and aspirations of the dispossessed. Conditioning critique on the conventions of bourgeois civil liberties, and in deference to specters of recrimination, abrogates any meaningful notion of political independence. To ignore those conventions, to engage the world based on a set of fugitive values, will necessarily frustrate those in power in ways that require protection beyond the scope of academic freedom" (2019). Given that democracy is a wicked problem (as we will explain in chapter 1), relationships may be more important than specific solutions to particular exigencies because solutions rarely scale beyond the specificities of a given moment, while relationships do. Civil communication practices enable, sustain, and develop specific kinds of relationships, just as uncivil communication practices do the same. To put it as clearly as possible, our attention to civility highlights the importance of relationality to democratic culture. We will argue that many of the things associated with democracy—in particular, argument and deliberation—are constituted by specific kinds of relationships rather than (just) forms of speech. To go one step further, we also argue that relationality—the form and meaning of relationships—lies at the core of our understanding of how social change is both produced and deflected. We form relationships in plural democracies because those relationships are critically important for driving social or political change. When we see democracy as a wicked problem, we realize how important relationships are in the process of finding imperfect solutions. Questions about how we treat others are often also questions about the ways that we want others to change. We may engage others in an uncivil manner; that may be an error on our part, or it may be a deliberate form of engagement chosen because of values or actions that we wish those others would change. Occasionally, uncivil people value civility. But even in his bitterness, Salaita's reflections indicate a complex attitude toward civility: "My tweets might appear uncivil, but such a judgment can't be made in an ideological or rhetorical vacuum. Insofar as 'civil' is profoundly racialized and has a long history of demanding conformity, I frequently choose incivility as a form of communication. This choice is both moral and rhetorical" (2015). Without endorsing his generalization about conformity, we find his notion of choice completely on target. By focusing on civility, we will also be asking questions about what kinds of communication practices can generate change. Our study of civility, therefore, is an argument that our obligations to and treatment of others constitute a core consideration for any democratic society, and the manner in which we enact those obligations or forms of treatment through communication can determine the course of sociopolitical change. The importance of the relationships between strangers is both a timely and timeless consideration for democratic societies—it seems especially timely given the fragile state of our current moment and especially timeless given the importance of communicative interaction to any democratic system.

Communication practices, whether civil or uncivil, do not happen in a vacuum. Context shapes the meaning of any communicative practice, and therefore, we are also making an argument about the contexts within which civility and incivility are enacted. More specifically, we claim that, at this historical moment, it appears that two overlapping social imaginaries create conditions for making sense of our communicative acts as civil or uncivil. On the one hand, a *deliberative social imaginary* generates a space in which collaborative decision-making becomes possible. Such a space utilizes a set of underlying assumptions that value relationships, practices, behaviors, and modes of interaction oriented toward compromise and connection. Deliberative spaces sanction some forms of interaction by regulating the shape and possibilities for communication. This happens by way of institutional rules, geography and architecture, social and cultural norms, laws, and the other kinds of social and cultural infrastructure that we all inhabit daily. In the deliberative social imaginary, civility is valued over incivility, given that it makes possible many of the goods of social life, and the shape of our environment is arranged in such a way as to promote civility. On the other hand, a *critical social imaginary* is a space of structural inequity that may only respond to conflict. Many figures, relying on the towering work of Karl Marx, have argued for the importance of conflict for producing social and political change. Sometimes that has been true. In a social space marked by structural inequality and oppression, we use discourse to identify, resist, or critique power, and thus there are moments when we might engage in forms of incivility in order to magnify and call out differences that make collaboration and compromise impossible. We may do so when civil engagement only serves to entrench oppression and inequality with the hope that only fierce opposition can generate material change.

In light of these two different imaginaries, we will argue that we ought to pay attention to the ways in which our communicative agency is positioned in, or implied by, a deliberative or critical context. Some assumptions of the imaginaries overlap, but they are in other ways inconsistent frames for interpreting the possibilities for relationships and actions in a given social context; some ways of interacting are constrained while other ways may seem more natural or desirable. In other words, attending to the social imaginary we inhabit can help us explain to others and ourselves why we communicate in the ways that we do and how constructing, maintaining, or changing our social imaginary influences our choices and habits as rhetorical citizens. For example, working from the assumptions of the critical imaginary, a call for dialogue between the powerful and the oppressed may sound like a tactic of the powerful for delaying change, while in the deliberative imaginary, it may sound like a productive moment of relationship building that can lead, eventually, to social or political change.

We will also make an argument about the details of civil and uncivil communication in public settings. We do not intend to offer a handbook of such practices, but we are invested in showing what the key features of civil or uncivil communication practices are. Our argument is that we ought to be able to find the balance between civil and uncivil ways of enacting our rhetorical citizenship and that we should be able to move from one set of practices to another, knowing when and where to deploy each to different ends. Too much emphasis on uncivil forms of interaction might threaten the fabric of a democratic culture, while too much civility may prevent robust or substantive critiques of power necessary for changing or driving public discourse. We also argue that we ought to develop our awareness of when the deliberative imaginary or the critical imaginary might be obscuring or orienting our attention in impactful ways. At different times, we inhabit each of these social imaginaries, and effective rhetorical citizens are able to move back and forth between them. In other words, we argue that we have competing obligations to the plural others we meet in our democracies, and finding the balance between those competing obligations is a necessary characteristic of a good citizen. This balance is only possible when we realize that relationships matter in democracies and that communication is just as much a problem of establishing, maintaining, or changing relationships as it is a matter of information exchange.

Communicative Agency

From our perspective, civility inheres in communication practices, and so before we proceed any further, it is important to unpack what we mean by *communication* and what is at stake when we view civility as a matter of communication. Some outside the field of communication studies may be inclined to see communication as a process of exchanging information. From such a perspective, the communication process involves a sender, a receiver, a channel, and some packet of information that needs to be sent over a distance. This is not our view in this book. We see communication as a process of forming, maintaining, building, fostering, and changing relationships, and through that process, meaning emerges within the relational spaces formed by our communicative interactions. This view is indebted to the pragmatist tradition of John Dewey, George Herbert Mead, William James, and others.[1] Such a view highlights the ways in which meaning evolves in tandem with the effects relationships produce on the participants in social interactions. In other words, we reject the view that meaning is a preexisting property of words, symbols, propositions, or bits of information but argue instead that meaning emerges through social interaction in which different agents come into relationship with one another. Attending to civility as a form of communication practice therefore requires attending seriously to the nature and quality of relationships that are formed within democratic cultures narrowly and social spaces more generally. Those relationships constitute meaning(s) in the communicative sense.

This concern with communication as relationality drove American pragmatism's interest in and prescriptions for democratic culture. In *The Public and Its Problems*, John Dewey (1927) argues that democracy is not simply a form of government or a set of political institutions. It is, instead, a social idea or a way of life. Put more directly, for Dewey, democracy is a set of social relationships of interaction between citizens. Shifting one's perspective from seeing democracy as a system of government to seeing it as a set of social relationships should immediately reveal the importance of a concept like civility. According to Dewey, "The strongest point to be made in behalf of even such rudimentary political forms as democracy has attained, popular voting, majority rule and so on, is that to some extent they involve a consulta-tion and discussion which concerns social needs and troubles" (154). Obvi-ously the quality of consultation and discussion matters, and in this book, we set out to extend Dewey's insights into social democracy by unpacking the importance of civility for the process of consultation and discussion that he identified.[2] Dewey's 1927 *The Public and Its Problems* shows that forms of associated living drove the development of the state as a set of institutions—institutions that could respond to the consequences of the varieties of associ-ated living that emerged socially. In other words, interaction and association came first and the state and its institutions came after, eventually coming to exist in an ecological relationship with one another. From such a perspective, democracy is primarily a matter of community life and secondarily a mat-ter of state functions and actions. At some moments, the state constrains possible relationships; in other moments, new kinds of relationships force institutions to evolve. For the latter to happen, democratic cultures need to be organized into communities capable of holding institutional officials accountable and engaging in robust, deep discussion of public problems. Social change emerges from social interaction.

John Dewey, like many others, favors a particular picture of what authentic or genuine relationships look like. In the concluding passages of *The Public and Its Problems*, Dewey suggests that the development of the "Great Com-munity" also meant the revitalization of the local community: "In its deepest and richest sense a community must always be a matter of face-to-face inter-course" (1927, 156). Place matters for community and democracy because interpersonal relationships and attachments are "bred in tranquil stability; they are nourished in constant relationships." Given these kinds of commit-ments, for Dewey, communication is a matter of both relationality and social solidarity. The vision of the "Great Community" advanced in *The Public and Its Problems* relies on the "perfecting of the means and ways of communica-tion of meanings" (155). We argue that one of the more important ways of determining how best to "perfect the means and ways of communication" is to consider the role of civility and incivility in forming relationships between citizens. Dewey sought ways for individual citizens to participate in demo-cratic decision-making so that they would realize the interconnectedness of the community to which they belonged. Democracy and community are tied together for Dewey by virtue of the role that communication plays in guiding deliberation and constituting relationships between citizens. These relation-ships matter a great deal for the prospects and possibilities of change within a democratic culture.

This emphasis on communication as relationality rather than information exchange can be expanded through the concept of *communicative agency*. Communicative agency generally refers to the ability to speak or to express oneself. Most succinctly, it is the ability to create rhetoric. This means that communicative agency exists as a kind of empowerment—it relies on the classical understanding of rhetoric as *dunamis*, a power or capacity. The meaning of *dunamis* is inextricably linked up with agency within the classical Greek world, either divine agency or human agency. It is an embodied concept, meant to highlight the different kinds of powerful capacities for doing that both humans and gods possessed. Communication, in other words, is a powerful capacity for doing, located within the potentialities of human agents; it is a form of power in its nascent state. Communication, very broadly, can be construed as the power to affect people through words, where the fact of communicating implies a relationship. At the same time, communication scholars have always been interested in and attentive to the ways in which communication broadly and rhetoric narrowly are also *tekhne*, or sets of rules and practices for the purposeful use of language. To learn these rules is to learn how best to communicate or to direct human agency through discourse. We go in search of the rules governing the practice of communication to better turn potentialities into actualities or to manage the effects we produce on others through language.

Aristotle, one of the original communication theorists, admits that communication as rhetoric is not easy to practice because it is complicated by the presence of an audience, enmeshed with the speaker in a web of institutions and purposes: "But since rhetoric is concerned with making a judgment (people judge what is said in deliberation, and judicial proceedings are also a judgment), it is necessary not only to insure the argument is demonstrative and persuasive, but also to construct a view of himself as a certain kind of person and to prepare the judge" (2006, 1377b21–24). Here Aristotle tells us that the words themselves are not the only part of the communicative process. Instead, the person enacting communicative agency and the audience listening are essential parts of the process as well. Or to put it more simply, a statement can only be persuasive, for Aristotle, "because there is somebody whom it persuades" (1365b25–28). No communicative agent, from Aristotle's perspective, has the freedom and power to simply impose an arbitrary and idiosyncratic vision of the world on an unwitting audience; the relationship is always already there, prefiguring the possibilities of influence. Hence the power of communication is relational; it does not belong to a subject but is activated in the relationship that a subject forms with an audience. The *tekhne* of communication, therefore, is not self-expression: what is inside cannot really travel outside. One's inner sense of self or inner ideas are not directly revealed through communicative action, and audiences are never simply wooed, amazed, or moved by a powerful speaker-as-subject. Instead, the *tekhne* of communication outlines a set of principles for managing a relationship, meeting the constraints of the agency of the audience in order to actualize the potential power of communication in the communal, shared interactions between citizens with agency. Power does not operate from one single point or person; it exists as a potentiality in between, and within, a community of citizens. Communicative agency belongs to both the individual citizen and the audience of other citizens, constraining the freedom of both while being enacted and embodied through discursive choices.

This view combines insights from American pragmatism with rhetorical theory in an effort to articulate what is at stake in the concept of civility. As agents, our powerful capacity for using discourse really amounts to a capacity to form relationships with other agents that will determine future courses of action. Our agency is never just a matter of imposing our will through persuasion. It is always more a matter of managing our relationships with others and with the cultural, social, and institutional context within which we find ourselves. In what follows, we try to outline some of the features of both the power of this kind of communicative agency—in particular, the power to create social change—and the *tekhne*, or set of principles, that could be used to practice civility and harness the power of communicative agency. The search for durable social change within the landscape of democratic culture is just as much a search for communities—replete with communicative agents skilled at forming, maintaining, and transforming relationships with other communicative agents—as it is a matter of a change in laws, advocacy for a specific agenda, or the power of a charismatic leader to create change by force of will. If we think of communicative agency as only a matter of good citizens that are able to persuade other citizens or able to be persuaded by other citizens, then we miss the ways in which both citizenship and persuasion are matters of forming relationships within social, cultural, and institutional contexts.

At the heart of the intersection of communication, agency, and civility lies a set of questions about intentionality and social change within democratic societies. Of course societies change. Can we change them on purpose? Can we help bend the arc of history that Martin Luther King Jr. invoked? What set of practices and what set of circumstances are most conducive to producing change? Does civility inhibit social change by constraining public discourse?

Does it advance social change by creating solidarity and common interests? What are the best available communicative means for generating change within democratic cultures? These are the kinds of questions that we hope to answer in this book by investigating the power and forms of civil and uncivil communication practices within our democratic imaginary. These questions also have ethical implications attached to them. Civility can be viewed as a kind of communication ethics by virtue of the ways in which it highlights the formation and maintenance of relationships. An ethical impulse fuels our desire and ability to treat others with civility, and that ethical impulse might be tied up in the ways in which we chose to generate social change. We can ask the simplest question: Why does civility matter? We suggest throughout that civility matters because it is an embodied way of forming and maintaining relationships, because it holds the potential to generate positive social change, and because it enacts a form of communication ethics—all of which potentially benefit our democratic culture. In order to develop this argument, we will first need to describe the competing deliberative and critical imaginaries within which rhetorical citizenship has been practiced; these imaginaries form the kind of structural scene for practices of civility and incivility.

Let us pause a moment and introduce some useful (though provisional) definitions for civility:

> *Weak civility.* A network of behaviors and norms intended to maintain the appearance of comity, ease, comfort, and belonging. Often equivalent to politeness, it may accomplish its goal by strategically ignoring or effacing uncomfortable differences of belief or practice.
> *Strong civility.* A network of behaviors and norms that can be used to engage differences in a way that will deepen a sense of community and over time help communities move toward nonviolent systemic change. Strong civility may include deliberations, deep listening, dialogue, confrontation, protest, and civil disobedience.
> *Pseudocivility.* The invocation of weak civility norms against strong civility behaviors, resulting in a refusal to engage on the grounds that engaging some difference is always uncivil, even if the difference is arguably of great public and moral importance.

We will reference and build on these definitions as we go on. Here we use them to highlight the ways in which civility is always already a consequential matter of communicative agency.

Alignments and Temptations

The arguments that we are making about communication as relationality, as agency implicated within a social imaginary, and as a matter of finding a balance between competing obligations are not radically new. We see deep alignments between this set of arguments and several other intellectual pre-occupations that have received sustained attention recently. In particular, these arguments are aligned with the resurgent interest in American prag-matism, with existing commitments to deliberation, with systems theory and human ecology, and with the burgeoning interest in rhetorical citizenship. Articulating the ways in which our arguments align with these currents will allow us to put considerations of civility into a broader and more substantive context and will help us rescue civility from shallower interpretations that reduce it to politeness. We must also confront the temptation to dismiss civil-ity, and democracy along with it, brought about by recent questions about just how useful deliberation is for generating change. First we turn to prag-matism and then to the temptation to dismiss democracy and civility.

The intellectual roots of American pragmatism stretch back to the end of the nineteenth century and, most prominently, to the work of John Dewey and William James. Dewey has remained the foremost advocate for the argu-ment that democracy is a way of life, and James has remained an essential proponent of an epistemology characterized by plurality, utility, and skepti-cism. In the forty years since the publication of Richard Rorty's *Philosophy and the Mirror of Nature*, pragmatism broadly and John Dewey and William James specifically have influenced a range of different fields, including com-munication studies. Neither James nor Dewey spent much time considering the relative merits or limitations of civility. They did, however, introduce the importance of communication, experience, inquiry, and relationality as core considerations for both epistemology and democracy. These considerations have been critical to pragmatism's resurgence in the last few decades, and they are critical to how we see the alignment between pragmatism and ques-tions about civility. What Dewey terms "moral democracy" captures a good deal about why pragmatism aligns so deeply with our conception of civility. In his *Ethics*, Dewey describes a kind of ideal society that was diverse while being harmonious and was a fully participatory enterprise in which the pow-ers and capacities of individual citizens were harmonized by their coopera-tive activities. This emphasis on cooperative participation (what we might call inquiry) shares much with what we will call later the deliberative social imaginary.

The finer details of the philosophy of pragmatism also point to the importance of communication as relationality that we develop in this book. Dewey's emphasis on cooperative activities in democratic life is supported by an epistemology that rejects realism and idealism (or any search for foundations upon which to base truth claims) in favor of an ecological and evolutionary account of knowledge. From a pragmatist perspective, truth is not the property of a statement or proposition; it is, instead, the outcome of a process or a set of practices. Our interactions with others and with our environment become constitutive considerations in the process of generating knowledge. This is why so many pragmatists focus on the relationship between experience and pluralism. If we foreground the interactive way that we experience the world, then we become committed to a kind of political and philosophical pluralism, which suggests that final determinations (Truth) about the world are impossible and that the best we can hope for are workable, though temporary, agreements between diverse ways of experiencing the world. Those temporary agreements are achievements of relationships. We know this because communities make the pluralism and uncertainty of our world, which are never easy, acceptable, and community becomes a central concern for all varieties of American pragmatism. Dewey neatly ties pragmatist epistemology to his commitment to democracy by suggesting that "knowledge is a function of communication and association" (1927, 158), by which he means a function of community life. In this book, we will ask what sorts of communicative practices are necessary for preserving relationships and holding communities together. We think considerations of civility are an intellectual entailment of pragmatism's focus on democracy and epistemology as matters of community life.

John Dewey's commitment to a social imaginary consistent with deliberation is not the only place to recognize the importance of deliberation in general. Many moments throughout Western history have endorsed peer discussion on important matters. Deliberative bodies of all sorts have often been thought necessary for democratic governance since as early as ancient Athens. Our moment has its own champions of deliberation, from Jürgen Habermas and James Fishkin to John Gastil and Amy Gutmann. But today's deliberation is not like that of classical Athens. For Athenian theorists of rhetoric such as Aristotle, democracy was not possible in anything larger than a small city-state because only a face-to-face society could allow the kind of participation—and relationships—entailed by deliberation. Structurally, modern societies may lack the necessary ingredients for deliberation: messages being exchanged interactively at length and under conditions of reflection. Nonetheless, we remain preoccupied with what might be necessary to cultivate and sustain a deliberating public because of the faith we have in its key role in democracy and to enduring social change. Our moment has turned to the broad idea of "deliberative reason" as an important process of people thinking together aloud and in public for the purposes of decision-making. But as we will surely show in this book, public reason can often be uncivil or built on false facts and specious assumptions. Therefore, we confront many challenges to the possibility of deliberation: declining space and time for interaction between strangers—we see Robert Putnam's (2001) work as an illustration of this—as well as the role of the media in creating distance and displacing actors in deliberation, the professionalization of deliberation by a powerful class of public officials and media personalities, and the ways in which emotion influences reason, to name a few. These limitations have not stopped scholars from continuing to champion deliberation as a necessary component of democratic life. Instead, many of these challenges have led to renewed and extensive efforts to rehabilitate deliberation as a potential cure for the ailments of our moment.

We do not intend to make any significant pronouncements about the current academic work on deliberation. We remain agnostic about the ability of inventions such as "national deliberation day" to rescue us from polarization and paralysis. However, attention to deliberation must also require attention to the ways in which we treat the others we are deliberating with. And therefore, we see questions about civility and incivility as bound up with questions about deliberation, perhaps at a different register of attention from where philosophers and political scientists orient their work. Deliberation puts people in close proximity on the assumption that decisions are best made when everyone is engaged in a decision-making process. Deliberative bodies, we argue, must always already attend to the ways in which people treat one another when in such close proximity, and this is ultimately a question about civility and relationality. For the kinds of collaborative and cooperative decision-making that theorists of deliberation imagine to work, we must consider how communicative interactions that foreground issues of relationality influence the processes that scholars of deliberation spend so much time describing and prescribing. Accordingly, the arguments we make about civility are also an attempt to extend the conversation about deliberation.

As communication scholars, civility is also a way of showing how important questions of communication are for our habits of citizenship. In that way, this argument also draws us closely to contemporary work on "rhetorical citizenship." Here we agree that our communication practices are just as important to our role as citizens as are the rights we are granted by our government. In other words, the term *rhetorical citizen* is meant to highlight the importance of communication in enacting our citizenship. But *rhetorical citizen* comes with a temptation to think ideally about communication as a strictly rational project. We might call this "rhetorical citizenship" after the work of Christian Kock and Lisa Storm Villadsen (2012). This view of rhetorical citizenship privileges the role of rational argumentation in our communicative encounters with others over relationality. But do rational arguments really change minds? Do they preserve the social fabric so necessary for cooperation and collaboration over difficult, pressing problems? This book attempts to extend the conversation about rhetorical citizenship (and about pragmatism, deliberation, and relationality) without falling to the temptation of thinking that the best citizens are the most rational ones.

While the alignments previously outlined may operate as good contextual resources for our arguments, we also need to avoid the temptation of losing too much faith in democracy and thinking that democratic deliberation cannot possibly fix the deep structural problems of racism, sexism, capitalism, and environmental disaster that we are presently living with. The rising tide of violence precipitated by white nationalism reminds us that many people who inhabit our public culture do not have any interest in living well with others. Fascism and demagoguery, we ought to remember, are antidemocratic by virtue of how they divide the world into an "us" and a "them" without any desire for an "us" to live well with a "them." Those who advocate for liberal commitments to social justice ought to be careful to avoid enacting the same rhetorical and political practices that lead groups on the far right to seek out ways of eliminating pluralism. We see increasing indications that those on the political right *and* left are losing interest in the central democratic problem of constructing temporary alliances between diverse kinds of citizens with a plurality of values. When the purity of one's political positions (whether left or right) becomes the criteria for evaluating the quality of arguments in public discourse, we can see the rise of antidemocratic forms of rhetoric that seek victory over troubling opponents instead of compromise or collaboration with others who hold views we find deeply offensive. We show some of the rhetorical strategies behind such forms of public discourse in chapter 4. When we are drawn toward arguments about the very limitations of democracy itself, then the stability of our political systems is endangered. In March 2017, Keith Mines (one of several experts that *Foreign Policy* asked to evaluate the likelihood of a second civil war in America) claimed that the United States faced a 60 percent chance of civil war over the next ten to fifteen years. Other experts predicted a range of 5 percent to 95 percent, with the median possibility working out to 35 percent. Why, in this moment, does the stability of American democracy seem so fragile? Mines cites five conditions that support his analysis: (1) entrenched polarization with no possible meeting place for resolution, (2) increasingly divisive press coverage, (3) weakened political institutions like Congress and the judiciary, (4) the abandonment of responsibility by political leaders, and (5) the legitimation of violence as a way to conduct discourse. The current U.S. president, Donald Trump, has enacted, encouraged, or fueled each of these five conditions. Democracies operate within a scene of robust social intercourse that is necessary for the kinds of cooperation, collaboration, and coordination that democratic political systems rely on for decision-making, and especially for relationships between relative strangers called upon to work together for a common good. In the social spaces of democratic life, we negotiate the shared process of making and contesting meaning. When that shared social process breaks down, then democracy, as a system of government, is susceptible to collapse and failure. The experts in *Foreign Policy* were not communication scholars, but each was pointing to the ways in which we engage one another as rhetorical citizens (i.e., citizens that communicate) as critical to the stability and viability of democratic governance and culture. If we are tempted to think that more democracy is not the answer, then our political system is surely at risk of collapse. Some might view this as a positive outcome, and the temptation to see that as a positive continues to stress the social fabric holding our systems together.

But why, for example, would African Americans or Latino Americans endorse even basic forms of strong civility when so much of their history and present is marked by structural and practical forms of oppression or domination? Why might viewing civility from the perspective of the marginalized lead us to doubt its efficacy and embrace a more radical politics? These are hard and important questions. Many on the margins are likely to have experiences that tell them that civility does not do any good. Author bell hooks, for example, has long offered trenchant analyses of oppression while endorsing modes of transgression that flout norms to help secure justice. We can cite many examples of excellent scholarship analyzing the depth and degree of forms of white supremacy and/or heteronormative gender discrimination. From such perspectives, any endorsement of civility will read like an endorsement of the status quo (with all the troubling forms of injustice so carefully and expertly made clear in both scholarship and the material realities of so many citizens in even the most progressive democracies). We want to resist the strong temptation to read civility as a mode of endorsing the status quo and discounting the forms of injustice that surround us. We can certainly think about relationality and ethics without tying those considerations to democratic deliberation. But to read civility as something other than capitulation to injustice and the status quo is to remember that, for example, African American women continue to play a central role in community organizing by virtue of their ability to mobilize family, friends, and communities.[3] Or we could look to Jeffrey Stout's (2012) lucid description of organizing practices by mostly Latino groups in the Southwest, replete with instances of strong civility at work in the building of communities capable of advocating and securing change. We recognize that we have, in part, a responsibility to show how and why strong civility might help even those on the margins who have suffered from the forms of oppression that characterize our present and past. This responsibility brings us to the heart of the politics behind this book.

A Liberal Stance

In an increasingly polarized United States, political stances are often fraught and subject to (often uncivil) dismissal. Even our very faith in democracy itself can be questioned by a variety of figures in all areas of the political spectrum. So we wish to close the introduction by putting our cards on the table and defending a specific kind of commitment to social change that aligns with the value of strong civility. In part, we wish to address the temptation to be skeptical of all that democracy can do as well as the temptation to see civility as useless for those on the margins. We are liberals. Not neoliberals, though that term (which mainly seems to be a term of abuse) will no doubt be applied to us. So we need to explain what kind of liberals we are and how that stance is consistent with other commitments we have made. In a recent book (which draws heavily on Richard Rorty's *Achieving Our Country*), Adam Gopnik (2019) summarizes the debates of the last thirty years or so and eloquently crystallizes the liberal position that aligns with our own self-understanding of our project. The gist of his account is that liberals believe a flawed democracy is still evolving imperfectly toward equality and away from cruelty. His story highlights a core of fallibilism and humility—shared by pragmatists—that tempers the expectations we can have of any actual democracy. Liberals believe that those further left and further right of liberals, while sharing some (or many) liberal ideals, believe too strongly in the perfectibility of politics. The lesson of revolutions, left and right, is that perfection is brittle and temporary and often comes at an enormous human cost. Hence the liberal tradition is focused on reform: "The foundation of liberalism is cracked in advance. . . . Its foundation is fallibilism—the truth that we are usually wrong about everything and divided within ourselves about anything we believe. Reform rather than revolution or repetition is essential because what we are doing now is likely to be based on a bad idea and because what we do next is likely to be bad in some other way too. Incremental cautious reform is likely to get more things right than any other kind" (Gopnik 2019, 26). Have there been successes in reform in the last 150 years (setting aside, obviously, the U.S. Civil War)? Indeed, many, and most were not achieved through just asking or "making a demand," as fans of Frederick Douglass like to say:

> Militant activism was certainly responsible for the achievement of many of these reforms. But it was specifically *liberal* activism. It wasn't trying to change everything at once. It was trying to fix what was wrong now. Civil disobedience, women chaining themselves to parliament offices, the bravery of the Chartists in Britain or the popular front in France or the Selma marchers. But in the end their goals were specific, not utopian, capable of being achieved by democratic means of democratic legislatures, even if only when the cost of not achieving them became too great for the powers already in place. (Gopnik 2019, 25)

The point of liberalism is to acknowledge that the complexity of the democratic experience, imperfect as it is, should make us wary about trying to perfect it. The apparent mushiness of liberalism, in its failure to perfect freedom or eliminate oppression completely, is a feature, not a bug: "So, the critical liberal words are not *liberty* and *democracy* alone—vital though they are—but also *humanity* and *reform, tolerance* and *pluralism, self-realization* and *autonomy*, the vocabulary of passionate connection and self-chosen community. . . . Liberalism *ends* in the center not because that's where liberals are always thinking the sanity is, but because they recognize that there are so many selves in a society that must be accommodated that you can't expect them to congregate in a single neighborhood" (Gopnik 2019, 14–15). Liberalism, in Gopnik's account, is primarily a set of practices rather than a credo, an orthopraxis rather than an orthodoxy: "Liberalism is as distinct a tradition as exists in political history, but it suffers from being a practice before it is an ideology, a temperament and a tone and a way of managing the world more than a fixed set of beliefs" (21). What are the practices of a liberal democracy that lead it, haltingly and imperfectly, to a more just and less cruel society? Gopnik cites a centerpiece of the civil rights movement: "Bayard Rustin, the great black and gay man who organized the march on Washington in 1963 and who, at the end of his long life, summed up his credo elegantly in the three simplest of distinctly liberal dance positions: 1) nonviolent tactics; 2) constitutional means; 3) democratic procedures" (21). Our point is that forceful, effective reform is consistent with civility. Of course, those being reformed may resist it, but the question is whether the *terms* under which they resist are sustainable or coherent over the long haul. One of the oddities of the Charlottesville marches by neo-Nazis and anti-Semites is their insistence that *they* are not the racists; other people are. The logic is twisted, but the premise should compel our attention: in 1918, it would not have occurred to a Jim Crow racist to deny being a racist—there was pride in that label. Now, however, we have all learned the lesson of the civil rights movement: racism is immoral and indefensible, so watching racists twist and turn to avoid the label is in fact watching a victory, albeit one in progress and not yet complete.

The purpose of our book is to offer a specific reading of civility that aligns with pressing issues related to contemporary democratic theory and practice and one that resists oversimplifying the kind of communication that can help preserve, enhance, and improve our democratic culture. Our obligations are not just to facts, truths, or processes (although we do have such obligations); we also have obligations to the other strangers that we meet in our democratic lives. Analyses of the possibilities for our encounters with others and the practices we use in those encounters can help us see what is at stake in the everyday interactions of democratic life. If democracy is a wicked problem (see chapter 1), then we face a new test every time we must weigh our competing obligations and productively interact with the many different others we meet. We will not be arguing that we must always treat one another with civility, but we will be arguing that we must always think about how we treat one another if we want to build and maintain a democratic society. That kind of concern is a matter for communication theory and practice, but only when we see communication as more than the transmission of information. That kind of argument also highlights the importance of civility in building and maintaining the kinds of relationships between strangers that are necessary for democratic life.

I

CIVILITY AS A MORAL QUANDARY
AND A POLITICAL NECESSITY

In the present argument, friendship is not an emotion, but a practice, a set of hard-won, complicated habits that are used to bridge trouble, difficulty and differences of personality, experience and aspiration. Friendship is not easy, nor is democracy.

—DANIELLE ALLEN, *TALKING TO STRANGERS*

On June 22, 2018, White House press secretary Sarah Huckabee Sanders and some friends went to dine at the Red Hen, a small farm-to-table restaurant in Lexington, Virginia. After the waitstaff recognized her, they contacted the owner, Stephanie Wilkinson, who lived close by and came immediately to the restaurant. The staff said they were uncomfortable serving Sanders, in particular because of her aggressive defense of President Trump's homophobic comments and policies. The owner asked the employees what they wanted to do, and they unanimously said they would prefer not to serve her. The owner asked Sanders to leave, and she and her party left, having offered to pay for the food they had already eaten; the owner responded that it was "on the house." On Twitter the next day, Sanders commented, "Last night I was told by the owner of Red Hen in Lexington, VA to leave because I work for @POTUS and I politely left. Her actions say far more about her than about me. I always do my best to treat people, including those I disagree with, respectfully and will continue to do so." Reactions were swift and predictable. President Trump insulted the appearance of the restaurant: "The Red Hen Restaurant should focus more on cleaning its filthy canopies, doors and windows (badly needs a paint job) rather than refusing to serve a fine person like Sarah Huckabee Sanders. I always had a rule, if a restaurant is dirty on the outside, it is dirty on the inside!" An unrelated restaurant in DC, sharing the same name, was subjected to vituperation and threats. Commentators pointed out the dubious truth in Sanders's rejoinder, given that she was often disrespectful of the press at her podium, and some considered her defense of transparent lies told by the president to be disrespectful of the American people. Still, it seemed shocking to some that an individual in her private life was being held accountable for her behavior in public office. And while Sanders couched her response in terms of "respect," the commentariat framed the episode in terms of civility.

What we would like to do in this chapter is begin by exploring some of the responses to the Red Hen incident and then take the measure of how civility is currently perceived by way of introducing our own approach to civility. The responses to the Red Hen affair will show how civility exists simultaneously as a norm and an antinorm. This leads us to consider Wilkinson's decision as an ethical one rather than something like a lapse in decorum. Understanding how civility is the site of ethical decision-making requires us to identify some conceptions and misconceptions about civility and consider what it means to cross a line into incivility. Finally, we sketch the potential role (to be filled out in the following chapters) of civility and incivility as a part of social change.

Overall, responses to the episode were disappointingly predictable. Some were offended by what they perceived as a lapse in civility and interpreted it in terms of the general decline of civility in American life. Conservative commentators were quick to bristle, wielding an obvious double standard (given that their president is regularly crude, rude, and insulting to an extent that embarrasses even some of his supporters). A *Fox News* headline read, "Left Setting New Standard of Incivility, Critics Say: 'This Is Very Dangerous'" (McKelway 2018). Katha Pollitt, in the *Nation*, complained bitterly of the double standard. She said that Wilkinson "could not have known how the incident would be blown up by the paranoid right, ever looking for proof that they are victims of 'political correctness.' . . . No matter how vulgar, gross, threatening, cruel, illegal, and insane the right becomes, it's always the left that is warned against piping up too loudly and in the wrong way" (2018, 6). And she concluded that it was time for liberals to stop tying their own hands: "It's like the old Jewish joke: Three Jews stand before a firing squad. Each is offered a blindfold. The first Jew takes a blindfold. The second Jew takes a blindfold. The third Jew refuses the blindfold. The second Jew elbows him and says, 'Moshe, take a blindfold—don't make trouble.'" A feature of many commentaries is visible here: comparing civility (in general) to passivity in the face of violence. Is this an apt comparison? Are the stakes for civility really that high? A number of commentators leapt to the claim that civility is a terrible thing, useless, that it suppresses dissent and protest and is ever the barrier to social change while being the ally of oppression. To take a different example, in the 1980s, the group ACT UP (AIDS Coalition to Unleash Power) popularized the slogan "Silence equals death," meaning that if we cannot talk about the uncomfortable subject of AIDS (acquired immunodeficiency syndrome) and its effect on the LGBTQ community, people are going to die in greater numbers. In 2014, a job offer to Dr. Steven Salaita was withdrawn by the University of Illinois over a series of angry tweets about the treatment of Palestinians. Pressure from donors was likely behind the withdrawal, but the public excuse was that Dr. Salaita was more uncivil on Twitter than a public university could tolerate. Merits of that claim aside, the controversy soon produced a graphic declaring "Civility = Silence / Silence = Death," which was followed shortly by buttons that read "Fuck Civility." When one of the authors asked a member of the Women's Studies Department about this pin, she replied, "Twenty years ago when I started working here, I was told by a male colleague, in the mailroom, that it was uncivil to have a woman on faculty. And I've hated civility ever since." A fair response on her part, even though this seems to be an indefensible use of the term by the male faculty member— refusing to acknowledge a colleague due to race, religion, gender, or sexuality seems definitionally rude and uncivil. Racism and sexism, as we shall see, are intrinsically rude (among other moral failings)—they do not count as just another difference among people to which we owe a civil tolerance.

This episode stands in for a whole class of cases where a misuse of civility—directly or as an explanation for a refusal to engage—is taken as a reason to reject civility. Hence in a sense, we are taking a contrarian stance in defending some version of civility while accepting that many academics position their endorsement of incivility as contrarian. We wish to take the measure of arguments against civility without rejecting it entirely. We have not seen a better rejoinder to rejections of civility based on the harm it might do in some settings than Aristotle's with respect to rhetoric: "And if it is argued that great harm can be done by unjustly using such power of speech, this objection applies to all good things except for virtue, and most of all to the most useful things, like strength, health, wealth and military strategy; for by using these justly one would do the greatest good and unjustly, the greatest harm" (2006, 1355b). Even if one thought that the main purpose of civility was producing comity, the fact that it can be used to produce division does not show that it is intrinsically bad or only productive of division.

Thinkers in the modern period disrespected rhetoric due to the evils it could produce, and only in the twentieth century did scholars try to recuperate it. Rhetoric falls into the category (with some justice) of things where the same word is used for the good and the bad (as Derrida pointed out for ancient Greek, *pharmakon* meant both medicine and poison). Wayne Booth (2004) suggested we use *rhetrickery* to describe rhetoric used insincerely or for ethically unsavory purposes and reserve *rhetoric* for more virtuous contexts and uses. In a similar vein, we might define *pseudocivility* as the pretense to civility that fails, in some contextually relevant sense, reasonable tests of civility. Since racism is uncivil, intrinsically, then objecting to it cannot be intrinsically uncivil.

The following cartoon is interesting in that the epithet ("You racist SOB!") in the second frame becomes the leverage for the accusation of incivility (see figure 1.1). Certainly the epithet seems impolite though understandable in the circumstance. But given the level of racism and the history of violence attached to the Ku Klux Klan, such a strong condemnation may well fall within the bounds of civility, if not politeness. In addition, the response of the KKK character is doubly disingenuous, since any "Death to . . ." formulation has already foreclosed the possibility of "meaningful dialogue." When the gentry of the antebellum South did not want to discuss abolition because it "wasn't civil," they were embracing pseudocivility. But that stance need have no claim on our current understanding of civility: though they also objected to abolition on the grounds of rationality, religion, biology, and culture, we need not give up on those on account of their misuse by justifiers of slavery. The deployment of a kind of racist pseudocivility, in all its hypocrisy, was highlighted by a shirt attributed to professional basketball player LeBron James (it was actually an altered photo) during the Black Lives Matter controversies, which said,

> *We March—y'all mad*
> *We Sit Down—y'all mad*
> *We Speak Up—y'all mad*
> *We Die—y'all silent.*

In the responses to the Red Hen incident, we also find comparisons between incivility/rudeness and direct-action tactics, and this comparison can be tricky to parse. Asking Sanders to leave the restaurant satisfied Wilkinson's conscience, but did it really constitute direct action against the Trump administration? Was there any chance that it would shame Sanders

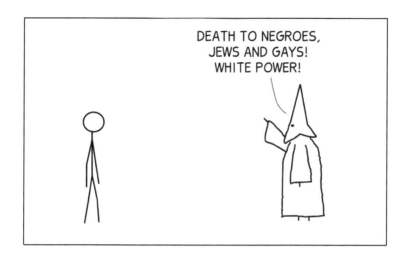

FIGURE 1.1 Pseudocivility in action

or Trump into changing their behavior? Even if not, it still might have been the right thing to do, but compared to direct action, from nonviolent to violent, it does not seem to be in the same league. In the title of the *Atlantic* article "A Template for 'Incivility': Today's Protesters Are Reviving the Tactics of the Anti–Vietnam War Movement of the 1960s and '70s—with Similarly Mixed Results," Julian Zelizer interestingly puts *incivility* in quotation marks, presumably because he thinks it is really nonviolent direct action. Clearly, violence is uncivil (even when justified), but it seems a stretch to include the Red Hen incident with the antiwar protests Zelizer recounts.

Continuing the theme of violence, others framed this incident as an incivility that finally struck a blow for liberals against a hated administration (one continually criticized for its crudeness and incivility). Perhaps the endless verbal assaults of the president had left people feeling battered and wimpy. Jelani Cobb, academic historian and *New Yorker* feature writer, confidently asserted on Twitter that "civility is the coward's favorite virtue" (2018). One hopes he only means this relative to particular settings; one can easily imagine examples where it might be a "cowardly" choice and ones where it is a courageous choice. Yet speaking up for civility, at all or in a specific case, becomes for some people prima facie proof of one's failure to "resist" a racist, sexist, and homophobic status quo and hence to be complicit: Doug Gordon, replying to Cobb's tweet, claims, "Civility in the face of tyranny is just another form of complicity." A legitimate question involves asking under what conditions incivility would actually constitute resistance or noncomplicity. Stokely Carmichael famously made a stab at an answer: "Dr. King's policy was, if you are nonviolent, if you suffer, your opponent will see your suffering and will be moved to change his heart. That's very good. He only made one fallacious assumption. In order for nonviolence to work, your opponent must have a conscience. The United States has none" (Olsson and Rogell 2011). This analysis seems like it would apply equally well to strategic or righteous incivility; uncivil protest (e.g., aggressive shaming) would only effect change if the targets could feel shame on the topic at hand. Legitimate questions remain, however, about the power of incivility. A separate argument is that not only is civility-as-complicity bad in itself but even engaging discussions about it can preserve the existing social order.

We might also conclude that appeals to civility in this case are simply a red herring. While Stephanie Wilkinson refused to serve Sarah Huckabee Sanders, the Trump administration was busy separating parents from their children after the families crossed the U.S. southern border. We might say that this policy is what really matters and the entire debate about the Red

Hen is a distraction from the "real" policy decisions that have material consequences. And if we were to genuinely address or respond to the complexities of Trump administration policies like the practices being implemented at the border, then civility would not be a sufficient weapon to resist or critique those policies. This amounts to the claims that civility is merely a naive consideration when confronted with the political challenges of the moment and that worrying about civility amounts to bringing a pen to a gunfight. Both of these objections rest on the belief that more serious, complex, difficult, or real considerations lie beyond our focus on civility or incivility in the interaction between Sanders and Wilkinson. But there is much at stake in this interaction, and there are significant consequences, both material and intellectual, to our treatment of others. The wish to genuinely change Trump administration policies and alter the course of the political events unfolding in any given moment is deeply implicated in questions of choosing between civility and incivility.

The Ethical Moment

The Red Hen responses highlight three questions: (1) Was the Red Hen incident actually uncivil?, (2) What goes into such a decision?, and (3) How do we understand its consequences? We believe that tough-minded answers to these questions cast doubt on much of the commentary and reveal a woeful gap in our understanding of and conversation about civility. This incident also returns us to the distinctions between weak civility, strong civility, and pseudocivility that we made in the introduction. Seemingly everyone who commented on the Red Hen incident presumed that this was an unquestionable example of incivility. On closer examination, however, this may not be so obvious. While perhaps not everyone will agree, we believe a case can be made that it was not an act of protest or political confrontation—but an act of civil confrontation. Wilkinson's decision was not hasty or visceral; she consulted with her staff and took their input seriously, including their feelings of righteous indignation. She recalled in the *Washington Post* the next day, "I'm not a huge fan of confrontation. I have a business, and I want the business to thrive. This feels like the moment in our democracy when people have to make uncomfortable actions and decisions to uphold their morals" (Selk and Murray 2018). She saw this as a political and moral decision—a complex one but one that had to be managed with civility. Wilkinson told the *Washington Post*, "I was babbling a little, but I got my point across in a polite and direct fashion.

I explained that the restaurant has certain standards that I feel it has to uphold, such as honesty, and compassion, and cooperation. I said, 'I'd like to ask you to leave.'" Sanders's party agreed immediately and offered to pay, which was refused ("it's on the house"). If this was a skirmish in a political war, it was surely a very polite one, as the *Washington Post* noted, "For all the angst that evening, Wilkinson said, everything had taken place with decorum. She had been polite; Sanders had been polite; the press secretary's family had been polite as they followed her out the door." None of this is meant to take away from how controversial the confrontation was, only to point out that it was grounded in civility.

Absent some more reporting, we cannot know exactly Wilkinson's thought process going into this decision. But we can still parse the possibilities as they are given to us in this quotation, which links "democracy" and "morals." Interesting moral decisions are ones that weigh various goods against one another; while choosing the good over the bad is easy, choosing one good while giving up others is fraught. Wilkinson was aware that she was being confrontational and possibly rude. However, she positioned her actions as a complex ethical choice justified, on balance, by the particulars of the situation. Which ones? First, Wilkinson cites Sanders's general track record in her role. Despite Sanders's claim of being asked to leave because of where she works, the fault seems to lie in how she does her job. Second, she explains the harm that Sanders represents to "democracy" in general, which flows from insincere or duplicitous communication from the White House. She appeals to the need to keep her business going, which means it is a risk to create wrathful customers or negative publicity or see her Yelp score drop precipitously (as it did). She mentions her sense of her employees as a group; since they would suffer any consequences, they should be part of the decision. Wilkinson highlights the particular affront felt by her staff as marginalized Americans ("they were mostly gay") in the face of Sanders's willingness to show complicity with the administration's decisions by defending or obfuscating about those decisions from the podium. (Interestingly, despite some commentators' desire to see it this way, the question of family separation was not the key issue, and Sanders had in fact refused to go the podium on the question the previous week, displaying some conscience about the issue.)

In rhetorical terms, we could say the decision exhibits both *phronesis* (practical wisdom) and *kairos* (timeliness in the context). The confrontation shows practical wisdom in that Wilkinson took action based on a moral judgment in the unexpected moment in which action was required; she did not shrink or temporize. Her judgment was timely in that since criticizing the president, by anyone, had proved ineffectual, the time was ripe for a non-partisan individual to confront a member of the Trump administration. Our analysis intends to reframe the meaning of civility and cut through the easy but unsatisfying opposition between civility as niceness and what is variously called civil disobedience, confrontation, protest, or resistance. Even terminologically, the continuity between civility and civil disobedience should be obvious. Yet as we shall see, an entrenched conviction has taken hold, especially of academics, that civility is incompatible with social change, and any discussion of civility is a distraction from the "real" issues. We are pretty much in agreement with such critics about what the real issues are, but we dispute how we should see civility in relationship to them. The fallout from the Red Hen episode suggests two salient insights to us. The first is that discussions of civility are far from irrelevant. The very critics who decry them have spent a good deal of time not only criticizing the administration for its vulgarity and crude macho aggressiveness. They have also wished that members of the administration, as well as its supporters, would listen to their complaints and arguments—which presumes a certain kind of background civility that operates in the condition of deep disagreement (what we define as "strong civility"). Second, and perhaps more alarming, are the calls for escalation of confrontation that came soon after. Not only will we assuredly see more incidents of service denied in restaurants and other places over Trump supporters' "Make America Great Again" ("MAGA") hats and the like, but they could turn angrier and even less civil—and potentially violent. This argument played out in the civil rights community in the 1950s between King and Malcolm X: Should the violence implicit and explicit in the current system be fought with violence? King questioned both the strategic and moral effects, and those questions remain. What will calls for escalation to outright violence produce? And what will their moral effects be, if those who imagine they hold the moral high ground decide, out of anger and frustration, to stoop to what they see as the worst of the "other side's" excesses?

Conceptions and Misconceptions About Civility

The Red Hen affair shows that civility seems to come in for uncritical praise (as a value) and some uncritical condemnation (as a practice). To clear the ground for a more substantive discussion, we should review some conceptions and misconceptions. They are, as one might expect, interconnected with one another and not fully separable.

Civility Is Just a "Preference for Order"

This objection must be answered at different levels of analysis and with some historical consciousness. Basically, it reduces the enormous number of norms that form our picture of how to interact with others to a fixed and rigid framework that, so the objection goes, exists either for its own sake or for the sake of those with privilege in a given society. A critic can easily find cases that fit this description. Yet civility, even in its weaker forms of manners and politeness, can be dynamic, complex, and evolving. For example, a long European tradition holds that women are the economic property or personal servants of their husbands. As this tradition was successfully challenged in the 1960s and 1970s, the problem arose of how to politely address women in a way that did not presume they belonged to someone else. Several solutions were tried ("Ms." won out in the end), and the transition was filled with a good deal of disorder—for manners and civility. Civility reflects a given order but can find within it the resources to challenge that order as well. Clearly, we should not accept social organizations once we realize their injustice, in that they are intrinsically racist, sexist, or homophobic. Racism, sexism, and homophobia are thus revealed as uncivil, and a commitment to civility demands that we avoid embodying them in our interactions.

Does this commitment also demand that we publicly shame those who persist in using forms that embody injustice? That question is trickier, since the correct answer is probably "yes, but appropriately." The qualification does not suggest "compromising" or temporizing with moral wrongness but rather taking into consideration how change happens and what the world will be like after it happens: ends do not always justify means. In opposing unjust social orders in the name of, and with the tools of, civility, we have to care about the effects of our mode of opposition. Martin Luther King Jr., in his most famous speech, identified both sides of the problem. For the sake of our common civic values, we need to shake things up: "There will be neither rest nor tranquility in America until the Negro is granted his citizenship rights. The whirlwinds of revolt will continue to shake the foundations of our nation until the bright day of justice emerges" (King 1963). However, for the sake of those same values (in his understanding, founded in Christian morality), we should be careful about our own moral status and the world we are making: "But there is something that I must say to my people who stand on the warm threshold which leads into the palace of justice. In the process of gaining our rightful place we must not be guilty of wrongful deeds. Let us not seek to satisfy our thirst for freedom by drinking from the cup of bitterness and hatred." That position was controversial then and may be controversial now, since it begs the question of moral hazard and moral corrosion *as well as* a question of what will be left to work with after the resistance is done. The specter of Jacobin excesses needs to haunt the work of reform.

We Can Assume Civility and Incivility Are Efficacious

We also need to think through the possible and actual outcomes of being civil or uncivil. This problem looks quite different if asked about local versus global actions and effects. In the local case, choosing to be civil or uncivil may have an effect on a specific relationship or interaction but no appreciable effect on the total level of civility in a community. However, the global effects of civility—which are the ones we are trying to defend in this book—are the result of patterns of local interactions; as with any system, if enough nodes change, a global effect will result. The global features of civility (or incivility) may also affect norms and expectations in local interactions; the interpersonal performances Erving Goffman (1959) wrote about are the products of local management of the situation, yet they rely on both a repertoire of behaviors and interpretive strategies from a culture or community and the normative force that comes from the community. However true this picture is, what are reasonable expectations about effects produced by civility/incivility? We can admit that civility matters while acknowledging that unreasonable expectations have been foisted on it.

To illustrate, let us consider the case of the fabled inappropriate holiday dinner; suppose an older relative, Uncle Jim, makes a remark that seems to you evidently racist, sexist, or homophobic. You have several (standard) choices, and it is worth remarking on how we understand the effects of each and hence what kind of choice each is. First, you could just ignore it, consistent with Harvey Sacks's "let it pass" rule: ignore mistakes or flubs in conversation unless they are serious enough to derail the purpose of the conversation (Sacks 1992). Many people fear the effect of this rule is a tacit approval of the racism or sexism, because having an enjoyable holiday meal is more important, at that moment, than pointing out the rudeness of what was said (hence the old saw "No politics or religion at the table"). We have to ask, however, for whom this approval functions. Does your silence cause Uncle Jim to believe he is right in saying these things? For that to be the case, Uncle Jim would have to be aware there was something wrong with what he was saying. He may not yet have figured out that it is rude to refer to LGBTQ people as "homos."

This returns you to the problem of how to respond to this violation: Is it severe enough to address in the moment? Do you decide to take him aside later? Or do you decide that based on your experience, he is hopeless? If you do decide to challenge him, you can do this politely ("Uncle Jim, I'm sure you mean well, but my LGBTQ friends have told me that word seems offensive—maybe we can try 'gay' or 'lesbian' instead?"). While you are not trying to make him feel shame ("I'm sure you mean well"), this may strike some as a discordant note for the occasion, especially if he decides to contest your correction, which will force you to decide whether to engage or let it drop at that point. If you do let it drop, have you accomplished anything for the cause of LGBTQ rights and general social respect? Perhaps. You might have planted a seed for Uncle Jim that will allow him to rethink terms on his own and then change his usage (perhaps gradually). Confirming the other guests' perception of your virtuousness might be a worthy effect of challenging Uncle Jim, depending on the company and the context. Does it serve the general cause of LGBTQ rights and respect? That seems less clear, since it is likely you are signaling because people present already agree with you. We could also describe this outcome as "hailing" in the semiotic tradition (addressing people in a rhetorically recognizable and codified manner) or what Richard Gregg (1971) called the "ego-function" of protest rhetoric, where the outcome is not to persuade others but to cement a group identity.

However, the challenge to Uncle Jim might be a little more direct and qualify as politically confrontational or actually uncivil. ("Uncle Jim! That's terrible. You can't say that—it's ignorant, disrespectful, and naive.") Notice here that the reproof of Uncle Jim, while provocative and not allowing him to save face, is premised on civility—respect for a group. Do you have a reasonable expectation that Uncle Jim will have his consciousness raised or an increased awareness? Not in general. Of course, the history of your interactions may be such that this may be a decisive turning point, but absent that history, it is equally likely that he just ignores you or even digs in his heels on the expression or the group. In terms of the others present, you may cement your status as a fighter for righteous causes, though some may resent you for introducing tension into the meal; there may not be a reliably predictable outcome. You may have mixed feelings, since you may feel good in some ways for having had the confrontation but regretful in other ways about your effect on the enterprise. Chapter 3 will explore how these same considerations play out in the public sphere, but the lesson we can draw from this thumbnail example is that there are multiple possible outcomes for civil and uncivil behavior, and particularly in the case of deliberate incivility, we cannot be sure in advance that we will get the desired effect.

Protest and Confrontation Are Uncivil

This claim follows from *weak civility*, which is an account of human relationships in public as mere politeness: following forms that are designed to make people comfortable. This level of politeness certainly exists and for everyday purposes can be a useful thing. But the vast system of manners, etiquette, and civility that has evolved historically (as we will describe in chapter 2) is far more complex and subtle than simply "making people comfortable." The norms of weak civility have the strongest claim on us interpersonally, but they generally give way to strong civility in public (and, to an extent, professional) contexts. We can easily imagine situations in which being polite makes someone uncomfortable; the phrase "kill them with kindness" describes such situations. Disagreements, especially about important values or ways of life, are often uncomfortable. Yet they can still be conducted, on both sides, in a civil way (nowadays, such interactions are sometimes called "difficult conversations"). Judith Martin identifies standard ways of doing this (she prefers to talk about politeness and rudeness rather than civility and incivility, but in this case, they amount to the same thing):

> Bigotry is rude. (Practicing it is immoral, but expressing it is rude.) Reacting against it in a civilized fashion is not rude [but] actually more in keeping with the basic principles of manners, dignity and respect, than is ignoring bigotry, *which may superficially—but deceptively—appear to be the polite response.* . . . Objections to bigotry should match the severity of the transgression, ranging from "Surely I must have misunderstood you" to "I beg your pardon!" to "How dare you!" to "You will be hearing from my lawyer." Properly used, however, all of these are perfectly polite responses to highly impolite behavior. (1999, 263–64; italics ours)

These remarks may appear surprising from the perspective of weak civility, which often aims to keep a dubious peace by ignoring actions, which in turn might cause conflict. Human relations, however, inevitably result in conflict, and the possibility of family, community, and state rest in the existence of skills that allow us to disagree without immediately being reduced to violence or broken relationships. Strong civility is thus necessary to an argumentative, deliberative public culture. Not every issue is arguable; some are not amenable to reason (people will never agree on the best music or the proper cooking of eggs), and some exist, at a given moment, beyond argument. In the first half of the nineteenth century, the morality, advisability, and practicality of chattel slavery were subjects of heated public and personal argument. They no longer are; aside from some fringe religious communities, slavery is so widely considered morally unacceptable that even when it is practiced, the participants deny that what they are doing is slavery. When President Trump responded to a neo-Nazi march in Charlottesville, Virginia, in 2017 by saying there were "some very fine people on both sides," he appeared to be, as it were, equivocating the evil and the just. But they are not the same; Nazis, by definition, are not fine people, because no just or morally acceptable claims can be made on their legacy.

While some issues of social justice and morality command a consensus, most of the time, we end up arguing about things because we do not have complete consensus (hence the need for argument), and this requires us to take a stance of some humility: "Of course even though *I* think I'm right about this, you probably think with just as much moral conviction that *you* are right." This stance requires effort, for we need to acknowledge that our beliefs and commitments, important as they are, are defeasible and corrigible. In a democracy, social and political change should (and often do) happen when we find common ground and accommodations that allow us to have enough of our commitments met that we can move forward together, knowing that these commitments and practices will change and evolve. Hence civility is tied to a kind of epistemic and moral humility (as well as the recognition of what Martha Nussbaum [1986] has called "moral luck"). Hence pitching every issue in absolute terms is civically disabling.

This cluster of issues lies at the heart of Patricia Roberts-Miller's (2010) *Fanatical Schemes: Preslavery Rhetoric and the Tragedy of Consensus*, which analyzes how Americans before 1850 argued about slavery. The abolitionists clearly believed that moral suasion might result in the end of slavery and pursued this end through books, pamphlets, speeches, and legislative exchanges. Roberts-Miller wants to know how those in the South defended what we now know to be indefensible, and she duly catalogs their twists and turns, logical contortions, evasions, self-contradictions, and prevarications. She is particularly interested in their attempts to refuse engagement, and one of their tactics was to claim hurt feelings, which they attributed to disrespect and incivility. Upstanding citizens in slave states were deeply offended to discover that abolitionists wanted to eliminate their primary economic system and hence their way of life and claimed the abolitionists were unkind for provoking such distress. In fact, they blamed the offensive rhetoric of abolitionists for their own unwillingness to engage abolition. In retrospect, this seems amazingly juvenile and self-serving, though neither the dismay nor the objection is particularly surprising. What is more surprising is that even though it is not crucial to her argument, Roberts-Miller codes the failure of persuasion as a problem about civility relative to the assumption on the part of the slaveholders that someone should care about what they think and feel. This, Roberts-Miller believes, is dangerous: "This sense of a public sphere of compromise and concession is often connected to privileging civility, a powerful, but very vague, concept. 'Civility' tends to be defined through negation: it is not emotional or abusive; it does not involve personal attack; it is not offensive. Offending one's audience, it is argued, alienates them, and persuading them necessitates moving them to one's side, not pushing them away" (5). Several important issues jump out from this passage. First, we would argue that the United States (at least) *needs* a public sphere of compromise and concession: they are features, not bugs, of a diverse representative and liberal democracy, consistent with Gopnik's account of liberalism discussed in the introduction. Granting that slavery was morally abhorrent and needed to be abolished, different paths to abolition were possible, and reasonable people might disagree about them; given how Reconstruction proceeded and the subsequent failure of the United States to build a system with full civil rights for African Americans, we clearly did not take the best possible path. Understandably, the idea of having a debate about slavery seems noxious in the abstract, but in the moment, it seemed to make a difference; requiring that others will automatically see themselves as wrong, beyond the need for argument, may be futile. Second, civility is no more (and no less) vague than any other important moral concept; it does not have sharp edges and clear applications—but neither do justice, equity, equality, and other concepts we need to understand and guide public life. Perhaps it is often defined negatively, but that is not necessary, as we hope to prove in the course of this book.

Yet her last point in the passage quoted is absolutely crucial. Is civility a necessary element of persuasion? (Roberts-Miller cites Aristotle's authority on this matter.) Perhaps, but the important point is not to collapse the difference between disrespecting or offending people and confronting them. This space is a difficult one; as in all rhetoric, a time and place for each exist. An audience can decide that any attempt at persuasion (on a particular topic) is intrinsically offensive, in which case her point is moot. At the other extreme, the persuaders may be blunt to the point where a claim could not fail to be offensive (hoping, perhaps, a moment of enlightenment or contrition may result from the offensiveness). In between is the wide space of civic argument: "With all due respect, you are wrong, and here's why" (with the respect given to the person, not the position). Engagements in this style may not produce persuasion in the moment, but they may generate arguments that, when circulated, can produce persuasion, as the abolitionists indeed showed, though they never won over the most intransigent (and Roberts-Miller is probably right that many people were never particularly open to argument anyway).

In her conclusion, Roberts-Miller returns to this theme, and she again points to civility (or more precisely, accusations of incivility) as the culprit, the fly in the ointment of abolitionist advocacy. Her analysis implies that without the burdens of civility, abolitionists might have been persuasive, might have carried the day in the great public deliberations leading up to the Civil War:

> To blame abolitionists for incivility is to preclude abolition. My grievance is not with the notion that public discourse ought to have certain standards and that billingsgate should be avoided—I hope it's been clear that I consider proslavery rhetors' reliance on smear tactics as juvenile, hypocritical, and destructive. The problem is that conventional notions of civility, which tend to emphasize whether the audience is offended, inevitably put an impossible burden on dissenters. While calls for social change might themselves call for more or less violence, they always necessarily involve criticism, and no one likes to be criticized. To prohibit anything other than "civil" political discourse, as long as "civil" is defined as discourse that does not upset anyone, is to prohibit social change. (2010, 231)

Roberts-Miller's faith in dissent is laudatory, and she may be right about civility under that definition: weak civility is incompatible with strong critique; notice the slide from "criticism" to "does not upset anyone." But respectful confrontation and criticism—including the ability to receive it as well as deliver it—is the essence of strong civility. Certainly some moments require one to think about whether it is the right time to offend an ally, though that is not every moment. An important corollary is that offensiveness per se does not constitute critique or engagement, as evidenced by the rise in troll culture—virtue signaling to one's community through angering or offending people on "the other side" (Harris 2018; Coppins 2018). Trolls probably do not mean to be persuasive, and they may not ever actually persuade anyone. If the audience reaction, either way, is not determinative, then we would need a set of tests for the civility of an approach so that we can account for the situation in which an audience is offended when it should not have been (in J. L. Austin's [1975] terms, a definition of the illocution rather than the perlocutionary uptake). In a similar way, someone might react to a speaker as illogical or unethical, even though they arguably were not.

Where Is the Line?

Slavery was and is the deep, primordial evil of the U.S. democratic experiment. In many ways, it is unlike most of our public arguments, yet it also highlights a moral and practical quandary that arises for many engaged in public deliberation. Objects of the most intense moments of public debate and disagreement (as the case of abolition shows) are framed in morally absolute or certain terms. In such cases, we are apt to draw a line that warrants our uncivil treatment of those on the wrong side of that line. In other words, we cannot be expected to treat slave owners with any degree of civility because of the noxious nature of their belief system. We suspend our commitments to civility when others cross a certain line because slave owners, Nazis, pedophiles, and cannibals are not worthy of our respectful attempts at dialogue and deliberation. But where do we draw that line? In the Red Hen case, the employees of the restaurant may have felt that Sarah Huckabee Sanders had crossed that line by virtue of her complicity with Trump administration policies. Perhaps—but that line cannot be crossed everywhere, all the time. Can we be constantly looking for occasions to draw and redraw that line?

None of this is easy. In writing about the vicious culture of denunciation and invective based on religious differences in early modern Europe (so similar to the culture wars of today), Teresa Bejan notes, "Still, whether in the service of toleration or uniformity, these early modern attempts to tame men's tongues through law reflected a widespread belief that societies neglected wars of words at their peril. . . . Yet, then as now, agreement on the importance of civility did not necessarily entail agreement as to who or what should count as 'uncivil.' Indeed, disagreements on this score could and did engender their own heat" (2017, 47). If we conceptualize our conversations about tax law, tariffs, health care premiums, or gun laws as moments of confrontation with evil people who do not deserve respect, then we have begun to overconfidently—and in the long run destructively—draw the lines of acceptable public engagement. In such moments, civil disagreement certainly remains possible, as long as we choose to treat those who hold opposing positions with some degree of respect. This does not preclude moments in which we can or should draw a line that would relieve us from the responsibility of careful, reasoned, respectful discourse. But it does remind us that we ought to be careful about where we draw such lines and that the more we consider beyond the line, the more we preclude possibilities for meaningful dialogue that could lead to social and political change. We do not know where the line should be, and we ought to acknowledge that such a line is a historical byproduct of ongoing conversations anyway. We may, in fact, engage in civil or uncivil arguments about where that line should be. But finding the balance and acting as good rhetorical citizens does involve an open degree of agnosticism about where that line should be and a willingness to resist drawing it wherever one sees someone with whom they disagree.

Let us extend this analysis by examining one analytic approach to the ethics of civility. What does it mean to be uncivil? Philosopher Aaron James (2012) argues that we can understand what an *asshole* (which we take to be a highly uncivil person) is or what makes a person an asshole by analyzing the concept through the lens of social philosophy. The difference, he says, is this: Consider a quotidian act of rudeness—say, cutting in line at the coffee shop. A *douchebag* may commit this infraction but experiences shame and perhaps verbalized remorse: "Hey, sorry, I just really need to get to work right away."[1] Assholes, on the other hand, have no qualms, because they proceed from an assumption that they are entitled to cut in line because they are Very Important Persons. The point of waiting in a line was that it seems to people in North American culture like a fair (i.e., civil, recognizing equal claims) way to manage the disorder of multiple people attempting to simultaneously order at one or two registers. James parses the assumption of entitlement as a question of social justice, but we are interested in another difference between these offenders. We are all going to be rude at some time or another. We may realize it or not; it may be purposeful or inadvertent; we may or may not apologize or make excuses. But at what point is one entitled to say one's rudeness is justifiable? Not often. In case of emergency, one might be excused, for example, for pushing people aside to tend to an injured person; medical triage is an exercise in disregarding the "first come, first served" rule. But the point here is that rudeness is not normally a morally justifiable action.

What is the implication of this distinction for civility? We will all say things, at some point, that are gratifying but that we know were unnecessarily at someone's expense; we may acknowledge the slight (or not), and we may apologize or make excuses. But what would we say to someone who deliberately causes an offense he or she thinks is justified—and what counts as a justification? Consider someone who refuses to refer to a transgender woman with female pronouns and insists (to her face), "It's nice you want to dress as a woman, but you are not one." Making a careless mistake (especially twice) about this person's announced identity seems douchey, but doing it deliberately seems to make one an asshole. What justifies this person's entitlement? It seems like the "really" is the clue; the person thinks because it is "true" that someone is biologically a man, then he is justified in ignoring the person's stated identity. So some notion of the "truth" trumps the respect due to another person. One can parse this fault both in terms of the offense given and the offense taken, depending on the setting.

Consider a second case, where a vegan makes other diners uncomfortable about the cruelty that produced their food. We can imagine a "just slipped out" version of this act ("I'm just so passionate about animal rights and welfare!") but also a very deliberate version. (Of course, vegans often make much more sophisticated arguments and frequently have a better sense of timing.) But what justifies the basic asymmetry of criticism, since the other diners (presumably) have not criticized the vegan's food choices as shameful? If you understand the world through the critical imaginary, the truth ("meat is cruel") and the duty to object to what one believes is cruelty justify the asymmetrical criticism because it is some form of consciousness raising: "If these people only realized the truth, they would stop eating meat, and if enough people did that, overall cruelty would be reduced, which obviously is a good thing."

While we might easily dismiss the righteous dinner companion (who probably will not be invited back), would the same behavior in the public sphere get the same judgment? It depends on what "the same" means here, because the context of public discourse is so different. Earnest editorials about the evils of meat (or more often, particular production practices for meat) are unobjectionable in newspapers or blogs in ways they would not be at dinner. These contributions project a vision of how life should be lived, and that vision does—and should—jostle with many others. They may even try to be very strategic and find strategies to appeal to carnivores. But what if their arguments imply that carnivores are cruel and evil people? Perhaps, then, there is a rhetoric of turning to veganism that is deeply uncivil, premised on denying, fundamentally, respect to the meat eaters because they have crossed "the" line. While we might presume a community of right-thinking "civil" people is the prerequisite for deliberation, the "deliberative imaginary" (see chapter 2) has enormous latitude in who counts in the discussion and what counts as discussable, on the assumption that we need to be very careful about kicking out anybody except murderers, pedophiles, cannibals, and others who cross a line (a line that may have evolved historically). The "critical imaginary," however, is more willing to circumscribe participants and topics once critique has shown them to be oppressive, either directly or systemically. We are thus faced with a kind of individual policy choice with a version of William James's (1896) dilemma about believing from "The Will to Believe." James points out that if you are easygoing about believing lots of things, then you have to accept that you will end up believing some that are false. If you are rigid in rejecting anything that might be false, you are bound to lose a number of actual truths in the process. So those buying into the deliberative imaginary are likely to end up discussing, inter alia, some oppressive things they should not, and those in the critical imaginary are going to refuse to deliberate some things they need to.

Ironically, a persistent fear (Lozano-Reich and Cloud 2009; Roberts-Miller 2010) is that acknowledging civility will result in pseudocivility being deployed strategically to prevent critics from getting specific forms of oppression into the conversation; without a doubt, this does happen, though with inconsistent results. This fear of silencing pervades the critical imaginary, since ruling people and topics out of bounds is how the status quo holds its rhetorical ground. The only question is who gets to do the suppressing; presumably, when the forces of justice and equity take over, racist discourses will be suppressed (we see a version of this in Germany's laws against expressions of anti-Semitism). From within the critical imaginary, this makes sense, but it turns critics, in essence, into virtuous oppressors who can only battle the system by dismantling it. But it contains, strangely, an implicit appeal to a larger deliberative setting in which oppression is battled by getting a hearing in that larger setting. So while in some ways critics see deliberation as the problem ("Don't debate racism; it's just wrong"), in other ways, it is a solution ("Discussing racism can raise consciousness and get people woke to changes that need to be made"). Black Lives Matter (BLM; discussed in chapter 3) might be understood as an uncivil means to civil discussion and some consciousness about how we would (collectively) act if black lives mattered as much to us as white lives. Black Lives Matter is a fragile negotiation between rhetorical forms of protest and challenges to the question of who is the "we" in "What should *we* do about racism?"

We return, then, to the question posed earlier about whether the demands of civility are absolute. Civility is a value—but it cannot be our *only* value. Incivility is a value—but it cannot be our *only* value. How can we understand, rhetorically and ethically, how to balance these? Scholars of rhetoric in the late 1960s wrote about the most electrifying rhetorics of the day, the various protest movements; in particular, they examined the protests at Columbia University, where students marched, clashed physically with police, took over a building, and in effect, held a university president hostage for a time. Scott and Smith subjected these episodes to some trenchant analysis. They see, in the actual rhetoric deployed, what they call a "Manichean" approach of good versus evil, us versus them, which they see as leading to a rhetoric that is the "rite of the kill"; having quoted Fanon on violent reactions to violent systems, they go on to describe the implicit rhetoric: "The enemy is obvious, and it is he who has set the scene upon which the actors must play out the roles determined by the cleavage of exploitation. The situation shrieks kill-or-be-killed" (1969, 4). They conclude that confrontation can be a totalizing or nontotalizing tactic. When it addresses systems of oppression that are total, then the protesters have no need of respecting or preserving the current system and have no qualms about "burning it down," so to speak. When confrontation is nontotalistic, it may allow us a chance to jumpstart change, to fix a broken system: "Student activists in the New Left vacillate in their demands between calls for 'destruction' of universities as they are now known and tactical discussions of ways of 'getting more into the system' to make it more responsive to student goals. . . . Drift toward non-totalistic goals . . . may also reflect a latent response to the embarrassment of affluent students, beneficiaries of the establishment, who claim the language and the motivations of the truly deprived" (6). Rhetorically, they say we "should observe the possible use of confrontation as a tactic for achieving attention and an importance not readily attainable through decorum" (7). But incivility as a tactic "poses new problems for rhetorical theory" (7). From a tactical or managerial perspective as well as from political legitimacy, they say, we have to see that confrontation sometimes reflects a real gap in traditional rhetorical politics: "Even if the presuppositions of civility and rationality underlying the rhetoric are sound, they can no longer be treated as self-evident. A rhetorical theory suitable to our age must take into account the charge that civility and decorum serve as masks for the preservation of injustice, that they condemn the dispossessed to non-being and that as transmitted in a technological society they become the instrumentalities of power for those who 'have'" (7–8). They make no normative claim here but a descriptive one: here are data for which we need to account—namely, the *charge* that civility serves as a mask for power. This passage does not endorse all confrontation or incivility as part of the cause of justice, and the article casts doubt on whether totalizing confrontation can achieve anything meaningful. James Andrews, writing in response and from his vantage point as a faculty member at Teachers College, Columbia University, is willing to provide a relatively negative judgment of the protesters' rhetoric, insofar as it privileges ends over means (a common ethical dilemma), but he ends by noting,

> To think, however, in this case, of "patriots" and "tyrants" is to oversimplify, to make an exceedingly skewed judgment that the facts hardly seem to warrant. This is no doubt the quintessential problem, for it hangs ultimately on the extent to which one may allow himself to go when condoning rhetorical strategies used in behalf of what *he* considers to be worthy causes. If rhetorical theory in the twentieth century must take into account the change described by Scott and Smith, that "civility and decorum serve as masks for the preservation of injustice," then rhetorical criticism obviously must also provide for the examination of those cases in which civility and decorum are discarded for ends that are not obviously and unquestionably just. (1969, 15–16)

So Andrews's conclusion is not that civility and decorum are intrinsically oppressive but that civility and incivility not only are caught up in a complex moral calculus of means and ends but also are understood against conflicting background pictures of what they mean in society.

Democracy as a Wicked Problem

We claim civility as an important theoretical and practical dimension of democratic life, but not without an awareness of its shortcomings. We are proposing not a utopian picture for the perfection of democratic life but rather a picture of one version of an imperfect one—for there are no others. All democracies are flawed, just in different ways. In a word, democracy is a "wicked problem." In 1974, the Australian public policy scholars Horst Rittel and Melvin Webber described a difficulty at the heart, as they saw it, of public policy practice. Policies are enacted to solve problems, but at least two classes of problems exist. Some are "tame" problems (sometimes called "hard," as in "merely hard," problems). Tame problems are ones where the problem is well understood: it has a widely accepted definition and is often quantitatively definable. Correspondingly, the solutions are also well understood, in terms of both how to implement them and why they are solutions. Building a bridge is an example of a tame problem. A road exists on either side of a river. The banks are a particular distance apart, the road needs to carry a particular amount of traffic, the geology of the banks has specific properties, and there is a latitude for the budget, safety codes, and so on. Building the bridge will be complex and time-consuming, but as a problem, it is pretty straightforward.

But Rittel and Webber point out that most problems of public policy are not like this. They are not just "harder" or "more complex." Rather, they are qualitatively different; Rittel and Webber call them wicked problems. Wicked problems are multilayered and elusive and characterized by interdependencies between attempted solutions and aspects of the problem in ways that make their best solutions deeply enmeshed in trade-offs; solutions to wicked problems are trade-offs "all the way down." Consider for a moment the "obesity epidemic" in the United States. How does one define obesity as a public health problem? Weight? BMI? Body fat composition? Each of these definitions is itself problematic and leaves some people in or out of the problem space. How would you know when the problem is solved? When no one is obese? That obviously will not happen. Suppose you pick a target that seems like an acceptable trade-off of resources and outcomes, say "No more than 10 percent of the population" (which assumes you have decided which kind of obesity you will tolerate). Obesity has numerous direct and indirect causes, and a solution that addresses any one of them is likely to interact with others. For example, one might say obese people should have a better diet—less processed food, less meat, more fruits and vegetables. Yet a lower income and the probability of being obese are correlated. Inner-city residents often do not have access to a range of foods but do have access to a lot of fast food and may juggle multiple jobs and childcare. So to solve the problem of a better diet (often portrayed as "making better choices"), one would have to address large systemic issues that structure food choices for people, and obviously poverty and housing discrimination are big problems in themselves.

This example helps highlight how much democracy itself is a wicked problem—every best version of democracy will have undemocratic aspects or dimensions. How can people govern themselves in an equitable and effective manner? The quip declaring that "democracy is the worst form of government, except for all the others" gets its bite from an underlying truth, which is that there is no perfect solution to the problem of self-rule; every solution we have involves painful (moral) trade-offs and simultaneously creates other problems. Rittel and Webber give the following characteristics for wicked problems:

1. There is no definitive formulation of a wicked problem.
2. Wicked problems have no stopping rule.
3. Solutions to wicked problems are not true-or-false, but good-or-bad.
4. There is no immediate and no ultimate test of a solution to a wicked problem.
5. Every solution to a wicked problem is a "one-shot operation"; because there is no opportunity to learn by trial-and-error, every attempt counts significantly.
6. Wicked problems do not have an enumerable (or an exhaustively describable) set of potential solutions, nor is there a well-described set of permissible operations that may be incorporated into the plan.
7. Every wicked problem is essentially unique.
8. Every wicked problem can be considered to be a symptom of another problem.
9. The existence of a discrepancy representing a wicked problem can be explained in numerous ways. The choice of explanation determines the nature of the problem's resolution.
10. The planner has no right to be wrong. (1974, 166)

This formulation seems apposite, since Americans commonly think of their democracy as an "ongoing project." We think that in the pursuit of perfectibility, failure is inevitable; the best we can hope for is a better set of trade-offs. So while civility is bound to be imperfect, we argue that its trade-offs make it worthwhile. What are, in fact, the desiderata of democratic life?

- equal participation
- good decisions
- the minimization of the tyranny of the majority or minority
- the deliberative character of decision-making at various levels
- inclusive institutions and practices
- appropriate trust and distrust in government

- the minimalization of the influence of money
- healthy supporting institutions
- healthy relationships with media

A longer list could easily be generated, according to one's political tastes, but this is a good start for norms and goals that form the constraint conditions on the problem of constructing a functional democracy. One could not even say that any of them is independently a tame a problem, since there are so many evident interdependencies among them. Jointly they exhibit a high degree of wickedness. Robert Ivie has argued that a functioning deliberative sphere will be "rowdy" (2002, 277), which one would expect if different stakeholders were attempting to simultaneously achieve different goals, reflecting different values systems. Democracy is also evolving and somewhat experimental; while some democracies have been more experimental than others in changing their frameworks to achieve a different set of trade-offs, even the United States has tweaked its system, sometimes modifying the Constitution (the Fifteenth and Nineteenth Amendments; the Seventeenth Amendment, which allows the direct election of senators) as well as through judicial decisions, federal laws (the Voting Rights Act of 1964), and local changes (Maine and California experimenting with non-winner-take-all voting systems). The United States has always had a sort of civil religion (Bellah 1992) that, while not quite a credo, amounts to a set of principles that can be referenced in evaluating trade-offs. The set of principles may itself be contradictory, but it nonetheless functions as a way of grounding arguments about how best to proceed. The United States has also been blessed with a tradition of local political experimentation that, importantly, does not scale, since having different solutions for different local contexts is itself a way of grappling with wickedness.

How does civility figure into all this? We are reminded of Karen Armstrong's quip about theology: "We often learn about God at about the same time as we are learning about Santa Claus; but our ideas about Santa Claus change, mature and become more nuanced, whereas our ideas of God can remain at a rather infantile level" (2010, 320). When we learn "manners" and norms of politeness as children, they are often framed in terms of a perfect world in which if everybody is polite to everybody else, we could all get along. Munro Leaf's charming book for children, *Manners Can Be Fun*, builds this sunny world out of a few basics. It is worth noting that even in miniature, he is giving a functionalist justification for manners—they must have evolved to make social life possible:

Having good manners is really just living with other people
   pleasantly.

If you lived all by yourself out on a desert island,
   others would not care whether you had good manners or not.

It wouldn't bother them.

But if someone else lived there with you,
   you would both have to learn to get along together pleasantly.

If you did not, you would probably quarrel and fight all the time, or—
   stay apart and be lonesome because you could not have a good time
   together.

Neither would be much fun. ([1936] 2004)

Leaf summarizes a certain set of background assumptions very well. Living
with others requires either fighting with them or getting along with them,
and each strategy has consequences. A good start, but this account bears little
resemblance to either the complex world of adult interpersonal relationships
or the wicked world of public discourse in a democracy. That does not mean
that civility (or even politeness) is irrelevant, just that we need to describe a
version of civility appropriate to a world in which we want to—and sometimes
need to—fight and argue all the time about pressing issues. If we begin with
the assumption that democracy is a wicked problem, then we can begin to
see how and why civility may be an important characteristic for those of us
attempting to navigate the complexities of our democratic moment.

Civility, Social Life, and Change

The Red Hen affair, then, is interesting for what it tells us about how people
think about public discourse and civility and how it illustrates their role in the
wicked problem of democracy. The problem here is to figure out how civility
works for—or against—ideas about social change through discourse: Does
civility enhance or detract from a culture of deliberation in which change
(toward social justice) can occur? For now we will say "culture of deliberation"

rather than "deliberative democracy" because it hews more closely to what those who disagree share in common. Consciousness raising and demonstrations exhibit the same faith as public debates and forums in that, in some way, what we say to one another may, eventually, influence changes in social relations and politics. But from that starting point, the pictures diverge about how and why talk matters and how we should understand the associated norms. One way to frame this problem is in terms of conceptions of *rhetorical citizenship*, a framework developed by rhetoricians at the University of Copenhagen. In the introduction to their recent book, Kock and Villadsen articulate it this way: "Rhetorical Citizenship as a conceptual frame emphasizes the fact that laws, rights, and material conditions are not the only constituents of citizenship; discourse broadly conceived among citizens (in other words: rhetoric in society) is arguably just as important. The concept unites under one heading citizens' own discursive exchanges, in public or in private conversation, i.e., the active or participatory aspect of rhetorical citizenship, and the public discourse of which they are recipients" (2012, 11). Thus we constitute ourselves as citizens in the discursive sense by communicating in ways that are consistent with our (diverse) civic values and goals. Rhetorical citizenship is maintained, systemically, by granting it to others, since it is a functional condition of public argument and is enacted through participation in a broad range of communicative practices. Civility is one among several obligations of rhetorical citizenship because it implicates and recommends specific communicative modes of interaction between citizens. One of the problems, from such a perspective, involves negotiating the extent of the substantive commitments required of rhetorical citizens by civility. Is civility simply a kind of superficial tone, or does it perform an agenda-setting function by parsing social interactions into categories? In other words, does it help make distinctions about what can and cannot be said or argued in public discourse? Those who endorse civility do so based on a picture in which it can be (mostly) neutral and that neutrality counts as a virtue in enabling rhetorical citizens to cultivate a deliberative culture; those who reject civility do so based on a picture of rhetorical citizenship in which civility is one of the barriers to a deliberative culture, a barrier that often excludes important contributions necessary for fulsome deliberation.

Why would one even try to salvage civility as a useful concept? At least two reasons present themselves. First, even conceding (as we will later) that civility can have perverse effects does not justify abandoning it altogether. While one can debate whether rhetoric should or should not be defined in a morally neutral way, Aristotle's point on this matter still seems valid, as noted earlier. Unless one believes that an endless rhetorical war of all against all is inevitable or desirable, then possessing an ethics of public discourse is a worthwhile goal. Hobbes is the touchstone here; in the preface to *Leviathan*, he distinguishes these politics from those in a civil society: "I demonstrate in the first place, that the state of men without civil society (which state we may properly call the state of nature) is nothing else but a mere war of all against all; and in that war all men have equal right unto all things" ([1651] 1994). However, the ethics must be realistic for the complexities of rhetoric and public reason; simple injunctions or principles ("be nice," "be rational," "be respectful") are not likely to be helpful. Second, we need a framework that allows people to be accountable to one another, both for their civil *and* uncivil communication. A parallel case might be truthfulness and lying (Toulmin and Jonsen 1988). In general, of course, truthfulness is a Good Thing, and it has a peculiar kind of normative character; it is not just good but also *necessary* in general, since it would be hard to get things done if, normally—as a default—one had to assume everybody was lying. Certainly we can identify shades and nuances, from "white lies" to euphemisms and face-saving, and certainly interactional settings where truthfulness is irrelevant might also exist (Sacks 1975). We could also think of times when lying, though wrong in general, is the right thing to do. The question is what kinds of situations trump the general and highly functional norm of truth telling: to save someone's life, certainly, but to save some money, certainly not—unless that money will feed your starving children, and so on. To us, this seems a much more fruitful and interesting territory on which to discuss civility than blanket, abstract praise or condemnation, however validating those may seem. What is lacking is an account of civility rich enough to allow us to talk about the trade-offs in view of holding our own and others' discourse accountable. While recognizing the limitations of civility, we can still analyze the complex play between agentic and systemic stances in useful ways.

To sketch the argument briefly, we claim that civility is not a simple or superficial consideration for life in democratic societies. Instead, it contains complex and meaningful details about our considerations, obligations, and treatment of others. Civility reveals the relationality at the heart of all deliberative cultures, or in other words, it points us toward the ways in which relationships constitute meaning and context, guide decision and judgment, and sustain the fabric of democratic culture. Civility, in other words, enables specific forms of relationships, just as incivility does the same, and these

can be analyzed in terms of the effects those relationships have on deliberative decision-making and life in a democratic society. By pointing us toward
relationality (or relationships), civility also turns us to the norms of practices
of communication that we use within our deliberative cultures and the centrality of those norms and practices for generating social change. This is
why we like the term *rhetorical citizenship*: we are interested in the ways in
which specific communication practices are capable, or incapable, of producing social change and whether improvements in communication practices might facilitate improvements in deliberative decision-making. In later
chapters, we will unpack specific civil and uncivil communication practices
in order to consider how such practices produce social change and shape our
deliberative cultures. A more nuanced understanding of civility and incivility, in terms of communication practices and social change, might allow us
to move beyond the shallow charges laid out in the debate about whether
we have too much or too little civility in our public culture. A more nuanced
analysis also requires that we place the debate over civility in a broader historical context.

The U.S. political system has always been characterized by change, particularly changes in mass opinion and action. One might think, for example,
of the women's suffrage movement and the Nineteenth Amendment, the
Civil Rights Act of 1964, and the Voting Rights Act of 1965. These political achievements were a product of changes in mass opinion and specific
political actions. One could, as historians and sociologists have done, explain
these changes through structural factors instead of rhetorical ones (the slow
collapse of the slave economy vs. the arguments of abolitionists, etc.). We,
however, would like to argue that, without discounting structural factors,
deliberation plays a significant role in social and political change in the modern era (for good or ill). In other words, democracy must constantly confront
the underlying discursive tensions between maintaining and changing community, even diverse, complex heterogeneous communities. We manage
that tension through institutional structures as well as discursive practices.
In other words, communicative practices play a significant role in shaping
the meaning of both the political actions and the underlying views that generate change. If, like John Dewey, we think about democracy as a way of
life and not just a system of government, then we can begin to realize the
role that rhetorical practices play in shaping that way of life. Dewey thought
of democracy as a mode of associated living to which communication was
central, and so any kind of change within those forms of associated living

had to be made through communication practices. This view underlies our interest in civility and conditions the meaning of civility historically and in our own moment.

Two main stories bear on the contemporary relevance of civility in personal and public life. The first is the emergence of the culture wars (Hartmann 2015; Sunstein 2009; Mann and Ornstein 2012). Since the 1960s, the tensions implicit in postwar America have, in part, worked themselves out through a discursive (and in some cases literal) clash of cultures. Liberal/conservative, red/blue, right/left—these have become the interpretive frames for understanding people's positions on anything from the cars they buy, to the salad greens they prefer, to the policies and candidates they favor. Andrew Hartmann traces one obvious story about the origins of the culture wars, while Jason Stahl (2016) specifically cites attempts to influence the overall rhetorical climate. As Hartmann (2015) shows, the culture wars emerged out of the tumult of the 1960s through the transmutation of policy disputes into philosophical disputes and then into differing worldviews. As we will argue later, this abstract framing damages our ability to communicate deliberatively. The adoption in English of the 1930s German term *kulturkämpfe*, or culture wars, was significant because it signaled the transposition of disagreements from institutional frameworks to any cultural form or product. The values that justified institutions—freedom versus fairness, say—were common values written into the American civil religion. But the 1960s brought so much change—demands for gender and race equality, recognition of sexualities other than heterosexuality, acceptance of alternative lifestyles, and more. These changes seemed to many to amount to a wholesale assault on the American culture they understood, not just a disagreement about economic policies. Yet culture seems to be exactly the kind of nebulous thing that is hard to argue or deliberate about.

The problem posed by the culture wars, as a rhetorical phenomenon, is their ability to prefigure people's responses to one another to the point of stalemate, which can produce both an entrenched anger or frustration and sometimes a kind of despair (Eliasoph 1998). If someone makes an argument to you about gun control, say, you may already know all the arguments on the other side, and you might believe that the disagreement goes "all the way down," that the interaction is probably pointless, and maybe that your interlocutor is "just a _____" (fill in the appropriate epithet). Obviously this can play out in all sorts of ways interpersonally, but in the news media, stereotyping abounds (e.g., "If you are a conservative, you must believe . . ."), and this cannot help but have an impact on the nature of interpersonal encounters.

Anyone foolish enough to interact on Facebook about political issues knows that when confronted with asynchronous friends or partial strangers, people are quick to emulate the stereotyping, aggression, and disrespect implicit in media treatments of political discourse. Expressions like *libtard* are less surprising than the freedom with which they are bandied about. These expressions are, of course, a symptom and not the disease.

As Hartmann points out, the culture wars should be seen as "a history of debates about the idea of America" (2015, 2). *E pluribus unum* is an ongoing process, not an eventual point of stasis, though a good many people engage the cultural wars as if there would be a point at which "the" American culture (however they conceive it) will dominate. Is America—and its values— "really" white, Anglo-Saxon, Protestant, heterosexual, and cisgender? Visions of America, in terms of not only identity but urban/rural, working class / bourgeois, and more, have been in dialogue, tension, and competition since the founding. The question, which Hartmann implicitly recognizes, is not how we resolve the disparate visions but the consequences of how we *manage* them—productively or destructively? In ways that become progressively more democratic, inclusive, and equalizing, or in ways that generate hierarchy, exclusion, and oppression? These ongoing debates have very real consequences; in 2016, the topic of "Black Lives Matter" versus "All Lives Matter" is bound up not only with the attempt to lay bare the roots of systemic racism but also with questions of violence and counterviolence.

What Jason Stahl's (2016) book *Right Moves* shows is a convergence of modern forms of mediated communication (including print, radio, television, and the internet), and the publics they help constitute have enabled an evolution in the concept of mass political influence that used to be called propaganda. As Michael Sproule (1996) has demonstrated, the advent of modern communication technologies and professions in the early twentieth century ushered in a wave of paranoia about the possibility of engineering or controlling public opinion that placed democratic political power in the hands of those who controlled the presses (like William Hearst and his newspapers) or those who controlled the messages (Ivy Lee and subsequent legions of public relations specialists). The moral panic inspired by the faith in a naive theory of direct media effects seems overwrought except for the underlying premise—that the quality of democracy depends on the quality of communication. Aside from the comic book scares and concerns about subliminal persuasion in the 1950s, Stahl shows that the 1960s brought a new, almost Habermasian twist on the question of propaganda. If ideas spread through public argument, then the way to make your ideas dominant, or at least in the mix, is to get your arguments out there. In his 1949 speech "The Plight of the Conservative in Public Discussion," rhetorical scholar James McBurney (1950) lamented that liberals (with whom he sided) were impoverished by a lack of public dialogue and engagement with conservatives, since in the post–Franklin Delano Roosevelt era, it was hard to find anyone to publicly challenge a monolithic liberal consensus (though that would change as Cold War rhetoric ramped up). Think tanks stepped in to to fill this need. The Brookings Institution and the American Enterprise Institute, among others, evolved to both create and disseminate arguments and argument frames that reflected a conservative worldview and challenged both traditional liberal views and emerging countercultural ideas and practices. This development is interesting from a rhetorical point of view. It backs away from the implicit authoritarianism in the propaganda mentality and seeks to work with a public sphere that is potentially civil and rational. And yet we have seen that the net effect is an escalation of hyperpartisan argument about what the "real" American is.

If America is an experiment, it is not only an experiment (just) in institutions but a rhetorical experiment in whether a country can be held together by a vision that is itself constantly in dispute and in motion (Meacham 2018). We would argue that civility names the strategies for managing the tension between challenging the status quo and preserving an ongoing community, since this tension cannot be overcome or eliminated. In a very simple way, this was the tension being negotiated in the Red Hen when Sarah Huckabee Sanders sat down to dinner. What management implies is that there will be no neat and easy answers or solutions (the wicked problem of democracy) and maybe no good guys and bad guys. Rather, we have to examine a set of rhetorical trade-offs that function as both constraints and affordances. In their role as constraints, they do not forbid certain kinds of talk in all circumstances but make some kinds difficult to justify. In their role as affordances, they enable communicative agency.

2

IMAGINING THE POLITICS OF CIVILITY

A civil society will allow the individual room to experiment, doing so most of the time from a position of mild relativism—that is, one that doubts the presence of a single set of universal rules about every aspect of behavior. . . . To say that recognition of difference is *shared* and the decision to live together is *mutual* is to note a background consensus, an agreement to differ.

—JOHN A. HALL, *THE IMPORTANCE OF BEING CIVIL*

Americans have the right, with some qualifications, to free speech, including the freedom to insult others in an uncivil manner. But is free speech enough to generate discourse fostering democratic outcomes? Certainly for democracies to thrive, citizens must be willing and able to express and exchange ideas among themselves and with their representatives in government to collaboratively weigh courses of action and potential consequences. But *meaningful* deliberation may have grown more difficult, despite our freedoms, with certain forms of legal speech serving to weaken the bonds of political and civil society. This means that freedom of speech may be necessary but not sufficient for a healthy democracy. We propose civility as a necessary component of democratic life because "strong democracies" (Barber 1984) also need citizens who are willing to listen to and respect others with viewpoints very different from their own—particularly on controversial issues. We argue that to reach a decision in meaningful discussions of information and policy choices usually requires some framework of civility. This chapter aims to explore why that is true, where commitments to civility emerged from, and what virtue civility might impart to the process of democratic deliberation. If free speech is all we have to support our deliberative procedures, then our democratic systems may be in danger—we have known this for some time, as civility has been with us as a preoccupation since the Roman Republic.

Deliberating public issues—by weighing opposing views, attempting to decide difficult questions, accepting majority decisions while honoring dissent, or looking to achieve broad consensus on values—is not a spontaneous form of behavior but requires instruction, skill, and multiple opportunities to practice. Occasionally instruction in the art of deliberation might happen in formal school settings, but it is also likely to be an implicit outcome of our social interactions anyway. In other words, we learn habits of interacting with others as we are socialized into the norms of our society or culture, something a broad range of social psychologists and communication scholars have shown. We ought to, then, look to the underlying social norms or assumptions at work, both historically and in our own moment, to better understand how we come to learn practices of deliberation. We will point to some of the more concrete practices and habits of communication that foster civility in chapters 3 and 4, but our focus here is less on the specific ones that individual agents might use for interacting in deliberative settings and more on the cultural or social scene within which deliberation takes place.

This kind of analysis requires retelling a particular intellectual history using theoretical tools from philosopher Charles Taylor, the "modern social imaginary," the deep set of assumptions about public and private life that help us explain to ourselves what it all means. Discovering how and why commitments to civility have emerged as components of thinking about democracy can help show what is at stake in civility and why our ability to engage in civil communication practices might be necessary for enriching and enlivening our present democratic experiments. The evolution of the modern social imaginary was part of what Norbert Elias (2000) called the "civilizing process" (at least for Europe, though other regions and cultures may not have been as much in need of change), and so commitments to civility, with varying force and in varying registers, have been woven into our social life for quite some time. Those commitments create a range of assumptions and implications—at times useful and at other times dangerous—that have guided our interactions with others. At the same time, historians, philosophers, sociologists, and psychologists have proposed ideals for imagining a form of social democracy in which our relationships with other citizens are the defining characteristics of good decision-making. In other words, a broad social imaginary committed to civil interactions among strangers emerged in the Western world as a consequence of the evolution of political life. Taylor argues that the social is a feature of modernity, which displaces family, tribe, race, and church in favor of nationality and community.

Modernity is itself multiple and contains multiple social imaginaries (Gaonkar 2002, 4)—economic, political, religious, and so on. We will follow Taylor's account of the increasing normative focus of social relations on equality. Unpacking the historical and theoretical features of his account will give us a renewed sense of the vitality, importance, and complexity of civility.

Social Imaginaries and the Civilizing Process

A social imaginary is relevant to public discourse because it gives a very abstract picture of how and why discourse works and how it can make a difference; it is the collection of background assumptions that make it possible for us to interpret speech in public life and relative to the actions of others. In other words, it outlines the ways in which language and other symbolic practices or systems (either formal or informal) can affect, constitute, or alter relationships between people; can manage or regulate how people interact with institutions or structures; and can form habits or cultural practices of meaning making. According to Charles Taylor, "[A social imaginary is] something much broader and deeper than the intellectual schemes people may entertain when they think about social reality in a disengaged mode. I am thinking, rather, of the ways people imagine their social existence, how they fit together with others, how things go on between them and their fellows, the expectations that are normally met, and the deeper normative notions and images that underlie these expectations" (2004, 23). Taylor identifies a set of background assumptions about a social world populated by people, ideas, discourse, choices, and the possibility of both influence and manipulation. While broad and somewhat nebulous, the social imaginary is still a useful concept because it shows that the habits or practices that we use to interact with one another are products of broad social and cultural forces. As Dilip Gaonkar notes, "The social imaginary is something more than an immediate practical understanding of how to do particular things—such as how to buy a newspaper, ride a subway, order a drink, wire money, make small talk, or submit a petition. It involves a form of understanding that has a wider grasp of our history and social existence. It is closer to Pierre Bourdieu's notion of *habitus* or what some contemporary philosophers, following Martin Heidegger and Ludwig Wittgenstein, call the *background*" (2002, 10). As communicative agents, the social imaginary reminds us that we are always already implicated within a scene of background assumptions that condition our possibilities for talk and for action. We are not taught the social imaginary as a theory or set of rules, but "the social imaginary can confer legitimacy on our common practices and pursuits and embed them in a normative scheme. Moreover, the idiom of social imaginary is distinct. It is expressed and carried in images, stories, legends, and modes of address that constitute a symbolic matrix that cannot be reduced to theoretical terms" (10). This is the background for our communication practices, and it commands our serious attention too if we are to understand why we choose to talk to one another in the manner that we do.

Taylor's conception of the "modern" social imaginary is in many ways continuous with a deliberative imaginary (the advance of the public sphere as detailed by Habermas) and with the conception of civility being advanced in this book. Historically, he argues, important changes in our understanding of our social world crystallized in the seventeenth century, about the time the Dutch philosopher Hugo Grotius developed a picture of social life that "derives the normative order underlying political society from the nature of its constitutive members. Human beings are rational, sociable agents who are meant to collaborate in peace to their mutual benefit" (2004, 3). The psychological and philosophical accuracy of Grotius's account aside, this develops into a picture of social life that places individuals and society into a particular kind of balance, where agency is possible but is turned "naturally" toward mutually beneficial relations with others. This moral order has become so ingrained for us that it operates as an assumption rather than a theory, and it has expanded in two ways, according to Taylor. First, many more people—or rather, many more kinds of people—are implicated in it. Rhetorical citizenship (who can speak and expect to be listened to) has been granted, in the United States, to more and more people as time has passed, by including women, African Americans, Catholics, Jews, and many other identities / social locations, albeit imperfectly and in ways that continue to develop. The second expansion has been in the intensity of what is demanded by these social relations: We are supposed to negotiate increasingly complex differences; the current struggle over how to talk with and about transgender and gender-fluid people is a good example. And we are expected to negotiate those complex differences with sharp and effective social skills. So the points of interaction and the topoi of conversation are expanding in degree, kind, and complexity while the number of participants in the communicative action of the social scene is also constantly expanding (in the founding era, for example, it was mainly just men of the landed gentry, all with similar educations, talking to one another). This may be one reason that meaningful deliberation has seemed to become more difficult over time. Within such circumstances, simply guaranteeing freedom of expression to all is not sufficient to create the conditions for effective deliberation.

This social order is also a moral order that, for Taylor, "goes beyond some proposed schedule of norms that ought to govern our mutual relations and/or political life" (2004, 12). A moral order has to create a picture in which it is clear *why* the norms are the right ones as well as the contexts and situations in which we can hope to realize morally right states of affairs; the moral order should contain directions for its own application. He contrasts this Grotian sense of moral order with older, more holistic pictures (which included God, the king, classes of people, and so on). In those, the individual emerges organically out of the larger system, whereas "the basic point of the new normative order is the mutual respect and mutual service of the individuals who make up society. The actual structures were meant to serve these ends and were judged instrumentally in this light" (12). The point here is that individuals and their interests and rights get equal balance in this picture, as opposed to a picture where the structure itself (classes, hierarchies, royalty, etc.) is the ultimate end rather than a tool. The new focus on individuals and their increasing equality makes possible the question "How are we supposed to treat one another?"—one that previously was difficult to formulate. In deeply hierarchical societies, proscriptions and prescriptions about role-based behavior made the politics and ethics of everyday interaction obvious. But the transition Taylor describes made such interactions gradually more difficult, and people began to worry enough about them that they wrote and read behavior manuals or etiquette books. When the social imaginary starts to become predominantly a matter of equal and mutually beneficial relationships between ever-growing numbers of different people, then questions about, and commitments to, modes of interaction become central. How should people treat one another? What forms of interaction are obligatory, and what forms are optional? How do larger social structures (with their commitments to and limitations on equality, among other things) get constituted in daily social intercourse?

The process of working through the set of problems related to behavior, etiquette, and equitable interaction began at least in the late Middle Ages; in thinking about civility historically, Norbert Elias (2000), in *The Civilizing Process*, was correct to insist on understanding civility as part of the civilizing *process*: an ongoing, evolving, transnational process. Before proceeding, however, we wish to acknowledge here that the history of civility we are offering is limited. We are leaving out a good deal, and we have chosen to focus on a particularly American version of this history because of the context it provides for later chapters. Our goal is not an authoritative account of the history of civility (and we have hardly taken up marginalized understandings of civility at all), but instead, we are using this historical account as context for our broader claims. This process dimension of civility can be hard to keep in mind. In order to create usable representations of social relations, people since the Middle Ages (as Elias shows in detail) have composed lists of "rules" or maxims that distill their understandings, though they often present these rules as timeless and universal principles of human relations. Perhaps the most famous ethical rule of this form is called the Golden Rule: treat others as you would have them treat you. This rule, some have argued, is the cornerstone of a kind of timeless and duty-based ethics. But there is nothing timeless about civility. Elias saw the civilizing process from the perspective of economic history, and we can usefully begin there.

In historicizing civility, we should understand how, even within that history, it is defined in relationship to a cluster or a family of terms, which are tangled and often in tension, with crosscutting relationships (see figure 2.1). The underlying thread tying these concepts together is the imagined transition from savage/wild to civilized, understood from ancient times as a movement from animalistic living to fully human—and thus social—modes of life.

We need to point out that this notion of "civilizing" has both figurative and literal dimensions (and of course is not unique to European history). As a fundamental form of "othering," it can serve as a way of creating ("better") norms in contrast to the imaginary others; this can operate externally (in reference to another country) or internally (dividing one's own group into better and worse, more and less sophistication). Europeans, in their colonial aggression, justified their horrific treatment of indigenous people on the basis that they were bringing them "civilization" and Christianity; even after they became "Americans," these justifications served as excuses for continued (and continuing) mistreatment of Native American populations. We do not wish to excuse, ignore, or underplay the role that "civilization" was made to play in these events. But we do want to highlight the irony that the "bringers" of civilization were so often savages in their treatment of others; the "civilizing process" we will emphasize is what we called in the introduction a liberal one, one that among other things diminishes cruelty and increases relative equality among people.

Some accounts of the process cast rhetoric as the catalyzing agent, in that the difference between humans and animals is the use of language. A telling

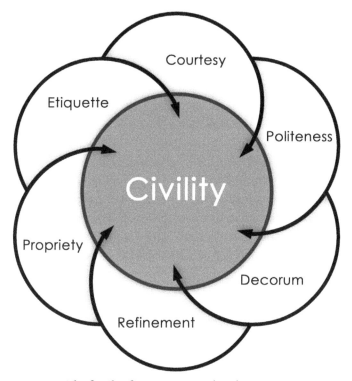

FIGURE 2.1 The family of concepts around civility

condensation of this picture is found in Cicero (1949, 1.2.2), *De inventione*, recounting how people discovered they could use language (rhetoric, eloquence) to govern themselves as opposed to force:

> For if we wish to consider the origin of this thing we call eloquence . . . we shall find that it arose from most honorable causes and continued on its way for the best of reasons. For there was a time when men wandered at large in the fields, like animals, and lived on wild fare; they did nothing by the guidance of reason, but relied chiefly on physical strength; there was as yet no ordered system of religious worship nor of social duties . . . no one had learned the advantages of an equitable code of law. And so, through their ignorance and error, blind and unreasoning passion satisfied itself by misuse of bodily strength, which is a very dangerous servant. At this juncture [some man] . . . became aware of the power latent in men . . . [and] through reason and . . . transformed them into a kind and gentle folk.[1]

Cicero paints here a picture of humans existing in a bestial state where might makes right. In such circumstances, individuals are at the mercy of both physically strong people and their own appetites. Teresa Bejan notes, "Scholastic translations of Aristotle, in which the difference between *barbaroi*—non-Greeks who babbled nonsensically and lived as wild men or slaves—and *polites*, or Greeks whose *logos* or reasoned speech suited them for political life, was rendered in Latin as the distinction between *barbari* and *cives*, that is, barbarians who lived a wild and nomadic existence and citizens who lived in settled communities under law (*civitates*)" (2017, 42). That wildness is reduced in the process of coming together into workable social arrangements, typified for the Romans in the image of the city: the *civis* is the citizen of the union or commonwealth (*civitas*) of people who possess the property of *civilis*, or civility. They have been gentled or tamed and are no longer wild and savage. In this sense, Elias claims that civility, at any given point in history, amounts to "imagining who we are" and hence what it means to be both human and social. Civility operates on both a dimension of the whole community (we Good People versus those Savage Others) and by defining people and cultures within the larger community. Hence the tensions between cosmopolitan and restricted conceptions of community (and thus civility) are always being (re)negotiated. We can see this process currently in various changes in manners, including the revolution in treating women as social equals to men in the last forty years or the accelerating acceptance of gay marriage into the norms of marriage. For other groups, we have yet to see exactly how they will become part of "us." For example, we are just beginning to learn how to interact respectfully with transgender people and those with fluid sexualities; it is unclear whether a version of our current (English) pronoun system will do the job or whether a more complex one will evolve.[2] But in any case, the struggle over pronouns is a clear indication of the way in which discourse works in light of a set of background assumptions to create a kind of social imaginary *and* how that process is not a natural one but an achievement of agents acting within that imaginary.

According to Elias, the civilizing process (his history begins in the Middle Ages) has several effects. It moves from the age of feudalism, in which kings exerted absolute control over territories, to the period of consolidated kingdoms, where kings and princes had domesticated the warring knights and princes into their courts. Similarly, Taylor describes "the transformation of the noble class from semi-independent warrior chieftains, often with extensive followings, who in theory owed allegiance to the king but in practice were quite capable of using their coercive power for all sorts of ends unsanctioned by royal power, to a nobility of servants of the Crown/nation who might often serve in a military capacity but were no longer capable of acting independently in this capacity" (2004, 33). In the early modern era, violence as an ever-present and unpredictable part of daily life began to recede into the background, since violence was increasingly monopolized by the state; at many levels of society, people no longer had to worry about being killed by an acquaintance or stranger in a fit of temper. Since might no longer made right as a part of daily interaction, new ideas emerged about how to relate to one another in ways that do not presume that they might be suddenly killed: "The new gentleman required not principally a training in arms, but a humanistic education that would enable him to become a civil governor. It was necessary to cultivate the capacities of self-presentation, rhetoric, persuasion, winning friendships, looking formidable, accommodating and pleasing" (35). Teresa Bejan notes that these styles were somewhat nationalistic:

> Elias credited Erasmus himself, in his *De Civilitate Morum Puerilium* [On the civil manners of children] (1530), for inventing the genre and reimagining classical *civilitas* to reflect new standards of "civilized" behavior and bodily propriety. Yet as numerous scholars have pointed out, Castiglione's account of *"la sapienza civile"* [the civil wisdom] in the *Book of the Courtier* predated Erasmus' manual by two years and subsequently ignited an international trend. These countless handbooks of *converzatione civile* were culturally particular and often contradictory. While the Italian *civilità* and *vivere civile* emphasized urban living, republican citizenship, and civic virtue, the French discourse of *courtoisie, civilité*, and *politesse* was more status conscious, courtly and aristocratic. . . . Civil worship, like divine, dealt paradigmatically with the performance of respect between unequals, usually from inferiors to superiors, including children to fathers and subjects to their sovereign. The proper performance of these forms was a sign of gentility, as opposed to the "rudeness" of "clownishness" of the rustic and vulgar. (2017, 42)

European and American societies were not (and are not) suffused with equality; modes of address and interaction evolved to allow people to show deference and condescension through language. People also learned to regulate affect—whether anger, lust, greed, or gluttony—in appropriate ways. The control of affect is part and parcel of how norms evolve through self-regulation and the regulation of others' behaviors by reference to norms, where *courtoisie* (courtliness or courtesy) designates the way people behave at court: "Civility was not something you attained at a certain stage in history and then relaxed into, which is the way we tend to think about civilization. . . . This change didn't come without resistance. Young nobles were capable of outbursts of mayhem, carnivals teetered on the thin line between mock and real violence, brigands were rife, vagabonds could be dangerous, city riots and peasant uprisings, provoked by unbearable conditions of life, were recurrent. Civility had to be to some degree a fighting creed" (Taylor 2004, 37). As civility became an entrenched mode of life, people had less freedom of behavior (to eat like an animal, beat other people up, be selfish) but needed to show increasing tolerance, which gradually created the freedom to have different beliefs, forms of worship, customs, identities, and so on. (Wendy Brown [2008] has critiqued this tradition for being too laissez-faire about "tolerance" for morally odious cultural practices, from racism to genital mutilation.)

The most important implication of Elias's account of the civilizing process is that there is a *functional* character to norms of politeness and civility. Civility has to address a basic paradox of modern sociality: How can we maximize our freedom to be different from one another and still manage to get along well enough to live and flourish together? Note that civility does not *assume* some kind of substantive consensus but rather is a framework to *manage* difference (Whittenberger-Keith 1992). This is an absolutely crucial point; civility's morals represent not the victory of a specific morality but rather the means to manage differences. Keith Thomas notes that "good manners, in the sense of considerate behavior and tactful accommodation to the feelings of others, continues to be widely regarded as serving an essential purpose. They facilitate communication between human beings. . . . Civility in the past has tended to be a conservative force, respecting social hierarchy and outlawing the expression of radical sentiments because they endanger social harmony. But courtesy and consideration need not imply abject deference. Civility is as important in an egalitarian society as in a hierarchical one" (2018, 252–53). It is just as important to take account of the affordances of civility and politeness as it is to weigh their constraints.

Of course, to be functional, civility would need to be flexible, depending on the situation and the need, and the temptation to reify or inappropriately stabilize it (*the* rules of civility) is constantly present. But as functional norms, civility and politeness do not assume we all agree with one another (or somehow require agreement) but instead begin from the assumed fact that we do not and need not have the same religion, tastes in food or music, politics, and so on. This emphasis on accommodating difference can be obscured by the fact that a significant stream of thinking about etiquette (though not as much about civility) is devoted to allowing people to show off their class status and privilege; this more superficial etiquette consists of not only being able to afford fish knives for your table but also knowing how to use them.

One can see in this version of the civilizing process continuity with the underlying dynamic of progress (the journey from eating with one's hands to using forks is a journey of successive refinements), but it also highlights a tension, since officially (in the United States, at least), the class structures that various etiquettes were meant to support do not (should not?) exist. In *Common Courtesy: In Which Miss Manners Solves the Problem That Baffled Mr. Jefferson*, Judith Martin argues that Jefferson worried about what an American etiquette would be like, since manners imported from Europe seemed to be almost entirely concerned with signaling status and class membership. While some etiquette manuals in the United States persist in worrying about how to correctly set a *service à la russe*, many are focused on how to manage social situations. This need to manage new or difficult situations flowed, says Taylor, from the understanding of equality implicit in the modern social imaginary: "Without engendering the full-scale contemporary notion of equality, the understanding of membership in society was broadened and detached from specific gentry or noble features, even while keeping the language of gentility. The extended understanding of civility, now called 'politeness,' remained directed to the goal of producing harmony and easing social relations, but now it had to hold together people from different classes and operate in a number of new venues, including coffeehouses, theaters and gardens" (Taylor 2004, 47). As Martin points out, in the American context, this has meant that in principle, people can expect to be treated (quoting her correspondents) "just as good as anybody else" (1999, 54). This version of the imaginary may explain why an overwhelming majority of Americans think they are "middle class." In principle, money does not make the difference between whether one is treated civilly (even if it sometimes does in practice), and economic class—as well as race, gender, and sexuality disparities of U.S. life—stands in strong and often uncomfortable tension with the general equality of treatment and opportunity we expect. One could argue that part of the reason for the relatively swift reversal of U.S. public opinion about LGBTQ marriage is that once LGBTQ Americans gained a measure of public (and private) acceptance, it became increasingly difficult to maintain a stance that they should not have the same rights as everyone else; the parallels with the civil rights movement are inescapable, and the presumption toward equality flows from the social imaginary, no matter how far we may fall short in practice.

Before we move on to analyze how this broad social trajectory affects forms of political life, we want to be clear about both the assumptions implied by the civilizing process and the consequences for communication habits. Taylor and Elias both show that the advent of modernity assumes individual agents, learning how best to live alongside an ever-expanding cast of others without recourse to violence and without resorting to coarse linguistic correlates of violent behavior. One of the central problems of modern life requires calibrating one's virtuous behavior, a matter of finding and practicing the habits most conducive to peaceful forms of coexistence with others (what some might call "social harmony"), since practices of fostering social harmony are necessary for forging a collective sense of "who we are." All of us will probably recognize or remember moments in which we were taught the virtue of being polite to others or getting along well with others, along with a lesson about the connection of this behavior to the social imaginary—that is, why it makes it possible for us to get along. Consequently, we must privilege specific kinds of social skills that promote harmony; these skills were, and still are, considered characteristics of a civilized person. But note that the value we place on such skills issues from a scene of uncertainty (produced by the transition to modernity) marked by diversity and the commitment to equality. What, then, is the connection between these important social skills and politics or forms of governance?

The Social Imaginary as Deliberative

How do these practices of equality connect to the political practices of democracy? Ancient Athens, that paragon of the democratic imagination and wellspring of much of what we think democracy means still today, did not face the problems or complexities Elias and Taylor point to. Instead, to be an Athenian citizen meant to be one of roughly thirty thousand native-born, land-owning men over thirty years old. Thus one of the "advantages" of Athenian democracy was its lack of size, scale, and diversity. Nonetheless, the social scene clearly and critically influenced political deliberation. Athenian citizens were divided into ten "tribes," and the practices of decision-making that governed the Athenian city-state were organized around participation in the tribes. The agora of Athens served as the central social meeting place, marketplace, and site of civic buildings for these citizens. As such, it served as the crucible in which political debates and alliances were forged. In fact, we do not know which came first: the agora as an open, social space or public speaking as the constitutive component of deliberation. We do know that the art of rhetoric was exercised within the public space of the agora in an effort to express political power and guide decision-making. The agora was a sloping, tree-shaded area surrounded by groupings of civic and commercial buildings. The philosophers and their students often sat in one of the stoas in small groups and practiced dialogue, a form of argumentation designed to discover the truth. Eventually, the Athenians needed a specific space for meetings of the ever-growing assembly, and so one was constructed outside of the agora, on the hill called the Pnyx (not for reasons of topography but apparently to separate the hierarchical form of oratory from the more socially level agora). Hence the agora was a key catalyst for the development of Athenian democracy.

The agora's design reflected two goals: intervisibility and interaudibility. Inward-facing seating, which made intervisibility possible, was a consistent architectural feature of the buildings designed for the public meetings of any of the levels of the demos; privacy was neither provided nor wanted in these spaces. The Athenian state commissioned and designed these buildings, demonstrating the value of intervisibility to their understanding of democratic processes. Organizing space this way was not necessarily an Athenian invention (other city-states in archaic and classical Greece employed similar architectural styles), but it highlighted the extent to which democratic Athens valued egalitarian interaction. In the Roman era, as republican forms of government were replaced with oligarchies, the original open-space agoras of a number of Greek cities were filled in with very large temples (buildings not well suited to mutually facing public meetings). In other words, "there is a historical association between democracy in Athens and architecture promoting 'intervisibility' and 'interaudibility'" (Ober 2007, 209). These spaces further allowed for the development of common civic knowledge, to be shared by all members of the polis.

We have paused here to dwell briefly on the Athenian example because it displays the connection between democracy and our social imaginary, since a democracy must promote, facilitate, and enact egalitarian social relationships as a fundamental component of developing deliberative decision-making practices. Think for a moment of the effort that the Athenians expended to make such social relationships possible: the innumerable public buildings, formal committees, and meetings. Yet the relationships fostered through these efforts seem, from our perspective, straightforward, since they were between members of the same economic class, same gender, and same ethnicity, which should make us realize why civility carries such a burden in a modern democratic society marked by increasing levels of pluralism and participation. Put more succinctly, the problem that Elias and Taylor outline was only barely present for Athenian democrats (they still had aristocrats, workers, and slaves, as well as a very limited diversity), yet they dedicated enormous resources to building structures, institutions, procedures, and rules that fostered egalitarian social relationships anyway, because they knew those relationships were the cornerstone of an authentically democratic state.

This context helps us understand the career of John Dewey as a political theorist: it was in large part an attempt to theorize the relationship between democratic principles and institutions and social relationships. As indicated in the introduction, Dewey championed participatory democracy, arguing that democracy was a way of life and not just a system of governmental institutions. In many ways, his political theory filled out a particular social imaginary that could animate the political institutions of governance by addressing directly the tensions and contradictions that complicate discursive and political equality. Dewey first became committed to these arguments while living in Chicago at the end of the nineteenth century: he worked closely with Jane Addams at Hull House, witnessed the violence of the Pullman Strike, and directly engaged with the ever-growing immigrant communities that settled in the city. These early experiences sparked an ongoing social and political activism and provided the impetus for his later works in political theory, most notably *The Public and Its Problems*. Dewey wanted a greater number of citizens incorporated into the life-affirming processes of participatory democracy, and he believed that doing so would bring out the best in both those citizens and the process of public decision-making. He was, along with Jane Addams, central to the articulation of the meaning of a social democracy, where the quality of our relationships with others determines the extent to which we could consider ourselves as participants in a democratic culture (Danisch 2015).

At the core of the concept of a social democracy lies communication. Just as the Athenians saw rhetoric as the indispensable instrument for managing political life and making decisions, so Dewey saw communication as the means of binding a diverse citizenry together for the purposes of collaboration and cooperation; for Dewey, we are constituted as citizens in the quality of our communication with one another. While rhetoric in the Athenian context typically took the shape of public speeches in the court or the assembly,

Dewey understood communication more broadly: "Men live in community by virtue of the things which they have in common; and communication is the way in which they come to possess things in common. . . . Communication is a process of sharing experience till it becomes common possession. It modifies the disposition of both parties that partake in it" (1944, 4). Dewey is struggling here to articulate the constitutive role of communication in the modern social imaginary. In many ways, Dewey is building on the work of George Herbert Mead, Chicago social psychologist and author of *Mind, Self, and Society*. Implied here is the idea that social life—participation in the social imaginary—generates both common ideas and symbols as well as individual personal development. Communication, while not always thematized as such, plays a role in how we get along within the social imaginary and how we improve ourselves by virtue of our participation.

In *The Public and Its Problems*, Dewey lays out a normative vision for the version of the modern social imaginary that would improve American democracy. This book was a response to Walter Lippmann, who had written both *Public Opinion* and *The Phantom Public* a few years earlier. Lippmann argued that average citizens were poorly equipped to live up to the ideal of deliberating citizenship in an increasingly technological and complex world that would not reward or support their participation. Lippmann thus endorsed a democracy augmented by groups of experts who possessed the methods of analysis and the data to inform good decision-making. Dewey, in contrast, approached the problem in a different register; he advocated democracy as a social ideal embodied in his idea of the "great community." If one views democracy as a set of social relationships constituting the social structures that we inhabit, then the key components of any democracy are discussion, consultation, persuasion, and debate. In other words, he outlined a social imaginary that puts communication practices in a critical position for all citizens. Democracy as public discussion is the best way to deal with conflicts of interest and the general conditions of pluralism in places like Chicago: "The method of democracy—insofar as it is that of organized intelligence—is to bring these conflicts out into the open where their special claims can be discussed and judged in the light of more inclusive interests than are represented by either of them separately" (Dewey 2008, 547). Forms of associated living, in fact, undergird state or government institutions, because those institutions emerge as responses to, or consequences of, those forms of association. (This represents an instance of the inversion between institutions and individuals that Taylor describes.) Interaction and association between free and equal agents came first, and the state came after as a consequence.

Dewey defines the public in the following way (and we could also call this an element of the social imaginary): the public is "all of those who are affected by the indirect consequences of transactions to such an extent that it is deemed necessary to have those consequences systematically cared for" (245–46). Loosely organizing all those people is an ongoing, plural, complex process that unfolds in light of the social imaginary.

Dewey argues in *The Public and Its Problems* that when the public is organized into a state, it acts through representatives and officers of the state, but the public also needs to organize itself into a community that can hold officials accountable and make the discussion of problems more robust. For Dewey, the institutional machinery of the state needed to be supplemented by an active community full of associated citizens, which is an achievement rather than a requirement of communication practices: "The perfecting of the means and ways of communication of meanings so that genuinely shared interest in the consequences of interdependent activities may inform desire and effort and thereby direct action" (1927, 174). In the concluding passages of *The Public and Its Problems*, Dewey argues that the development of the great community, the community of the imagination, is also the development of the local community: "In its deepest and richest sense a community must always remain a matter of face-to-face intercourse." In other words, places matter for community life because interpersonal relationships matter; associations and attachments are "bred in tranquil stability; they are nourished in constant relationships" (140). This is why the Athenians built the infrastructure of the agora in the way that they did—and the consilience of their vision of democracy with Dewey's strikes us as fundamental. Only in face-to-face associations could citizens of a community engage in dialogue about pressing problems. But the challenge Dewey faced, the one that was made so clear at Jane Addams's Hull House, is the diversity and number of interpersonal associations that needed to be maintained and fostered within a large democracy like the United States; scale is the enemy of the very relations that constitute the condition for democracy itself.

Dewey makes a normative argument about the conditions for the development of the great community, an argument that we ought to heed. He is not terribly specific about the form of the communication practices that meet these normative conditions, but we will argue later in this book that civility is a necessary dimension of them. He is clear about what they need to accomplish, allowing people to inquire and deliberate as well as reach revised decisions. The most famous passages from *The Public and Its Problems* are normative endorsements of a kind of vision of a deliberative social imaginary: "The essential need . . . is the improvement of the methods and conditions of debate, discussion, and persuasion. That is *the* problem of the public. We have asserted that this improvement depends on freeing and perfecting the process of inquiry" (1927, 208). In what follows, we will argue that the public also depends on developing civil dispositions in public communication. Dewey does make a vague assertion about the significance of communication for building the great community by claiming that it relies on "perfecting the means and ways of communication of meanings" without telling us how we ought to perfect those means and ways. But effectively Dewey seeks the methods of communication that would allow individuals in a democracy to participate in decision-making and activate the interconnectedness of the community to which they belong. In light of this argument, we can appreciate Dewey's most famous proclamation from *The Public and Its Problems*: "It [democracy] will have its consummation when free social inquiry is indissolubly wedded to the art of full and moving communication" (184). Whatever the "art of full and moving communication" is supposed to be, it must directly address the problems in the modern social imaginary that emerge in the story that both Taylor and Elias tell us. That means that the art of full and moving communication must be a matter of civility if relationships of equality are to be preserved and strengthened through deliberative participation. Dewey's added emphasis on the process of "social inquiry" must also deeply rely on the practice of strong civility for the purposes of generating new knowledge. Inquiry points to the importance of collaboration between strangers with different values and different knowledge bases into important issues. That collaboration cannot just happen without modes of communication that would allow for the process of inquiry to unfold as it must in order to gain new insights and produce new knowledge.

Across the United States, people explored both the concerns and the remedy Dewey proposed in the early part of the twentieth century. Problems of scale and diversity seemed devastating to democracy. Many people in the 1920s, for example, were highly concerned about the twin effects of immigration and the shift of the United States from a majority rural country (in 1880) to a majority urban country (by 1920); both of those anxieties are still visible. Public forums were in part intended to address the perceived permanent loss of the affordances of small-town democracy (Keith 2007). While the original town meeting was probably never close to what nostalgia made it, the homogenous assembly of neighbors as the ideal for local democracy remained as important to Americans as their image of the Athenian assembly remained the lodestar for state and national government. Yet the realities of scale meant that intimate local government was beyond the reach of most Americans. The advocates of the forum movement proposed a variety of practices to embody the values and meanings they feared were slipping away. First, they created spaces ("forums") and gave them a function ("having a forum"); some forums were privatized (i.e., you had to join an organization to attend), but eventually, most were public. Using the term *forum* (corresponding loosely to the Athenian agora, both being public spaces) had the effect of signaling that these spaces were sites for public discussion and discourse but also not directly part of a government institution. The forum/agora allowed classical citizens to find out about and discuss the issues of the day in a dialogic, interactive space. The modern forums meant to re-create this ability in an intentional manner. People would overcome the diverse and estranged character of urban life by attending forums in which they would discursively engage one another.

But what would the nature of this engagement be? It could not be making laws or other decisions, since those institutions already existed. They settled on a notion of adult education, specifically civic education, and forum attendees would learn two kinds of things. First, they would indeed learn about the issues of the day from experts. Forum leaders were recruited from academia and the remnants of the chautauqua speaking circuit of traveling orators and entertainers who attempted (with varying degrees of success) to translate complex current issues for people with a variety of educational backgrounds; recall that it was not until the 1950s that a majority of U.S. eighteen-year-olds graduated from high school each year. Second, attendees would learn *how* they should talk to one another, specifically that they should be discussing rather than merely arguing or debating. "Discussion" was the attempt to marry Dewey's ideas about democracy as constituted by interpersonal relations into a teachable set of techniques that rapidly became normative. In the event, it really did not matter that the forums, which ranged from local programs to a network of federally sponsored ones, were not perfectly diverse and did not involve much easy, improvisational interchange. What mattered is that they were animated by the democratic social imaginary.

We have tried in this section to describe the importance of Taylor's "modern social imaginary" to understanding democracy. The Athenians understood the importance of social relationships for decision-making but did not face the same challenges as modern large-scale democracies. John Dewey returned us to the same considerations that drove the creation of the agora, but he did so without access to the same physical spaces. The forum movement tried to imagine and build such spaces and even thought seriously about the communication practices necessary for functioning in them. In each case, we get a normative picture of what would be necessary for a social imaginary to form associations between strangers for the purposes of building a kind of social democracy. Danielle Allen (2006) makes this point at the end of *Talking to Strangers* when she describes democracy as containing a kind of obligation to build trust and friendships with others that you do not know and might not agree with. These same challenges helped construct the discourse around civility and help us see the normative value of civil communication practices. But forms of association, inclusion, and relationship building contain a multitude of challenges, and analyses of civility reveal just how complex building a deliberative imaginary can be.

The Problem with Civility in the Social Imaginary

Civility, in spirit if not name, has recently been mobilized for deliberative culture by Robert Ivie (2002, 2005) and Robert Asen (2017, 2018; Asen and Brouwer 2001), whose theories seek to preserve the possibility of deliberation while acknowledging its complexity, contentiousness, and rowdiness. The difficulty for a positive account of civility, no matter how nuanced, is that civility must perpetuate certain exclusions (something or somebody has to turn out to be uncivil) or it is not doing its job. Perhaps Dewey never saw this point clearly; many of the things proscribed by civility are ones that in general we would not miss because they still generate exclusions. Which exclusions can we accept and which are actually virtuous? Responding to someone, in public or private discussion, with name-calling, slurs, and so on will not enhance the possibility of productive argument. An example of people trying to functionally self-regulate on the fly will illustrate this point. In the midst of proposed budget cuts in 2015 to the University of Wisconsin System, a Facebook page laid out the case for their enforcement of civil behavior:

> Reposting: Please remember to keep the dialogue in the comments civil. Any comment found that threatens and/or attacks people will be deleted.
>   Evidence-based arguments and personal stories are welcome. Tensions are high and we understand the frustration and the anger that

comes with all that's been proposed, but instead of using that anger to devolve into name calling, let's use that energy to organize and find constructive ways to fight these proposed policies.

And, as a good friend pointed out, talking about Walker's college record or not having a degree is counterproductive. It feeds into the narrative that educators are elitists, it's divisive, and it detracts from our focus. Personal attacks on Governor Walker help him and hurt us.

The goal of this Page and of the website is to salvage our awesome education system from K to post-grad and to reach out to any who have benefitted from these institutions—including those with whom we may disagree on other political issues. This Page is open to any political persuasion if you support the UW and the notion of public education. (Save the Wisconsin Idea 2015)

Their case, interestingly, is more tactical or functional than moral: "Stay focused and let's not alienate the people we are trying to productively engage." As we saw in the case of abolition in the last chapter, the weight of the competing obligations to critique and to muster allies is decided by the specifics of the case.

But here is the rub on things excluded (what we called "the line" in the previous chapter): What if the very thing that almost everyone agrees is over the line shades into the actual subject of the argument? Suppose you want, like Steven Salaita, to criticize Israel, but your opponents respond that this criticism is intrinsically anti-Semitic and *therefore* intrinsically uncivil and over the line. Or if "intrinsic" is too strong, they genuinely believe there is always a bit of anti-Semitism in it, and they want to highlight that and call it out. So arguments about policies get reinterpreted as anti-Semitic pro-nouncements, and right-thinking people pile on with condemnation, and when the dust settles—well, the dust never settles. Now you are in a bind, since it becomes hard to get a hearing with well-meaning people if they buy into the idea that critics of Israeli policies can be dismissed as anti-Semitic. Analytically, of course, these are separable, but in the heat of public engage-ment, the toxic character of accusations of anti-Semitism (or racism, sexism, and similarly for other cases) may result in criticisms of Israel not seeming to get a fair hearing, which in turn could explain Salaita's frustration and ver-bal escalation. Dewey does not anticipate these issues in his call for the great community (he never contemplates disagreements that cross the line), and thus we can start to see some of the complexity of forming social relation-ships with those who advance positions that may or may not be beyond the

bounds. Civil communication relies on distinctions between the appropriate and the inappropriate and in so doing attempts to produce an equitable
social order with a community marked by solidarity. How hard would it be
to produce such solidarity without communication practices that marked off
borders or limits for what can or cannot be said?

Civility needs to have things that are over the line or out of bounds, but
in limited cases, this requirement turns from a feature into a bug. Whether
this would justify (to switch metaphors) throwing the baby out with the
bathwater is less clear. In a *New Yorker* comment on the Salaita affair, Hua
Hsu concludes, "The problem with civility is the presumption that we were
ever civil in the first place. This is why calls for genteel discourse from on
high always feel like deeply nostalgic fantasies offered in bad faith. There
should be nothing controversial about everyday kindness; civility as a kind
of individual moral compass should remain a virtue. But civility as a type of
discourse—as a high road that nobody ever actually walks—is the opposite. It
is bullshit" (2014). Given the actual history, this represents a shallow understanding of civility as a tradition. Particularly in the Trump era, it should
be clear that the last half century has had many points at which things *were*
pretty civil—politicians and public figures had attempted the high road, and
their failures stood out as exceptions. The weakness of this all-too-common
objection is that it takes a highly controversial example—is there *anything*
that can be said about the Israel-Palestinian conflicts that does not outrage
somebody?—and notices that a lot of incivility is involved and then concludes that civility is useless or pointless. This is somewhat like saying that
if we have controversy about the controversial cases, then norms have no
useful application.

In addition, does Hsu's distinction between kindness and "a type of discourse" have any bite? In a precise sense, no (kindness is discursive, among
other things), though in a larger sense, Hsu is right to criticize nostalgic
appeals to civility, as if appealing to a golden age when people were always
nice to one another (superficial renderings of Athenian democracy sometimes paint it as a bunch of equals being reasonable, which, as even Pericles
allowed, was true only in the Athenian imagination). Yet so what? We would
not dismiss any discussion of ethics or other normative frameworks because
there was never a time when everyone was perfectly ethical. But we can also
understand that Hsu may be rejecting the deliberative social imaginary in
toto (an alternative considered in the next section).

Suppose that, in the last fifty years, there has been a real coarsening of public discourse (which is possible, even knowing that in the nineteenth century,

American discourse could be very crude and even violent). What has been gained, and what has been lost? Taboos have been cast aside. Some we will not miss at all; we can now talk about the beauty of same-sex love, the intelligence and the competence of women, and the nastiness of racism in ways that would have been difficult one hundred years ago. We also have culture wars (Hartmann 2015), increasing polarization (Brownstein 2008), Gamergate (*Guardian* 2015), and doxxing (S.-W. 2014), among other things. Why uncritically accept the latter as a consequence of the former? Because that is how things "really are"? People engage one another all the time, in various contexts, in ways they think are civil. Our question in this context is not "Can there possibly be a standard to which the University of Illinois can hold Salaita?" (This is a legal question, and the answer is probably no.) The right question is "Is there a standard to which Steven Salaita could hold himself, subject to discussion and query by others?" The answer ought to be yes, and a previous quotation shows that Salaita understands this while making a conscious choice for incivility. Is, however, there a perspective from which civility is not just "bullshit" but actively harmful to the process of social change? We will try in the next section to outline a broad alternative to a deliberative imaginary, which we will call a *critical imaginary*.

The Critical Imaginary

As a social space, the deliberative imaginary embodies the spirit of collaboration and coordination between or among conflicting, plural agents, a space in which social harmony and political friendship, in the midst of deep differences, are possible and desirable components of public decision-making. This problem is deeply built into the history of civility, as Bejan (2017) notes, "While supporters stress civic associations, critics take their cue from Norbert Elias and Sigmund Freud in order to highlight the dark side of stability. A synonym for civilization, as in Samuel Johnson's definition of 1755: 'freedom from barbarity; the state of being civilized,' civility would seem to be irredeemably imbricated with colonialism and Empire. Against this backdrop of the displacement and oppression of the 'savage' by the 'civilized' in the conquest and colonization of the New, and then the Known world, appeals to stability today take on a decidedly more ominous cast" (9). In addition to structural inequity, politics is also a matter of "us versus them," and resentments between competing classes, collectives, or groups can ground critical rhetorical practices of conflict. These conflicts conjure and reinforce disagreements between competing interests. A variety of perspectives have endorsed the utility of conflict for social change, and the rhetorical practices that support discursive conflict are often imagined as central components of progressive political achievements (justifiably so, in some cases). Karl Marx is perhaps the most famous and enduring proponent of intrinsic conflict as a driver of change; he offers rhetorical scholars and political theorists a way of identifying, critiquing, and resisting ideological power that can be quite effective when deployed in some political circumstances. The ways in which we use discourse to identify, resist, and critique power are central considerations in what we will call, by way of contrast, the "critical imaginary." In other words, the kinds of linguistic moves one makes and the ways of enacting one's agency within the critical imaginary differ in kind from those in the deliberative imaginary, being oriented toward different results and practices of citizenship. Our goal, however, is not to make evaluative judgments about which set of moves is better or more virtuous but instead to track some of what is entailed by these different moves, and at the core of these differences lies a debate about civility and incivility. On the one hand, civility can be read as acquiescent to structures of power or distorted ideology. From that perspective, incivility is virtuous due to its character as a resistance to the status quo. On the other hand, incivility can polarize situations, make deliberative compromise or collaboration effectively impossible, and can escalate conflicts without resolving them.

To be productive, critique and discursive conflict—argumentation— require instruction, skill, and multiple opportunities to practice. We might learn how to engage in this kind of critique in formal school settings, but we also learn how to engage others in argumentative ways through everyday social interactions and hence actively engage underlying social norms and assumptions. Oppressive norms and assumptions (and their often exclusionary and oppressive character) form the center of the critical imaginary. We will have to do some unpacking to understand how—and why—we as citizens might want to deliberately and rhetorically construct "us/them" binaries through forms of incivility. (We will more concretely analyze the rhetorical practices of incivility in chapter 4.) In this section, our concern is with the underlying social scene within which we might think uncivil, critical interactions *ought* to take place. Just as we did in the first part of the chapter, this kind of analysis requires the retelling of a particular intellectual history to discover how and why incivility has emerged as a virtue in democratic life. This will allow us to weigh claims to civility against claims to incivility in a form of comparative rhetorical criticism in which we can understand what is at stake in the different kinds of social imaginaries that support these different kinds of communication practices.

Let us consider the role of rhetoric in social change. Suppose that you were saying things so politically radical and threatening that you felt others were refusing to hear you at all. Others might reject you by claiming that you are "irrational," "crazy," "rude," "un-American," and so on. If your views are sufficiently radical, then you would need to alter the discourse just to engage others. At different points in U.S. history, many groups have found themselves unable to be heard. Rather than accommodating, you could also decide to just opt out of the whole project of civil discourse entirely. The functional question of "the line" was explored extensively by rhetoricians in the late 1960s and early 1970s. In "The Diatribe: Last Resort for Protest," Theodore Windt shows not only that there are situations in which this makes sense but also that such behavior is part of the rhetorical tradition, not alien to it. In protests over the Vietnam War, said Windt, "The question of obscenities weighed almost as heavily on some sympathetic minds as did the fact that protesters insisted on the absolute righteousness of their cause" (1972, 2). Following the lead of Noam Chomsky, protesters (in particular, some affiliated with the Youth International Party, or "Yippies") said they would not debate because there was nothing to debate; the Vietnam War was as wrong as the Holocaust or the Soviet invasion of Hungary, and debating implied there were two sides. Surprisingly, the converse of this move (creating an artificial debate) is central to those who would challenge mainstream science, whether about vaccination or evolution or climate change (Campbell and Meyer 2003; Ceccarelli 2011).

The means of refusing debate were intentionally not civil; Windt quotes a writer from an underground newspaper who claims the following as a just riposte of the protesters to their critics: "What difference can there be between shoving liberty up the ass of Vietnam and giving America love in the same way? When you are up against the wall the gun may loom larger than the man" (1972, 1). The idea that a willingness to engage has already conceded too much is extremely powerful; used freely, it would lead quickly away from any rhetorical citizenship and a discursively engaged public sphere, and rhetorical scholars in the 1960s worried about a slippery slope away from the whole rhetorical tradition. But is engagement really a slippery slope?

Windt traces the problem and the solution back to Diogenes and the Cynics. Diogenes had little patience for conformity, since "to live by men's conventions is to embrace the death of person[hood]; to defy society is to embrace life" (1972, 4). The Cynics deliberately rejected the standards of civilized

Greek life, and their eccentriciy "symbolically reinforced the commitment to a different way of living, even as it repudiated the conventional way in which men live." But how would they repudiate it rhetorically? By refusing persuasion in traditional ways and instead employing the *diatribe*, a speech or secular sermon that aimed, by haranguing the audience, to wear them down and rub them the wrong way (*diatribe* comes from a verb meaning "rubbing"), making an audience question convention without actually engaging convention: "The diatribe is to conventional speeches what Alice's adventures in Wonderland are to conventional life. Logic is inverted; assumptions are reversed; the unexpected is not unusual. . . . To reflect the *ethos* of society is to reflect civic corruption. Many must be cleansed of unclean expectations and thoughts. . . . The diatribe, then, is moral dramaturgy intended to assault sensibilities, turn thought upside-down, to turn social mores inside-out" (Windt 1972, 6). Windt documents how vigorously war protestors had reinvented this genre without realizing it. Predictably, as rebellion and dissent became commodified modes of cultural expression and consumption (Frank 1997), the rhetorical dimensions of cynicism enjoyed a resurgence. They were (and are) satisfying tactics; the pleasure of being a nonconformist is easily won and resonates with the American love of the underdog and the outcast. But even this tactic circles back inevitably to central questions in the deliberative imaginary: Whom *should* you talk to? In the antiwar movement, once protestors had raised their fists or middle fingers to "The Man," they had to negotiate a multitude of differences about the theory and practice of ending the war and addressing the (indigenous and international) injustices that attended it. If everybody refused to talk to anyone who disagreed with them, then the antiwar movement would itself fall apart from the inevitable disagreements within it; moral purity can be the enemy of cooperation and community. So those who opt out of one system of civility tend to find themselves inside another one, or sometimes the same one, just in a different register (Polletta 2002). This movement accompanies, though, the general construction of an inside and an outside, or a border between ways of seeing the world. The critique leveled by the diatribe reinforces a distinction by rejecting a whole way of being as not worthy of direct discursive engagement.

Margaret Renkl (2018) argues that if we want large-scale social change on racial issues, white people need to talk to their racist friends and relatives. Her argument is that those conversations should not start with accusations of racism, however, but proceed from common premises about fairness and tolerance and willingness to engage arguments. She points out a rather obvious rhetorical truth: "O.K., they're definitely all racists. But here is the thing: They do not believe they are. And the problem with writing off people who do not recognize this country's pervasive and enduring culture of white supremacy, much less the ways in which they themselves benefit from it, is simple: Being called a racist almost never causes a racist to wake up. Being called a racist almost never causes a racist to say, 'Oh, wow, you're right.'" She clearly is not talking about the rhetorical situation of walking up to a neo-Nazi or KKK member at a rally and beginning a polite conversation. She is talking about approaching people you know, people you know to be generally good-hearted people, and engaging them about racism without throwing up a barrier by way of a word that is such a slur, it shuts off dialogue. This proposal was met with fury and derision in some quarters for addressing a deep system of racism with "polite conversation." Damon Young (2018), for example, rejects her distinction between everyday racism, a kind of willful ignorance, and "vicious white supremacists," whom he thinks actually *are* the people you meet every day, not just the people marching as neo-Nazis in Charlottesville. Obviously, Young and Renkl are proceeding from different life experiences, but we are not willing to concede the uselessness of having "that" conversation over and over again; "that conversation" can be both civil/deliberative and civil/critical in an effort to generate some degree of change.

By the second decade of the twenty-first century, rather than being disruptive and courageous, the cliché of blaming the uptight status quo for repressing one's radical truths is everywhere (and that holds whether your truths are libertarian, conservative, liberal, or progressive). Since the 1960s, many in the public sphere have derided civility as a stance of cowardice and capitulation. Social media allowed the swift dispersion (in the wake of the Salaita affair) of apothegms like "Disruption is civil, patriarchy is uncivil," and "Fuck civility." Laurel Thatcher Ulrich's line "Well-behaved women seldom make history" has become a popular bumper-sticker and T-shirt slogan; it might mean "Don't worry if people don't think you're well behaved," or it might mean "You'd better not be well behaved if you want to make history" and maybe "Profanity is an essential tool in disrupting patriarchy" (Eltahawy 2019). A version of *parrhesia* (which originally meant speaking truth to power when that speech put oneself at personal risk) has become the default stance of many in the public sphere, even when all they risk is snarky commentary (Gehrke 2013). When no specific institutional or political power to be resisted exists, sometimes "civility" is mobilized as a stand-in for the institutional force of the status quo. In the critical imaginary, the forces of power and privilege work endlessly to silence the brave voices that would unmask their injustice. This is a powerful and compelling picture and, like the deliberative imaginary, has an appealing amount of truth to it. How did this imaginary evolve?

The story is complex, but a plausible starting point for a thumbnail sketch might be the waves of political change that convulsed Europe after the French Revolution. Both the power of popular change and its excess, demonstrated in the Terror following the French Revolution, made a great impression on culture and theory. The Revolutions of 1848 reinforced this impression, as did the evolution of a Gilded Age capitalist system that seemed to emulate the worst outcomes of the old monarchical system while possessing a wildly different structure. Marx acutely diagnoses the flaws and contradictions in capitalism, and given Taylor's account of the evolution of the modern social imaginary, with its increasing equality and mobility, it seems logical that at some point, workers would rebel. But they do not. Why not? The critical imaginary has evolved in tandem with answering that question (setting aside the problems of Leninism and Stalinism). The basic picture is something like this: the overt use of force and the political story that held monarchies in place have been displaced by the structural conditions of modern life, some economic, some discursive. These structures are not simply continuous or coexisting with an utterly inequitable and unjust status quo; they (in the critical imaginary) actually constitute it.

We can distinguish here between things like regressive tax laws (which directly make the rich richer) and the larger question of why nonrich people continue electing legislators who do not change such laws, the crucial question in a free democracy. In the deliberative imaginary, the answer to that question might be a failure of participation or some way in which deliberation is lacking. In the critical imaginary, such explanations seem naive, since all deliberation is already tainted by the economic and discursive structures that hold the status quo in place. In the critical imaginary, as Richard Rorty (1998) notes, democracy is the problem rather than the solution. Rorty rightly notices that the socialist-Deweyan version of democracy he likes looks a bit absurd in the critical imaginary. Yet in a different sense, he is wrong, because at least *some* version of democracy is key to the critical imaginary, even if it cannot be realized until the economic and ideological changes are complete. What does social change look like in the critical imaginary? What is the point of critique if not to open minds to the truth of an oppressive system in hopes that they will work to change it? In *Prophets of Extremity*, Allan Megill (1987) shows how Nietzsche, Heidegger, Foucault, and Derrida, in various ways, theorize "unmasking," stripping away the appearance of reason, rationality, comity, and tradition to reveal the will to power that resides in us all. Some version of "It's just power all the way down" is a truism of the critical imaginary. The massive expansion of mediated communication—from movies to broadcast to electronic communication—has not improved the situation, from the perspective of the critical imaginary. Georg Lukács theorized the role of literature and culture in the maintenance of a capitalist system, but the philosophers of the Frankfurt school really began to fill out our understanding of the critical imaginary by theorizing how capitalism must form a totalizing system that somehow makes it impossible to envision or deliberate alternatives to itself. Max Horkheimer, Theodor Adorno, and Herbert Marcuse all set the pattern of theorizing at deeper and deeper levels the ways in which economic and cultural structures of oppression are structurally "written into" our lives, with respect to what we do, consume, enjoy, and so on.

The critical imaginary, while often associated with leftists, also seems natural to those in the U.S. conservative tradition. Barry Goldwater's statement that "extremism in defense of liberty is no vice" is surely intelligible only by conservatives understanding themselves in light of the critical imaginary. In fact, the culture wars are only intelligible against the horizon of the critical imaginary (Hunter 1992). The existence of the culture wars dating to the 1980s (or even the 1960s) is proof that this imaginary is quite consistent with conservative politics, as commentators try to probe even more deeply to see how liberal ideologies are expressed or reinforced through virtually every facet of culture (David Brooks has made a career out of snarky conservative cultural analysis in this vein, such as *Bobos in Paradise*). Allen Bloom's *Closing of the American Mind*, while written from a conservative stance, clearly appeals to the critical imaginary in its prosecution of American culture and education for rejecting, subtly, the values from classical philosophy that are responsible for Civilization As We Know It. Conservative foundations, pundits, and theorists find the critical imaginary just as hospitable as liberal or leftist ones; William F. Buckley, Albert Nock, and Richard Weaver are just of few conservative thinkers for whom the critical imaginary makes the slipping away of modern life intelligible. The historiography is different, but the gist is the same: the conservative critique since the 1960s has been that the liberal ideas, institutionalized in New Deal policies and programs, have made it impossible for people to see how thoroughly we have fallen from our ideals and see the ideas that must be critiqued.

The extent to which the critical imaginary can be inhabited by both the left and the right signals just how diverse this imaginary is on the ground.

We could offer a fuller typology of actors within the critical imaginary and how those various actors use critique to assert moral superiority and resist specific forms of power. The critical imaginary does not just grow out of Marxism and does not oppose the development of democracy. In fact, the critical imaginary, in all its diversity, grows out of the civic republican tradition as well. Jeremy Engels (2015) maps a version of this story in *The Politics of Resentment*. In all the varieties of the critical imaginary, society is assumed to be divided into the few and the many, the mass and the elite, the rich and the poor. This is just as true in democratic Athens and Republican Rome. Josiah Ober (1989), in *Mass and Elite*, shows just how deeply a critical imaginary existed alongside the deliberative imaginary in Athens that we sketched earlier. The distinction between the few and the many must be managed within democratic states, and that process of management becomes a core consideration for any democracy. What we learn from approaches to the critical imaginary is that oppression is an ever-present danger that citizens must constantly be vigilant against. In this vision of democracy, which Engels defends in *The Politics of Resentment*, resentment is a core democratic emotion that plays out in a variety of ways in the social imaginary. One can easily see resentments manifest themselves in Facebook arguments over who is in and who is out. Engels shows how Cicero, who wanted to tame democratic resentment, praised *otium* (quiet) as a powerful rhetorical emotion. A great statesman, he says, has the power to quiet a resentful crowd, and once democratic citizens recognize this, they begin to fear attempts to quiet their emotions. For many, in the critical imaginary, civility may seem like just such an attempt. But this is the same critique of civility we see in all versions of the critical imaginary—a statesman who quiets the crowd does so to preserve the status quo, and civility is a practice relied upon for that quiet.

We want to further acknowledge here that at several points, the critical imaginary overlaps with the deliberative imaginary. In other words, the two imaginaries are not always opposed. Many scholars advocate critique and also hope to promote deliberation (Wilson 2016; Hartnett 2010), and it can certainly be useful to combine these imaginaries in our efforts to produce social change. In one version of the alignment between the two imaginaries, Marx thought a kind of socialist democracy was the political system that would succeed the prior ones with their contradictions, and the corruptions of Marx's thought by Lenin, Stalin, and others into bloody authoritarianism stands as a challenge to this account. So the critical imaginary indeed posits a democratic, deliberative future as an ideal, unrealized goal to be achieved in an unspecified future; the attractiveness of that imaginary as a goal is what might justify disregarding it in the here and now. Civility is appropriate to a stage that comes after our present one, in which we seem to find that every step to a just society (nonracist, nonsexist, nonhomophobic, etc.) uncovers new forms of power operating to maintain the status quo. Perhaps the best illustration of the critical imaginary's vision of a possible deliberative future comes in the closing lines of Guy Debord's classic *Society of the Spectacle*. After spending the bulk of the book making a sharp diagnosis of how the visual and verbal fads and fashions of contemporary life disguise its inequities, Debord says,

> Self-emancipation in our time is emancipation from the material bases of an inverted truth. This "historic mission to establish truth in the world" can be carried out neither by the isolated individual nor by atomized and manipulated masses, but—only and always—by that class which is able to effect the dissolution of all classes, subjecting all power to the disalienating form of a realized democracy to councils in which practical theory exercises control over itself and surveys its own action. It cannot be carried out, in other words, until individuals are "directly bound to universal history"; until dialogue has taken up arms to impose its own conditions upon the world. ([1967] 1994, 221)

Once the unmasking is complete, then society, in relative maturity, will be ready to deliberate its future in a genuinely democratic way. Civil, rational deliberation may be waiting at the end of ideological critique, but critique must come first.

What does it look like to condemn civility from within the critical imaginary? The classic case for rhetoricians is an article by Dana Cloud and Nina Lozano-Reich that responds to calls by feminist rhetoricians for an "invitational" rhetoric, one that supplements the traditional masculinist rhetorics based on conflict (Ong 1981) with a feminist alternative, which they claim both circles back to traditions of civility and is, at least sometimes, effective at creating change and solving problems (Lozano-Reich and Cloud 2009). Lozano-Reich and Cloud's piece represents a prototypical example of how the critical imaginary responds to those who make arguments seemingly consistent only with the deliberative imaginary, since that is clearly the frame from which invitational rhetoric proceeds. According to Lozano-Reich and Cloud, there are only relations of power, and since the deliberative imaginary assumes that participants can interact as relative equals, it fails to grasp reality and therefore perpetuates the oppressions of the status quo. To the extent that power can be impacted by discourse, they quote Frederick Douglass: "Power concedes nothing without a demand. It never has and it never will" (223). (Demands, however, can be perfectly civil, while threats are not; it is unclear how a "demand" makes a difference to those with the power to ignore it.) Lozano-Reich and Cloud find those who would introduce civility or "invitational rhetoric" into public discourse somewhere between naive and malicious. They allow that "in some contexts, such as the pedagogical situation and in discussions among material equals, invitation is appropriate; in others, however, this approach can be disabling to the oppressed" (222). They also introduce critiques of civility made by others. "Historically, dominant groups have repeatedly enacted civilizing strategies to effectively silence and punish marginalized groups (e.g., labor; women and people of color; the poor; and lesbian, gay, bisexual, transgender [LGBT] people). Indeed, nineteenth-century notions of propriety and civility were used as cultural ideals to place legal, political, and physical restrictions on women thereby relegating women to the private sphere" (223). This second claim is well established, though within Taylor's historicized version of the deliberative imaginary, it has a different meaning. Rather than licensing an inference from "this happened" to "this always/necessarily happens," we might take it, in the deliberative imaginary, as a stage in an evolving system that has moved toward inclusiveness and equality, which indeed it has; though the evolution is still incomplete and imperfect, hot-button issues about words for LGBTQ and African Americans show that exclusion and casual cruelty are no longer considered civil. Cloud and Lozano-Reich's critiques of the invitational account are mainly that it is a naive and misguided approach to the *realrhetorik* that could possibly respond to the "systemic obstacles to individual agency in the context of oppression and inequality" (222). The focus of civility tends to be on the accumulation of individual interactions; they claim, with some justice, that systemic oppression prefigures each interaction. So they are tempted to say things like this: "To refuse persuasion is to refuse participation in real-world encounters marked by material and antagonistic interests. . . . While voting is indeed civil, radical social change has not occurred in voting booths, but results, instead, from democratic grassroots tactics" (221). Counterexamples to the former claim are not hard to find, but such claims are better understood, as indeed are many pieties about the goodness of civility from the deliberative imaginary, as windows into a way of understanding the world rather than generally true claims about history.

For the critical imaginary, the problem with advocates for civility is that they just do not understand how the world *really* works, and that failure of understanding, per se, makes things worse; in fact, maybe one should assume that actually incivility is what works. In a 2018 article on "uncivil tactics" in the *Atlantic*, historian Julian Zelizer looks at the apparent excesses of the antiwar movement and concludes, "The tactics that they used were far less 'civil' than anything that President Trump's opponents have done thus far, yet that lack of civility was also integral to their effectiveness. Without dramatic tactics, they would not have gained as much attention." We can wonder exactly what the evidence here is for effectiveness. Many different media and voices were converging on the Vietnam War, and it would be hard to say the exact level of impact these tactics had compared to (among other things) print and television press coverage, discussions in churches, and Martin Luther King Jr.'s public condemnation of the war. This is not to say the student protests did not resonate through the deliberative system of the United States—they were clearly having an effect—but it might be easy in retrospect to overestimate their role in change. This may also be a moment where the combination of critique and deliberation, or the working in tandem of the two imaginaries, was a catalyst for effective change.

Just as critiques of civility might be brushed off as uncivil, questions about the critical imaginary may be brushed off as uncritical. Michael Hogan and Dave Tell (2006) have some interesting thoughts about these parallels. While taking Patricia Roberts-Miller to task about the idea of demagoguery, they point out that her attempts to define demagogic rhetoric (which most would grant is intrinsically uncivil) have too much political content and end up just rejecting a politics she does not like more than condemning a set of rhetorical tactics that might be used by any political perspective. They gently suggest that those on the side of social justice actually do make most of the same "demagogic" moves, just with a different justification; one could understand debates about political correctness as being about how internal leftist critiques get disciplined. In the end, of course, pretenses to scholarly neutrality will receive a critical drubbing, because in the critical imaginary, no defensible stance of neutrality is possible. In the deliberative imaginary, partisan people can enact a kind of constrained neutrality, believing they will benefit if others behave similarly. All this is to say that just as some notion of civility is foundational to the deliberative imaginary, in the critical imaginary, civility will inevitably represent a dynamic oppositional form to whatever the demands of social justice appear to be.

Agency and Its Implications

Our goal in tracing these two competing imaginaries is to highlight the ways in which our forms of communicative agency are always already embedded within a social and material scene. Attention to the deliberative and critical imaginaries reveals the ways in which discursively constructed conditions constrain the ways in which individuals, groups, texts, or artifacts act within systems of power. The constitutive relation between a social imaginary and agency ensures that the mode or means of action within systems of power will interact with larger social systems through which individual and collective bodies experience differing degrees of power and privilege. The individual agent in this context is implicated through the discursive construction of identity and subsequent embodied performances of such identity that sustain, maintain, re-create, or revise such constructions within systems of power and privilege. Both imaginaries reveal useful and important insights into the social and material structures of our moment. Both also provide and recommend sets of practices for negotiating meaning and power in those imaginaries. Civil forms of communicative agency may seem weak and useless from one imaginary or necessary and desirable from another. We ought to be aware of how and when we are being positioned, as communicative agents, by the unfolding scene within which we are operating. Good rhetorical citizens have this level of awareness and use it to make critical decisions about modes of interactions with the strangers that we, out of necessity, must interact with in our democratic systems. We may even be able to imagine a form of critical deliberation that combines communication practices from both imaginaries to leverage a broad range of possible strategies for creating social and political change. In the next two chapters, we will turn more fully to the range of communication practices available to us, but all those practices are always already implicated within the social imaginaries that we inhabit.

As a description of our current democratic culture, the deliberative and critical imaginaries overlap, intersect, clash, and sometimes complement one another. Conceptualizing our moment without either can seem, in some ways, fantastical or impossible. This is why we argue at the end of this book for "finding a balance." To persistently inhabit and live by the practices within one or the other of these two imaginaries might forestall or make more difficult political and social change and might threaten the social fabric of our democracy. In some ways, the hard work of democratic life is in finding the balance between our competing impulses to change the minds of those with whom we disagree (and to change the conditions within which we find our-selves) and to form connections and relationships with the varied others that make up our social and cultural worlds. This work requires responding to disagreements or conflicts about values, facts, morals, and truths. If the bal-ance tips too far in one direction or the other, we risk violence either way (the violence that attends the preservation of unfair conditions or the violence of rebellion against those who hold opposing views). These competing imagi-naries remind us why democracy is so fragile.

3

CIVILITY IN THE DISCURSIVE PUBLIC SPHERE

The civility of manners is a set of conventions that allows us, according to the philosopher Cheshire Calhoun, to "communicate basic moral attitudes of respect, tolerance and considerateness." Its counterpart runs deeper: It's the matrix of principles and obligations that undergirds our social pact.

We must behave as though everyone shares a common stake in the flourishing of the civic whole.

—Z. Z. PACKER, "WHEN IS 'CIVILITY' A DUTY AND WHEN IS IT A TRAP?"

Civility, Argumentation, and Publics

Civility matters most when the quality of public discourse matters. According to Joseph de Maistre's famous saying, "Every nation has the government it deserves," and the same may be said of its public discourse and of the rhetorical citizens who engage it. Ideally, public discourse serves (at least in part) as a means for public deliberation, the substance of a deliberative democracy. Having examined the (Deweyan) understanding public deliberation as a scaled-up face-to-face discussion or parliamentary debate, we wish to move to a more sophisticated view of it as a complex discursive ecology, with massively diverse inputs, multiple channels and media, and complex and incomplete feedback loops. From interpersonal conversations, to consumption of televised news, to posts and discussions on social media, to thriving print media, to organized public deliberations and more, we have a system of deliberation massively more complex than the town meetings, coffeehouses, and pamphlets of two hundred years ago. The temptation, which must be continually resisted, is to reduce public deliberation to a single form, genre, type of interaction, or relationship; any one of these looks, of course, is insufficient to bear the weight of what we expect from deliberation as a total political practice. A reductive account makes it all too easy to miss the strengths and weaknesses of public deliberation as well as the diverse ways civility supports it. Public discourse needs to be *systemically* or *ecologically* deliberative, and the system is complex.

Public discourse may serve many functions, entertainment not the least of them; not all discourse needs to display fitness for deliberation, though we assume civility, in general, is one mark of deliberative discourse. But the regulation of the discourse ecology by civility is subtle and diffuse; the norms of civility are ethical rather than legal; civic norms are less about what is permitted or forbidden than developing and adhering to generalizations about which discursive choices, on balance, holistically enhance public discourse and deliberation. Norms are in play with one another, but that does not make them arbitrary. Honesty has a kind of transcendental status in human communication in the sense that the presumption of honesty is a condition for the possibility of communication at all (this is part of Paul Grice's point, as we will see later). We do not assume people have to be honest, even most of the time, but we understand deception as a deviance from the norm. As a thought experiment, we can ask what human interaction would be like if we presumed that people were lying and that being honest was a deviation from that norm. One wonders how we would get anything done. In the case of civility and its presumption, historically, groups of people have treated others as presumptively not deserving civility (enslaved people, often servants, those conquered in war). But the point of Taylor's story about the evolution of the modern social imaginary is that the number of such groups has shrunk and continues to shrink as we discover, collectively, new dimensions of inclusiveness.

Given the interlocking layers of purpose and outcome, no simple account of norms and discourse will work. Civility might be the framework, but that does not foreclose the possibility that, at the right time, uncivil choices may be just as good, or better, than civil ones for promoting overall goals of deliberation. Just as honesty is a good norm in general, specific occasions may require some deception in service of better communication—but not every instance can be that occasion. Equally, just as some kinds of deception are normative ("Your hair looks great!"), not every instance can be that occasion. Deliberation does not require understanding civility as a fixed set of rules or as prescriptions of mere politeness, governing only the genteel tone of discursive contributions and engagements. Tone matters, surely, and we do not want to discard it. Hence we can stipulate a distinction between weak and strong civility. As we saw in chapter 1, weak civility is "mere" or superficial politeness, accomplished by following rules of decorum and being "nice" or avoiding giving offense. These rules work well for daily interaction, and many "rules of etiquette" grow out of them. Their usefulness has been long recognized in the European context: Norbert Elias quotes a relevant couplet from a sixteenth-century behavior manual: "Non dicas verbum / Cuiquam quod ei sit acerbum" (Say no word / which might be harsh; 2000, 86). Weak civility corresponds roughly to the grammar and usage sense of classical rhetoric's *to prepon*, or propriety, saying the "right" thing, which had linguistic and contextual dimensions. Proper syntax and decorous uses of words make one's language refined (for the author of the *Ad Herennium*, a popular Roman rhetoric textbook, a *solecism* was poor grammar and a *barbarism* the misuse of a single word), but refinement by itself is insufficient to produce civil language. Many languages have only a contrast between "mere" politeness and being civilized at all: *Höflichkeit* (courtliness, courtesy) versus *zivilisiert* in German, *høflighed* versus *civiliseret* in Danish; these do not capture a stronger sense of civility as used in "civil disobedience" and "civil rights" (though modern Greek and French have that contrast, ευγένεια [well bred] versus πολιτισμένος [of the civil sphere / political], and *le droit civil* or *la loi civile*).

Strong civility aims to capture a more robust functional sense of how relationship norms sustain and enable (and maybe constitute) a deliberative discourse. Strong civility amounts to communication choices that simultaneously exemplify tolerance and ethical judgment, giving others respect while both acknowledging and engaging with real and perceived differences of belief, values, practice, and more. As Michael Gerson points out, "Democracy is not merely a set of procedures. It has a moral structure. The values we celebrate or stigmatize eventually influence the character of our people and polity. Democracy does not insist on perfect virtue from its leaders. But we can articulate a set of values that lends authority to power: empathy, honesty, integrity, and self-restraint" (2018). Strong civility allows for confrontation that nonetheless does not deny the other's humanity; it goes beyond defending a right (which is a sort of formality) and engages suspect positions and points of view. It is closer in spirit to the quotation from the Roman playwright Terence, "Homo sum; humani nihil a me alienum puto" (I am a person; I consider nothing human strange to me), in engaging, to an extent, rather than shunning those with morally objectionable practices and views. Strong civility is the stance that in principle one can engage any point of view, if only to dispute or reject it.

A valuable concept here might be the principle of charity, popularized by Donald Davidson.[1] Davidson is concerned about the impossibility of communication due to radically differing conceptual schemes—what if people used such different vocabularies that they could not make sense of one another's actions and descriptions of the world? Davidson, unlike Willard V. O. Quine, thinks that conceptual schemes cannot differ too radically, since we actually do communicate (if imperfectly) across language, philosophy, and culture; he calls this "radical interpretation." Davidson proposes that communication in general is predicated on our willingness to be "charitable," which is to interpret one another's speech in a way that maximizes what is true and rational in it. We do this all the time in ordinary situations; language is a flexible, multilayered instrument, prone to ambiguity and multiple meanings; in Davidson's view, the task of interpreting a foreign language is not different in kind from interpreting people in our own linguistic community. So we are continually employing charity (and closely related principles like Grice's cooperative principle or "steelmanning," which is the attempt to give the best version of someone's argument, the opposite of a "straw man"; Cook 2009) as part of normal communication. However, we can identify easy cases and hard cases, where there is (so to speak) a greater distance in language, culture, and belief. In hard cases, we have to consciously work to exert charity, and that, we claim, is a mark of civility. One may call it "cutting people slack" or "giving the benefit of the doubt," but we do it when we are trying to get along and to make a relationship work over the long haul. Charity does not entail eventual agreement or convergence of belief and action (and is perfectly compatible with doubt and critical appraisal) but rather shifts from escalating to a kind of understanding that might develop into appreciation of difference. For example, one of the reasons the Romans were initially hostile to early Christians was that they took the Mass literally and thought it was a cannibalistic ritual (Wagemakers 2010). Finding out that it was a symbolic practice put it in the realm of understandable and acceptable religious practices, paving the way for more tolerance.

Ezra Klein (2018) recently pointed to an uncharitable habit that attends social media, calling it "context collapse." When texts circulate through a discursive network, they leave behind their original context; of course, as Derrida (1988) famously proved, crossing to new contexts is an inevitable consequence of the nature of writing. Yet even if utterances are functional in many contexts, we can recognize a kind of rhetorical charity where we hold people accountable to them relative to their original contexts (and even if "original" is a messy concept, it can still be useful). Klein is worried about things said/written as part of a joking or ironic context that then get imported into another context as completely serious. He points to the hashtag #killall-men, which circulated for a while as an ironic counterpoint to #notallmen (as in "not all men are harassers or rapists"). Without doubting it being in poor taste, it would be uncharitable to think the participants actually wanted to kill all men; they do not but were exploring a stance that would give feminists a chance to push back generically against a certain kind of excuse making. We could debate whether the original hashtag was in poor taste or unhelpful without pretending we cannot see the difference between internet banter and actual threats of violence.

Strong Civility and Argument

Strong civility is thus much more than simply saying "Let them speak" (sometimes while fully intending to ignore whatever they say), since it implies authentic engagement. Hence strong civility requires a sort of discipline, a set of intentional dispositions toward those with whom you disagree. Some characteristics of this discipline are outlined by David Zarefsky (2014) in his discussion of a "culture" of argument:

1. Importance of the audience
2. Uncertainty
3. Conviction amid uncertainty
4. Justification rather than proof
5. Cooperative argumentation
6. Risk taking

Zarefsky also identifies tensions in an argument culture, places where the demands of situation and exigence pull simultaneously in two directions, requiring us to find a balance between them:

Contingency and commitment. Speaking/advocating from one's commitments but being open to the impact of changing evidence, argument, and circumstances.

Partisanship and restraint. Arguing for one's side but observing limits (ambiguous and shifting as they may be).

Personal conviction and sensitivity to audience. Believing passionately that one is right while acknowledging that the audience also believes they are right.

Reasonableness and subjectivity. Using the resources of identity and experience but letting them be subject to reasonable critique.

Decision and nonclosure. Making decisions while being aware that those
decisions are seldom completely final or unambiguous, but they are
still worth making.

The tensions Zarefsky outlines belie the stereotype of civility as a set of rules
for being nice; civility looks instead like a set of tools for maintaining relationships in the face of conflict and conflicting ways and styles of resolving these tensions. In particular, these tensions and civility are stretched to
the breaking point if you believe you are in possession of the Truth about
something. Why be tolerant, restrained, or reasonable with those who are
simply wrong? We may feel justified in being disrespectful to flat-earthers,
but do "gold bugs" (people who believe that healthy monetary policy requires
the return to the gold standard) deserve this treatment? Beyond science
and policy (which may not be special cases), we will always confront disagreement in moral judgments. For those who do not believe in absolute
moral truths, consensus serves as a handy stand-in; since virtually everyone
agrees that slavery and racial oppression are wrong, then espousing such
views is uncivil. Yet coarser versions of this attitude are familiar enough:
epistemic might makes moral right, and tolerance is a virtue only for losers.
On similar grounds (and perhaps somewhat unfairly), Richard Rorty (1994)
declares all appeals to religion to be "conversation stoppers" because, he
alleges, all religions presume to have a Truth that makes conversation with
outsiders pointless.

Rorty may be overstating the case with respect to religion, but the communicative challenge of epistemic certainty is real (Gibb 1961). Within
a certain picture of how knowledge works, we have no reason to engage
other views once we actually know something. And while the notion of
"settled science" (i.e., issues that cannot be reopened without an enormous
amount of effort and evidence) is an extremely useful one, it is probably
not a good model for public discourse about wicked problems. If we really
think the best solutions to wicked problems are democratic (combining
deliberation about values, relative to stakeholders, with facts), that "we"
need to work together to find solutions to, then Rorty is right—we cannot
completely preempt conversation. The problem is pragmatic in both the
ordinary and the philosophical sense. We cannot have a conversation if
the very topic is beyond question; in any conversation, some things have to

be taken for granted. So we have to navigate between Scylla of absolutism and Charybdis of chaotic, incoherent commitments.

Strong civility implies an epistemic stance that is corrigible and foundationless, attentive to the fragile and transitory nature of our knowledge claims in many domains; it encompasses a kind of epistemic humility. The right image may be "Neurath's boat," a metaphor developed by Viennese philosopher Otto Neurath, with its emphasis on both the holistic and the nonfoundational character of belief and knowledge of change over time: "We are like sailors who on the open sea must reconstruct their ship but are never able to start afresh from the bottom" because the boat would sink. Neurath gives the following formulation in his 1944 *Foundations of the Social Sciences*:

> Imagine sailors, who, far out at sea, transform the shape of their clumsy vessel from a more circular to a more fishlike one. They make use of some drifting timber, besides the timber of the old structure, to modify the skeleton and the hull of their vessel. But they cannot put the ship in dock in order to start from scratch. During their work they stay on the old structure and deal with heavy gales and thundering waves. In transforming their ship they take care that dangerous leakages do not occur. A new ship grows out of the old one, step by step—and while they are still building, the sailors may already be thinking of a new structure, and they will not always agree with one another. The whole business will go on in a way that we cannot even anticipate today. That is our fate. (quoted in Law 2014, 118)

While over time we may replace every plank of the boat, enough of the boat has to be in place, at any moment, to keep it afloat in the meantime. We might eventually change our minds about everything—but not everything all at once. Notice also that this is a social project—we sink or swim together.

Practitioners of weak civility need not have such qualms about maintaining a stance of certainty; they can be polite about disagreements, avoiding anything difficult or ugly, all the while thinking, "Of course that person is completely wrong/misguided/irrational/deluded." Sometimes that solution works well at the interpersonal level. We should choose our moments and do not need to have knockdown fights over everything, in every interaction, and we should maintain friendships with those we disagree with. However, at the level of public discourse, weak civility cannot be scaled up and so cannot become more than mere tolerance (which has its own value). The argument culture outlined by Zarefsky can only advance our understanding because it is capable of fostering real, difficult engagements, and to engage, arguers must, to some extent, bracket the Truth of their positions. But not always. True, we may have an ethical duty not to be tolerant of bad arguments in cases where we know harm will follow inaction; cases like the sick children of Christian Scientists and anti-vaxxers challenge universal claims about tolerance.

We need to then consider the structure of argumentation, as composed of both reasoning and relationships, in this setting. Roughly, the answer lies in the difference between product and process (O'Keefe 1992). Arguments are (more or less) discrete units that can be assessed or critiqued independently of their producers and their audiences. Argumentation is the process of reason giving and reason critiquing that goes on between two or more people. So while one can say, "There is an argument circulating about why our relations with Russia should be strengthened, and here's why it's a bad argument," that "argument" is separate from any dialogue about it. The argument, so abstracted, might be intrinsically uncivil (because, say, it appeals to the *Protocols of the Elders of Zion*, a thoroughly discredited anti-Semitic tract) or might be neutral in that regard.

Argumentation, on the other hand, is the creation and maintenance of relationships in which the reciprocal engagement of reasons is meaningful. These relationships can be interpersonal or constituted by stranger relationality (i.e., stranger sociality), the kind of relationship you have with people you do not actually know—for example, people who consume the same media you do, cheer for the same sports, live in your town, voted in the same election—even if you have never met them and never will (Warner 2002). The argumentation dimension is important because, even in weak forms (e.g., explanation), it forms the substance of the deliberative dimension of public discourse. It matters less that "my arguments will persuade you" than "we create the possibility that these reasons can be influential, within and beyond the interaction." That possibility requires a particular kind of relationship, a relationship that has a mutual commitment to its own possibility.

To illustrate the problem of stretching and breaking relationships, consider Godwin's law, which states that as an online discussion grows larger, the probability of someone making an unjustified comparison involving Nazis or Hitler approaches certainty; corollary forms of it include a version that states that once the Nazis or Hitler have been inserted into a discussion, the discussion is functionally over (i.e., no progress can be made and the thread should be closed), and whoever did this is declared the loser. The early days of online discussion and debate brought a flood of people unaccustomed to navigating strong disagreement in a zero-history relationship, and the online setting seems to strip away face-to-face restraints. Lacking appropriate skills to maintain one's position *and* maintain the relationship with a diffuse audience, the discourse degenerated quickly. Calling someone a Nazi effectively ends an interaction, since, if true, such a person is beyond the pale of civility and probably beyond the reach of reason and, if false, is so unfair that it breaks the relationship. Perhaps some people are, in fact, equivalent to Nazis, and arguing with them may be pointless. But *in general*, labeling those with whom you disagree as Nazis will not help the process of argumentation. The problem is not just a matter of being momentarily offended but more of whether the relationship can sustain disagreement—is there enough trust and respect that engagement could lead to evolving beliefs on each side?

What is the nature of a relationship that sustains argument? Clearly arguers cannot simply hate, despise, or have complete contempt for the other person and his or her views, for then there would be no point in engaging, whether we argue to convince, persuade, explore, or test ideas and positions. Here are some candidates for the dimensions of this relationship:

> *Confirmation (vs. disconfirmation).* Participants can confirm or reject the legitimacy of others in an interaction; many expressions of politeness and civility confirm, despite disagreement or conflict, that someone else has the right to be fully engaged. Disconfirmation can be accomplished through sarcasm, mockery, changing the subject, personal attacks, questioning motives or credentials, and many other ways.
>
> *Respect (vs. disrespect).* A relationship of mutual respect is one where each party grants the other a basic degree of dignity, honesty, and competence. Disrespecting another person makes it difficult to sustain the presumptions of argument, since literally everything would be in question.
>
> *Recognition (vs. mis- or nonrecognition).* People bring themselves and their histories to an argumentative engagement, and they have a reasonable expectation that their interlocutors will acknowledge their identities as well as the knowledge, perspectives, and moral commitments that come with them (Taylor 1994).
>
> *Cooperation.* H. P. Grice introduced the "cooperative principle," the idea that communicative interactions are cooperative; he meant this less

as a norm of behavior and more as a norm of interpretative practice. Other things being equal, participants should interpret the contributions of others as contributing to the apparent ongoing activity (even if that activity is shifting and under negotiation).

Most people understand more or less how to maintain a relationship and in fact know the maintenance strategies by the name of "being civil." Popular commentary often refers to this relationship management as "tone," though usually as a criticism (if people object to being disrespected, they are accused of "tone policing"). Sneering, smirking, sarcasm, belittling, using stereotypes, and the rest corrode or destroy it, as well as most things that one would call poor sportsmanship (Rorty's "conversation stoppers"). What makes these relationship attributes so important? No matter how conflictual, argumentation is fundamentally also a cooperative activity between people. Part of the cooperation is logical (as Douglas Ehninger [1958] points out, you have to be talking about the same issue, working with similar ideas of evidence and reasoning, etc.), but part is relational: someone has to be willing and able to engage you. That engagement may be hostile and adversarial, it may be friendly and constructive, but engagement is required if argumentation is to take place. Interaction makes deep disagreement possible. Jim McKenzie (1985), in "No Logic Before Friday," argues that even on the strictest standards of logic, while proofs might be possible in isolation, logical *argument* is fundamentally interpersonal; Robinson Crusoe might do mathematical proofs but could not have an argument until Friday showed up. The key element is that the possibility of inconsistency arises in dialogue, and logic (in his view) is supposed to detect and remedy that flaw.

From Interlocutor to Audience to Public

So far we are imagining the basic situation or context of argument as interpersonal, something like a conversation or a debate. But that is only one form that interaction can take. We do not want to reprise here the history of mass communication and how "audiences" are created by various forms of technology; instead, since they all exist simultaneously now, we want to consider the analytical transitions among them. Returning to Daniel O'Keefe's distinction between argument as product and argument as process helps clarify where the relationship dimension lies. You can "make an argument" (a product) by just uttering or writing it, but that is not the same as an activity involving engagement, the process of argument. Moving from face-to-face conversation to the public sphere requires shifting one's communication to mediated modalities—basically to print or digital communication. In the immediacy of face-to-face communication, so prized by Plato, the feeling of deep connection (which happens in heated as well as pleasant arguments) falls victim to the asynchronous character of most mediated communication. If this communication is public, asynchronicity is equivalent to circulation; the relatively tight patterns of face-to-face interaction, laden with continuous feedback, evaporate. Like a message in a bottle, to write a letter to the editor is to lose, in that sense, control of one's message—to communicate with strangers to whom one is still socially connected.[2]

In the public sphere, this distinction between synchronous and asynchronous engagement bites deep. Launching a post (say) into the blogosphere may or may not result in any engagement. It may just exist, like debris circling the earth, never touching or engaging anything. Engagement in the public sphere is attenuated but seems often to devolve to a form ("dialogue" is maybe too generous a term for it) of angry rejoinder, the flame war. The dispersed relationships of cyberspace often do not seem capable of sustaining anything else for very long. So the usual rhetorical concept of "audience" (i.e., the "target" of a speaker) is dissonant with our interactional and relationship-saturated account and perhaps not very helpful. What exactly do we think the public sphere is like, and how is the metaphor cashed out? The modern social imaginary has barely caught up with the public sphere documented by Habermas, which included not only eighteenth-century coffeehouses but pamphlets, books, and magazines and has yet to grapple with the vast resources of digital communication. So we will need an account of "audience" that goes far beyond "the intended target of my message" or "the receiver of my message."[3] Accounts of the public sphere often do not represent how deliberation is realized in practice, as if dueling editorials or think pieces responding weeks later to speeches are "just like" chatting in the coffeehouse or debating in a club. Overlapping similarities exist, certainly, but we need to explore some fundamental differences.

Let us look in more detail at an intersection of the deliberative social imaginary and argumentation. In the imaginary, interpersonal argument is continuous with public argument (friends *or* strangers chatter at the coffeehouse), and much of Habermas's analysis of the evolution of the public sphere assumes some continuity; it also seems like a commonsense insight that public-speaking instruction presumes a connection (Habermas 1991; Keith 2007). However, just as a bullhorn changes one's voice, even though that is still the "same" voice used in conversation, the rhetorical roles and forms in the public sphere, understood in Warner's circulatory sense, have a different constitution and different consequences than the same roles interpersonally. The main reason for this is stranger sociality: your relationships with interlocutors in the public sphere are with relative strangers, and the demands of civility seem weaker with them than with acquaintances, friends, and intimates. These weaker relationships attenuate both the harms (you have not been personally insulted) and benefits (you do not develop a personal relationship to sustain argument) of civility. Another stance may be available for professional political communicators: "It's nothing personal." They just need to circulate arguments among those who agree with them already, and too bad if the arguments are partial, hostile, insulting, and so on.

A representative anecdote can illustrate this point. In a profile of conservative media personality Erick Erickson, *Atlantic* writer Molly Ball finds herself shocked at how nice he seems in person, noting that he has

> an eagerness to put others at ease that helped explain why so many people spend hours in their cars listening to him. Above all, he was polite. Which was interesting, because Erickson is famous for saying things that are not polite. There was the time, in 2009, when he called retired Supreme Court Justice David Souter a "goat fucking child molester." During the Occupy protests, he said his heart was gladdened by "watching a hippie protester get Tased." He nicknamed Wendy Davis, the Texas state senator, "Abortion Barbie." And in a blog post considering whether President Obama was "shagging hookers," he called Michelle Obama a "marxist harpy." (2015)

Ball also notes, "Erickson dismisses criticism of his vulgar taunts as pearl-clutching by politically correct prigs with no sense of humor." Since in the public sphere (and in cyberspace, in particular), the bar is lower for civility in general, this sort of shocking talk is less surprising than it should be (the current theory is "toxic disinhibition").[4] And it should be shocking for what it implies about the relationships fostered, tolerated, and favored in the public sphere (Mangu-Ward 2018). A favorite and surprisingly sexist way (for both male and female writers) to marginalize and dismiss civility concerns is to relegate them to "pearl clutching," implying that a manly realist would not flinch from the hurly-burly of public exchange (there are class overtones as well, hearkening to the historically genteel dimensions of gentility and politeness). This is not a helpful or defensible stance; rejecting toxic discourse is not a failure of virility but a recognition of productive boundaries (which are of course open to dispute). We need to understand as well as condemn toxic discourse. Hence we need to understand more about how argument works in the public sphere, and rather than see civility as homogenous, we should analyze it rhetorically.

The right question to ask may be, What worlds are we creating with our modes of address, with our public performances? We propose as a useful framework the *theater of public discourse*. This connects to a rich tradition of dramatistic rhetorical theory connected to Kenneth Burke and symbolic interactionism.[5] *Theater* is meant not to trivialize discourse of the public sphere but to highlight the performative range of rhetorical roles that people take on when they communicate there and the difference those roles make from the perspective of public argument. What this metaphor does for public argumentation is allow us to name and analyze the relationships that define argument; without understanding the relationships, we cannot understand how the arguments function in the larger ecology of public discourse.

Let's consider the example of the phrase Black Lives Matter, which has served, since 2013, as a metonym for a cluster of arguments about the relationships between African Americans, police, and state power in general and as a moral objection to the indifference of the U.S. justice system to state-sanctioned murders of African American men in particular. It would be easy to lay these arguments out, as many journalists have done, in terms of claims and evidence. But these arguments can mean something different depending on who makes them, since the person who makes them may take on different rhetorical *roles*. For example, an *advocate* and an *inquirer* differ rhetorically, not just in the things they say or their ethos but in their potential effect on what is (in effect) a system of argument (i.e., a system of social/political/communicative relationships).

The BLM advocates for police reforms are roughly making an assertion that they expect others to validate in order to hold institutions accountable for their treatment of African Americans. The same evidence and claims deployed by someone who wants to "explore and understand the issue" has a quite different force, since this person wants to advance some kind of understanding about the relationship between race and policing. The audiences for the theater of public discourse are the various publics for the discourse. Assuming Michael Warner is right, and publics come into being constitutively through the circulation, production, and consumption of discourse, then we are asserting that this discourse can have a structure derived from the relationships between producers and consumers of it.

A theater of public deliberation will have players, plots, and scenes, the essence of a dramatistic approach (Burke 1969; Nichols 1952; Duncan 1968; Goffman 1959, 1967). The players will be those who speak in specific roles. We should acknowledge that these roles will have blurry boundaries and a good deal of flexibility and can be expected to mutate and evolve in response to circumstances. The plots will strongly resemble the argumentative topoi of classical rhetoric, serving as malleable but practical templates for understanding how the rhetoric, for particular citizens and issues, can play out. To really be faithful to the analogy, we would have to acknowledge that the theater of public deliberation is fundamentally improvisational. Longform improvisation (the way it is practiced, e.g., at Second City in Chicago) involves combining templates and moment-to-moment creation to develop full-length stories from an initial suggestion. Good improvisation balances intelligibility with novelty and formal satisfaction, and the best public deliberation may be quite similar to it.

The first step is to identify the "players" (*argumentum personae*, as it were); these are the generic roles, along with their typical goals and motivations in public discursive engagement. To illustrate how the theater of public discourse works, let us explore some examples in detail. BLM has emerged as a movement, a group, a philosophy, an argument, a trope, a meme, a locus of argument and contest, and much more (see Biesecker 2017; Langford and Speight 2015; Mackin 2016; Taylor 2016). BLM began in the aftermath of George Zimmerman's 2013 acquittal for the murder of Trayvon Martin in Sanford, Florida. The verdict was widely perceived to imply that it was acceptable to kill a young African American man whom one found threatening just for being African American (Zimmerman's justification for firing was that Martin was wearing a hoodie and hence "reasonably" posed a threat). The obvious inequity between the value the legal and justice system placed on black and white lives (since the killing sits in the tradition of lynching) prompted the hashtag #blacklivesmatter, which itself quickly attracted a following. The phrase has had a cyclic life in public discourse but has sometimes become a focal node in a system of symbolic protests and, for example, has clear connections to the NFL protests where players kneel during the national anthem, most notably (ex–)San Francisco quarterback Colin Kaepernick. The BLM phenomenon is especially interesting because the phrase itself can so easily circulate as a token, becoming metonymic for a number of things, especially to opponents (who wish to reject "angry" African Americans, the "radical left," and so on), and because it has both been *used* and been *taken* as having many different kinds of force.

Table 1

Role	Stance	Goal	Method	Virtue	Danger
Inquirers	Neutral, undecided	Explore ideas, arguments, and evidence	Consume multiple sources; ask questions; generate data	Expand available knowledge and arguments	Undirected; no basis for action
Discussants	Provisionally committed	Engage ideas, arguments, and evidence; possibly change	Engage a variety of arguers; use discussion to both inquire and advocate; take multiple positions	Engage in more democratic inquiry and advocacy	Without structure or purpose, will go nowhere
Advocates	Committed certainty	Rhetorically fight for specific ideas/claims; convert/persuade	Use all available arguments and means to support the favored ideas/perspective	Discover and make the best case	Zealotry blinds advocates to their own errors or virtues of others
Critics	Provisional certainty	Expose structural causes of oppression, etc.	Use analytic tools to strip away appearances and masks, both linguistic and structural	Frame/reframe arguments and claims in systemic/structural terms	Armchair analysis not connected to action or change; can cause debilitating pessimism
Witnesses	Committed	Bring personal stories/perspectives into public space	Tell and retell compelling stories to a variety of audiences in various media	Add narratives/perspectives to debate, expanding and humanizing	Narcissistic cry for attention; can encourage thinking outliers are the norm
Warriors	Committed certainty	Defeat other claims, perspectives	Use all available arguments and means to defeat opposing arguments/arguers	Discover weaknesses of opposing views and opponents	Caustic/toxic effect on discourse; can result in dysfunction flame wars
Trolls	Ambiguous—may pose as friendly or hyperpartisan	Enrage those on the other side through taunts, insults, and inappropriate contributions	Use personal insults, absurdities, non sequiturs	May define a center	Exhausting and distracting, corrosive

White Americans have commonly understood the phrase Black Lives Matter to imply that "white lives do not matter," leading to counterformulations such as "All Lives Matter" and "Blue Lives Matter" (attempting to reframe the issue in terms of the courage of police officers rather than systemic racism). Certainly "White lives do not matter" would be an uncivil thing to say, but it is, of course, not an implication of the original phrase and undoubtedly a rude inference to draw; even though the deliberative imaginary positions everyone as equal, everyone knows by this point that this equality has not been realized. If they somehow do not know this, a civil person would be moved to say, "Of course they should be—how have we fallen short of making them matter?" Some commentators suggest "All lives matter" may well arise from the discomfort of confronting one's complicity in a system of policing that has similar outcomes to those seen during the lynching era.[6] We will have to return to the question of whether saying true things in a public space that create discomfort is inherently uncivil; even though it might be impolite in a particular interpersonal setting, the thrust of our analysis is to disentangle public civility from interpersonal politeness. Of course "call-out" culture exists, and we can have a lively debate about how uncomfortable to make people who say things offensive to you in a personal setting (Friedersdorf 2017; Herzog 2018; Eschoe 2018). But for now, we will focus on discourse meant for the public sphere.

Inquirers

The idea that one should acquire facts and knowledge before entering an argument or coming to judgment is an old one. People may find themselves in a position where they do not know anything about an issue or they feel they do not have enough knowledge to form a basis for having an opinion. Thus inquirers enter public discourse with a relatively neutral stance; while they may have political and ethical commitments that shape the nature of their inquiry, they attempt to be neutral within the context. The force of inquiry is often exploratory. That is, the questions asked are in service of finding out what is known and what others think. Hence inquirers are required to consume multiple sources, and they often operate by asking questions and follow-up questions.

The virtue of inquirers lies in expanding the available knowledge and lines of argument for the specific subject. A part of their method may be to ask big questions and then to engage in deep listening, which sometimes helps different parties to the issue come to understand one another better.

However, in the midst of a contentious argument field, inquiry may seem like a retrograde contribution or a subversive way of undermining others' arguments by questioning already well-established premises. On occasions, when a particular issue is relatively new (e.g., the beginning of the AIDS epidemic), the public really does not know what is going on, and inquiry is necessary before coming to a judgment. But even in well-established areas, like the American struggle with issues of racism, people gain "consciousness" at different times and therefore become inquirers in a staggered fashion, depending on where they grew up, where they live, their educations and social groups, and so on. Engaging inquiry is not uncivil per se, though it can seem that way to people who are engaged in a very different dialogue. But within the larger discourse system, there will be many different communities and different points of entry, and so there is no real way to see an argument field as having advanced to a particular point where no one can enter from the beginning. The danger of remaining at the level of inquiry is that one can continue inquiring and never actually form an opinion and move to advocacy or action. So sometimes inquiry seems to be a way of blocking, deferring, or delaying action.

In the case of BLM, many Americans seemed genuinely surprised by the statement. Some, obviously, reacted with anger. But some people were truly bewildered, so they asked honest questions about why BLM rallies were held and why the organizers and the organization needed to say such things. In response, the BLM organizers came up with an infographic, the "Campaign Zero" agenda.[7] This graphic has the caption "We can live in a world where systems and structures do good, not harm" and has ten boxes, each of which has a simple image and a title that names a recommendation for new policy: (1) end broken windows policing, (2) community oversight, (3) limit use of force, (4) independently investigate and prosecute, (5) community representation, (6) body cams / film the police, (7) training, (8) end for-profit policing, (9) demilitarization, and (10) fair police union contracts. This remarkable graphic performs several functions simultaneously. In essence, it prefigures the response to BLM as being about the notion of personal psychological racism—that is, the common response on the part of the white majority that racism is an isolated individual defect of persons and therefore not a social justice issue. The Campaign Zero chart directs attention instead to the systemic causes of violence against civilians by police. It assumes inquirers understand the total scope of killing; it focuses on how policies, practices, and regulation foster the environment in which minority shootings are so very common. Unsurprisingly, while some people received this chart as educational (and a very neatly packaged bit of learning), others took it to be a sinister "leftist" statement attacking fundamental aspects of the U.S. system (Baker 2015). Of course, it *is* also an attack on a system. But it does not function that way for everybody in public discourse.

Discussants

Discussants seek to *engage* others on an issue. Discussants try to learn about themselves and others through engagement, without preconditions or prejudgment. They differ from inquirers because they do not simply ask questions but take provisional positions "for the sake of argument" that allow them to test and explore the arguments for and against a particular issue. Discussants are often subject to the same critique as inquirers relative to their provisional neutrality. Some may wonder whether one can actually be provisionally neutral, whether the neutrality is in fact a cover for an agenda of advocacy, or whether there are particular issues on which one should *not* have a position of neutrality—where a position of neutrality is itself potentially unethical.

People engage in discussion to change their own minds or help to influence the minds of others. A characteristic of discussion or dialogue, as pointed out by Henry Johnstone and many others, is that you should enter into the discussion or dialogue willing to change as well as be changed. Discussants, as a function of their role, are open to ideas, evidence, argument, and stories relevant to the issue or topic at hand. One of the advantages of discussion is that it does not have a fixed process or set of rules, which means it can range over many types of arguments and freely switch back and forth. By the same token, one criticism of discussion is that it is so free-form that its shapelessness contributes to circling around the same arguments and ideas over and over again or never arriving at a place where a conclusion can be rejected.

Discussion has the advantage of positioning those engaging one another as equals; if discussants are not positioned as equals, then discussion fails. Hence the Dewey-inspired interest in discussion in the 1930s, where discussion was seen as the most appropriate kind of discourse within a democracy: an open give-and-take, with people who were willing to let provisional commitments shift and evolve as evidence and ideas presented themselves (Keith 2007). Discussion makes the notion of the "devil's advocate" seem most appropriate. Discussants may take multiple shifting positions as part of their effort to explore ideas and arguments and take them to their limit before making up their minds on the issue.

In the case of BLM, one can see the potential for the phrase, circulated through social media, T-shirts, bumper stickers, and other things, to spark discussion. The organizers of BLM, given their very clear convictions that they stand by steadfastly, seem to be disseminative. That is, they allow the phrase Black Lives Matter to circulate without attempting to strongly control the kinds of discussions that it could provoke. Clearly, the organizers have thought ahead to the kinds of discussions they would like to have, but instead of producing (say) a ten-thousand-word manifesto with everything other people should think, they rely on process. This is an intriguing strategy, and it dovetails well with the phenomenon of virality, which has become so common through social and other kinds of media. Compared to straight-up persuasion, discussion has advantages. If you make a pitch to persuade someone, and he or she does not accept it, you have failed. If you throw something out for discussion, and somebody disagrees with it, then he or she is still discussing; he or she is still engaged, and the possibility that the back-and-forth could dialectically make a difference to what that person believes or how that person acts is still present.

We should not forget, as well, that in the theater of public discourse, the line between observer and participant is seldom clear. Someone may hear about BLM; after that, every time it appears on Twitter, in his or her Facebook feed, or in the local newspaper, then in a certain sense, he or she is participating in discussions around BLM simply by noticing and attending. Probably at some point, this leads to casual conversation about BLM, which may or may not be as robust as the discussions that that person is witnessing. We should not discount the engagement that could come from being an audience, from grappling with ideas and arguments that one finds unfamiliar or uncomfortable, even if most of that grappling is inside one's own head.

Advocates

Advocates are those seeking to *convince* others (and sometimes persuade) on behalf of a correct view, mostly through argument. Advocates have a considered position on a public issue and must present evidence and reasons for it. When people think of public discourse as an ongoing debate (rather than a conversation), then most often they are thinking of advocates. Advocacy is in some senses controversial, because while it serves as an ideal of public discourse and deliberation, it seems to be so rarely engaged and practiced. Advocates are not seeking to make up their minds, and they are not necessarily interested in changing them. Their engagement is often not so much with specific audiences as it is with the attempt to get arguments in circulation.

The Campaign Zero graphic is an interesting example of a contributor to advocacy. Advocates typically have a change in policy or practice for which they advocate; without that, they would tend to lose focus. This infographic gives, in a brief form, some policy ideas that would tend to reduce the killing of African Americans by the police. All the suggestions are practical, affordable things that could be accomplished in the near and medium term. What is missing, of course, are the arguments that justify each of the items and the arguments that tie them all together.

Advocacy asks to be judged by its success in changing minds, which can raise doubts about deliberation based in advocacy (the critical imaginary imagines discourse to be extremely efficacious). Consider Occupy Wall Street (OWS), which was a rhetorical hybrid in that it clamored for the recognition of a specific issue without, as many on all sides complained, a specific policy proposal (the latter being the condition of admission to public discussion, apparently). OWS attempted to bridge the critical-deliberative imaginaries by reimagining deliberation as a fully inclusive activity. Perhaps they were not fully successful on either count. Here is a 2017 exchange between *New Yorker* editor David Remnick and Mark Lilla, just after the publication of Lilla's controversial 2017 book arguing that identity politics is antithetical to true liberalism:

REMNICK: The slogan of Occupy Wall Street was "We Are the Ninety-nine Per Cent." That's a pretty big tent. What did you think of Occupy Wall Street?

LILLA: Well, as I mentioned, nearly forty per cent of the country is Southern. One out of every four Americans is evangelical. I didn't see those people represented there. You know, I thought it was, the fact that—

REMNICK: But that's what the discussion was about. It was about class.

LILLA: It was about class, but it was bourgeois activists who were there. And that's fine, because at least someone was expressing outrage by the bailout of the banks and what happened after the crash. So I was happy that someone was saying anything. But it was theatre, right? And it doesn't lead to anything else.

REMNICK: Was it helpful theatre?

LILLA: Well, it was helpful in the sense that it certainly got liberals talking more about this, and it was just there that people were protesting. But by the time it descends into the drummers in Zuccotti Park, and people arguing into the night about which groups are being represented when they go up on the platform and speak, that just illustrates what's wrong with us.

We would argue that Lilla's comments, while in some ways trenchant in questioning the inclusiveness of the "99 percent," misunderstand public discourse and deliberation in a common way. OWS was not a failure because no laws were passed (it was not intended to foster legislative solutions). Consistent with the critical imaginary, it was intended to raise consciousness about the issue of income inequality, which it did: most national candidates now feel obliged to position themselves with respect to the issue of the 99 percent and, no matter how reactionary their policies, acknowledge that they want to do something to help the 99 percent. For Lilla, a "hardheaded" political stance sees this as just theater, an evasion of real action ("less marching, more mayors"). Yet our position is that *all* of it is theater, and all of it can matter. OWS certainly (pardon the pun) set the stage for a productive national discussion of income inequality, even if that discussion has not really happened—yet.

Critics

Critics seek to *reveal* the truth of a situation or a system; their contributions are typically posed in terms of "what's *really* going on here." Critics use analytic tools, often drawn from philosophies or political theory, to show that seemingly innocent or "normal" ideas or practices are shameful and reprehensible or try to draw attention to underappreciated evils in the public eye. Critics differ from advocates in that the only thing they advocate is awareness of a problem rather than a specific proposal or solution. The rhetorical exigence to which critics respond is "If people only knew . . ." They differ from discussants in that they are already sure they know what the correct analysis is, and they want to get it into circulation. The critic sees his or her role as uncovering what is otherwise hidden by the normal flow of discourse or to make sense of some problem by giving that problem a meaning that might not be immediately obvious to other participants in the theater of discourse.

The critic is often exemplified by the opinion writer. Sometimes people write op-ed pieces to advocate for specific programs, but most of the time they are trying to give an interpretation of current events. This can involve giving context, but more often the context is in service of a critical appraisal of the event in light of a picture of how things are getting better or (more often) how they are getting worse. Since much of public discourse is related to problems and their solutions, critics make a valuable addition by identifying and analyzing problems; this role can be complementary to others (with, for example, advocates supplying plans in response to problems critics have identified). Critique may have the purpose of paving the way for action or may become an end in itself, accompanied only by a hand wave toward what this knowledge or awareness would bring. That is not necessarily illegitimate, since once in circulation, critical arguments may interact productively with discussions, advocacy, and so on. Critics may or may not be dialogically oriented. They may feel in some cases that their critique represents the truth and is not really open to discussion or modification; in other cases, they may want to refine and revise critiques in circulation.

Critics often write as if people changed their beliefs rationally, based on exposure to critical reason. Without a doubt, this sometimes happens, though several strategies allow one to reject arguments or information that contradicts one's current beliefs or positions. If you decide not to change them, you can simply decide to live with the contradiction; while it may be hard to justify when challenged, we all live with a certain amount of contradictory information, though our tolerance for it varies. You can also adjust your beliefs about the contradictory information, using what philosophers of science call "auxiliary hypotheses" (supporting assumptions), deciding that the contradictory information is false, biased, or part of a conspiracy and disabling it. You can also decide which beliefs you want to adjust. In Willard V. O. Quine's famous metaphor, we all have a "web of belief" that grows link by link, with those at the edges being easier to give up than those at the center (which would require cutting up the whole web); thus, he argues, it might be easier to change your mind about the capital of North Dakota (since not much depends on it unless you are a resident) than the basic truths of arithmetic, which are implicated in many, many other beliefs (Quine and Ullian 1970). As noted in chapter 1, in "The Will to Believe," William James (1896) argues that you can take two stances toward unfamiliar or unwelcome information or arguments, with different trade-offs. You can be very skeptical, choosing to believe the side with the more rigorous evidence while knowing that it means you are more likely to fail to believe some truths that might have been important to you. Or you can choose to be credulous, believing as many things as you find reasonable, knowing that this probably means the portion of your beliefs that will be false is higher than it would be if you were skeptical. James suggests not that a correct position exists but rather that the consistent application of these "belief policies" would result in different belief systems in the face of similar inputs. Thus the variability of the way people respond rationally to information suggests that critics can never be sure how their thoughts will be taken.

Witnesses

Witnesses seek to tell their stories. Stories and witnesses come in several varieties, but their goal, as explained in Bradford Vivian's incisive 2017 book, *Commonplace Witnessing: Rhetorical Invention, Historical Remembrance and Public Culture*, is to create and cement public memory so that it becomes a context for public argument and discourse. What is important, he says, is "how and with what sociopolitical consequences, idioms of witnessing have infused the public discourse of ordinary citizens, politicians and public institutions in recent decades. . . . The rhetorical commonplaces associated with the public goods of witnessing allow such subjects to think and speak of themselves as witnesses obligated to preserve collective memories of past injustice or tragedy while preventing the onset of similarly devastating injustices or tragedies in the future" (2). Hence the rhetorically interesting feature of witnesses may be less the impact of their stories on themselves or an immediate audience and more the impact they can have when circulated and appropriated by others. Witnesses and their testimony become evidence, inventional or probative, in others' discussion and advocacy. The essential feature of witnessing is speaking from the authority of personal experience, not theoretical or fictional (important as those can be) but personally experienced and communicated. Christian witnessing in the evangelical tradition is generally telling the story of one's transition from sin to salvation; one may have a duty to witness without assuming it will be persuasive or effect conversion.

To witness in the public sphere is thus to construct a story that confers truth on events and ethos on the storyteller. This requires the story not just have a particular structure—sometimes hopeful, sometimes tragic—but be embedded in a particular kind of rhetorical context or network. Let us briefly sketch a couple of these from the current moment. The #metoo movement emerged in October 2017 in response to the credible and multiple accusations of sexual assault against film producer Harvey Weinstein. "Me too" began as a meme on Myspace from activist Tarana Burke in 2006 as a way for people to build solidarity as a response to abuse and assault; it was translated to Twitter as #metoo by actress Alyssa Milano in 2017 and soon snowballed. #metoo seems like a basic form of witnessing: "You are not the only one." This contribution is meaningful individually but even more so as it forms a public and becomes a minimally interpretable set of texts that circulate through an expanding circle of attention.

Christine Blasey Ford's testimony at Judge Brett Kavanaugh's Supreme Court confirmation hearings seemed to hit a different register. She was not a witness but rather someone who was asked (after considerable public pressure) to share her story for the consideration of the committee—and thus a national audience. Her story was not a slick piece of public relations, as expert testimonies so often are. Instead, it was presented as heartfelt and earnest, its veracity enhanced by its unembarrassed gaps and elisions, and it created shockwaves, not enough to fundamentally change the politics of the moment (i.e., the strategic value of voting in a young and conservative justice to the Supreme Court) but enough to make people on every side acknowledge its power. Interestingly, Kavanaugh framed his response as defense and apologia, more appropriate as responses to an accusation or charge and curiously out of sync with the raw honesty of Blasey Ford, who clearly had not tried to make a case against him, just to tell her own story. An interesting correlate emerged in an incident the day after. Lame-duck Arizona senator Jeff Flake was accosted by two women in a stairwell on his way to the hearing. Flake presented himself as a person of conscience (he claimed he decided not to run for his seat again because of the state of the Republican Party) and was widely perceived as a swing vote at the very partisan hearing. One of the women, identified as Maria Gallagher, said to him, "I was sexually assaulted and nobody believed me. I didn't tell anyone and you're telling all women that they don't matter, that they should just stay quiet because if they tell you what happened to them you are going to ignore them. That's what happened to me, and that's what you are telling all women in America, that they don't matter. They should just keep it to themselves because if they have told the truth you're just going to help that man to power anyway." As Flake listened, visibly uncomfortable, she continued, "Don't look away from me. Look at me and tell me that it doesn't matter what happened to me. That you will let people like that go into the highest court of the land and tell everyone what they can do with their bodies" (Malveaux and Stracqualursi 2018). This is not a pure type of witnessing (since she is also confronting him and critiquing his actions), but the witnessing part ("Look at me") did seem to make an impression on Flake, who decided he would not vote for cloture without an "investigation," which in the event was cursory and simply provided cover for his vote. The lesson of both these examples is that the true power of witnessing may be in its circulation rather than its immediate effect on the audience.

Thus the (not always intentional) effects of witnesses are multiple, but at least two are worth mentioning. First, witnessing humanizes abstract ideas and remote facts and circumstances. As we know from countless charity commercials, hunger and animal abuse are just abstract stories until we meet specific people or dogs and learn their stories. These stories make them available for our sympathetic engagement; as Richard Rorty argued repeatedly, you probably cannot reason your way into someone's sympathy—connecting with them through a story is far more likely to succeed. Witnesses thus provide the raw material for advocates and discussants to forge connections across radically different life worlds. The stories of witnesses also provide evidence of typicality: a particular kind of situation, with causes and effects and impacts, becomes typified rather than just a random, chaotic thing. Shifting to new typifications (as from stranger rape to date/acquaintance rape, which becomes a new type of sexual assault with its own typical story depicting its etiology, circumstances, and results) can result in whole new perceptions, arguments, and policy orientations. Once types are established, they can be reproduced on their own; creating new types requires a critical mass of stories circulating within and helping to bring a public into being. Witnessing implies a sacrifice, a cost for coming forward. The witness's is thus also (like the critic's) a close cousin to *parrhesia*, frank speech in the condition of risk (little or no moral courage attaches to speaking frankly when you have the power).

Warriors

Warriors are those participants in public dialogue seeking to defeat those with wrong views by "any means necessary." Their armament may include vociferous argument (which they share with advocates), typically paired with shaming, silencing, and personal attacks on credibility or moral worthiness. When a specific tactic is positioned as coming from a warrior, it often may be characterized as uncivil by both parties—the warrior reveling in the incivility (or accusation of it) and the recipients condemning it. If the point is to make people angry, you can only know you have succeeded. This may be part of the meaning of Vann Newkirk's claim that "protest isn't civil" (2018). He might mean one of two things: Even though the protest may be arguably civil (peaceful, nonaggressive), it cannot achieve its goal unless it makes someone uncomfortable enough to (perhaps mistakenly) call it uncivil. Or the slightly stronger meaning would be that you do not have a legitimate protest unless the target actually finds it uncivil, which implies that warriors need to get ever more aggressive until they get a reaction—and thus are more likely to cross into actual incivility. Many of the BLM protests fall into the first category. Simply asserting that Black Lives Matter is not uncivil (if all lives matter, then so do black lives); taking it as implying, against all denials, that white lives do not matter is uncharitable at least and uncivil at best.

Yet it can serve as a warrior's tool, since people apparently do (correctly) find it shaming and react to that shame with accusations of incivility. The reaction, which is unnecessary in reacting to (say) an advocate or discussant, can become weaponized by warriors once they know it exists (if pursued for its own sake, this amounts to trolling). Warriors are generally attacking because they believe that real or perceived incivility can create some kind of change. This might be a change in what people believe or perceive, though warriors might not be justified in expecting a response like "Wow! You're totally right! I never realized it before." Warriors often characterize their tactics as justified by urgency; they know that (so to speak) the house is on fire (as in the image from the Shakyamuni Buddha's Lotus Sutra), so change and action are imperative. A common refrain is "If you're not outraged, you're not paying attention." Warrior tactics of attacking and shaming the "other side" might serve as a wake-up call to potential allies. During the Trump era, it seems many people who oppose him have behaved as if ramping up their attacks on his character will produce a result they desire. Sometimes that result is framed as antinormalization, since keeping outrage fresh may prevent people from accepting what they see as an unacceptable president. Sometimes the result is framed in terms of people who are "on the fence" or "unaware," even though we cannot always tell how many such people exist that would also be paying attention to the warrior's provocations.

Consciousness does get raised sometimes, and warriors may well be right that, as they circulate through a variety of publics, their provocations have an effect. But we should note that this effect makes the most sense from within the critical imaginary. The attack on false consciousness is central to the critical imaginary in that critique itself is supposed to uncover the workings of power that people, if they but knew of them, would organize against and resist. Warriors attempt to engage the urgency of this project, fueled by a moral wrath; for warriors, the ends justify the means due to the moral seriousness of the situation. Hence warriors tend to dismiss other roles (discussant, advocate) as weak and morally compromised. To see this, consider a common warrior tactic: comparing the situation or a specific behavior to something that is universally acknowledged as reprehensible (slavery, Nazis, the Holocaust) and asking people to consider whether they would merely discuss or advocate it in the face of (what we now consider to be) unmitigated evil. Obviously, this tactic is meant to aggressively shut down discussion, and for the warrior, continuing discussion provokes fresh outrage as those in less aggressive roles appear to temporize with evil.

Civil disobedience often (but not always) is a warrior tactic. The best way, in theory, to protest unjust norms and laws is to refuse to obey them. This action raises, for its opponents, the professed slippery slope that the willful violation of one norm will result in the erasure of all norms. To forestall this objection, the practitioners of civil disobedience in the 1960s tried to be scrupulously polite, even as they were disobedient. In the critical imaginary, the warrior is the enemy of civility. In the critical imaginary, injustice and oppression are systemic; while individual acts may be judged to be contributing to or remediating oppression and injustice, the actual roots are in a system that produces unjust or oppressive relationships between people. In its Marxist origins, that system was an economic one, while latter-day critical theorists (following the Frankfurt and Edinburgh schools) have focused on the interaction between political, economic, and especially cultural systems. The systemic analysis may be correct, but it poses a rhetorical problem in that systemic relations are hard to *see*; as (for example) Spike Lee's film *Do the Right Thing* demonstrates vividly, while it is easy to see people rioting or smashing things, it is harder to see the systemic exclusions and oppressions that produce the anger leading to the riot. In the frame of false consciousness, people simply need to wake up to the systems that oppress them; in fact, the situation is usually complicated by the fact that everyone is systemically implicated, and so people may be relocated to acknowledge systemic oppression in which they are implicated. The warrior's aggressive tactics may be an attempt to shock and shame people into acknowledging their role in injustice and oppression. Fair enough, though we can still ask, "At what cost? With what result?" The warrior's vision tends to be totalizing and obscures these questions, to which we will return in chapter 5.

Trolls

The origin of the term *troll* for an online provocateur is a bit mysterious. Whether derived generally from the Scandinavian ogre or more specifically the Norse story *De tre bukkene Bruse* ("Three Billy Goats Gruff"), in which the troll prevents travelers from crossing a bridge, its meaning is wrapped up in both behavior and intent (Hardaker 2010). We may usefully compare Aristotle's discussion of "rhetorician" and "sophist" (2006, 1354b), where he points out that while one counts as a rhetorician even when using both good and bad arguments, what makes the sophist is not the ability but the choice—that is, intending to make bad arguments. So while one may offend or disrupt discourse inadvertently in the course of enacting any of these roles, trolls seek to offend or disrupt as their purpose. The phenomenon of trolling (at least the version that gave rise to the term) began in the 1990s in Usenet communities. These were organized around specific interests and beliefs, and those who did not share them would post to the discussions outrageous and offensive comments, driving the members into anger and disarray. These interlopers became known as trolls; they were not there for the legitimate purposes of the community's discussions but just to anger and outrage them; whether this was motivated by ideology or the pleasure of creating chaos was often hard to discern.

From the perspective of the deliberative imaginary, the troll is a provocateur, seeking to disrupt the norms and commitments that might hold deliberation together as an extended, dispersed process. From within the critical imaginary, the troll is a kind of terrorist whose attacks on norms and identities are indistinguishable from the forces holding the oppressive status quo in place; even if trolling is done "for its own sake," it still, in this view, serves the same function as intentional attempts to suppress critique. In a sense, trolling is parasitic on other roles, since it seeks to undermine those roles and deliberation in general through an exaggerated expression that attempts to reduce an opposing character in the theater of public discourse. Could it become, however, a dominant role in its own right? A game-like culture exists among conservatives in particular (especially high school and college students) in which taunts and bullying, only successful when the reaction is outrage, have become their primary way of engaging political discourse (Harris 2018). In this group, liberal outrage is the only worthy goal, and they will use anything necessary to accomplish it. In this they resemble warriors (who similarly prize ends over means), except that warriors fight for something outside the fighting itself. Yet it seems clear that some conservatives who espouse trolling do so from within the critical imaginary. Imagining themselves the repressed victims of a domineering liberal establishment, their use of trolling as a tactic of disruption is meant to empower them (cf. David Horowitz's *Progressive Racism* [2016] and *The Art of Political War* [2000]).

In "Trump's Right-Hand Troll," journalist McKay Coppins (2018) documents the career of Stephen Miller, youthful advisor to President Trump, as embodying a new kind of public rhetoric (new, at least, for the presidential orbit—it would not be hard to argue that Newt Gingrich has used it since the early 1990s). It seems rhetorically obvious that competent trolls have to deny being trolls for their technique to work, and Miller is nothing if not competent: He insists that he believes every word he says and that he is not a fan of "provocation for its own sake." But after some reflection, he admits that he has long found value in doing things that generate what he calls "constructive controversy with the purpose of enlightenment." Yet, says Coppins, Miller's entire career gives the lie to this assertion: He has been courting infamy since puberty. From Santa Monica High School to Duke University to Capitol Hill, his mission—always—has been to shock and offend the progressive sensibilities of his peers. He revels in riling them, luxuriates in their disdain.

Unlike the other roles, which each have their place in a complex system, we struggle to imagine the positive role that trolling can play in the overall system of discourse and deliberation. Trolling *seems* to fall into the same category as uncivil versions of protest and outrage; on the most charitable reading, these are designed to advance the discourse by disrupting it, though trolling seems hard to fit into that space, given its game-like quality. "Liberals" definitely annoy conservatives, but that does not seem to be trolling in the same way, since liberals often offend conservatives passively, by virtue of things they are and do—namely, their "lifestyles" (diverse, gay, etc.), which in the conservative imagination, amount to an attack on the treasured status quo. Liberal warriors are so common, they have a label ("social justice warriors"), but these people are sincere and sincerely "in your face" about what they want. Trolling requires masquerade, so they flourish in online spaces that preserve anonymity, though they can pop up as plants at rallies.

Roles in Practice

Let us focus on how these roles seem appropriate to (or are appropriated by) the deliberative and critical imaginaries. Obviously, participants in the public sphere can occupy different roles at different times, and sometimes a single post or speech or editor may have characteristics of more than one role. The roles can roughly be divided into the *dialogic* roles (inquirers, discussants, advocates, witnesses) and *monologic* roles (warriors, critics, trolls). Without evaluating these roles, we should note their differences. Those speaking in dialogic roles structure their rhetoric to not only allow for but often invite response, while those who speak or write in monologic roles do not generally open themselves to engagement. This roughly corresponds with an epistemic distinction as well. If you are in possession of the Truth, you may feel less of a need to dialogue or inquire and more inclined to fight and criticize those who resist your knowledge, while if you hold a corrigible or even skeptical attitude toward your commitments (in short, a Deweyan stance), then you are more likely to think they are improved through engagement.[8]

Clearly, the deliberative imaginary privileges the dialogical modes, and the critical imaginary privileges, in general, the monologic modes. Why? In the critical imaginary, the structures of capital, ideology, and consciousness render most attempts at inquiry or dialogue inauthentic and probably fruitless, since they are structured to only allow for the reproduction of the status quo. Yet bringing people to consciousness, in the public sphere, will not be accomplished by engaging them. An example of this point was cited earlier in terms of climate change. Climate change is real, and action needs to be taken. One can draw, from the deliberate imaginary, resources to assert, "Oh, there are always two sides; we should hear from both sides." And while debate is engaged—likely a debate with no clear resolution, where one side is arguing in bad faith—nothing gets done about climate change. Probably attacking and critiquing opponents of climate change is likely to be more productive than engaging them. But this is a judgment about a particular case, not a justification for every case. Of course, someone invested in the deliberative imaginary will say that reasonable people can disagree about this, and those appealing to the critical imaginary will doubt the force of "reasonable."

Returning to the question of civility, are any of these roles inherently civil or uncivil? Not inherently—but they have tendencies. The dialogic roles require building a relationship, and if relationships depend in part on civility, then these roles may have more resources to enact it. But the belligerent, bullying inquirer, in the tradition of Socrates, is also possible. The monologic roles' requirement for civility is thin (since the audience is diffuse and are "strangers" to us); with sufficient effort, one can muster it, though it is clear that very often, the effort is not there. Warriors can be civil; one way of understanding civil disobedience is in terms of a warrior who decides to be civil, breaking an unjust law but not otherwise attacking anyone. But warriors often come out swinging, using disruption, belligerence, and personal attacks. Critics in this sense do not engage opposing points of view as much as they undermine them by analyzing them; once a person or a view is revealed as just an effect or a worldview or as indebted to a particular institution, then that view can be safely dismissed. Relative to the critical imaginary, incivility in this sense is valorized; disruption and personal attacks are not just legitimate but even required techniques. All the roles are compatible with various publics and counterpublics in civil and uncivil modes, resisting any easy generalizations. In fact, incivility can be constitutive of one public/ community while rejecting another; glitter bombing a politician who does not support gay marriage might mostly just annoy the politician and her supporters but may please LGBTQ groups.

Some complaints about civility accuse it of too often collapsing into pseudocivility; by design, or maybe just functionally, it blocks certain roles, especially warriors. Pseudocivility typically works at the level of disciplining others' behavior explicitly rather than silently controlling one's own behavior; pseudocivility invokes politeness or manners to sanction acceptable behavior that nonetheless makes one uncomfortable. Of course, the root question (addressed already in chapter 1) is being able to find workable criteria for "acceptable" that are not based on an individual's subjective reaction. Consider current objects of discomfort, such as same-sex couples kissing in public or public breastfeeding. Part of strong civility is being able to separate one's reaction of discomfort from a recognition that your reaction does not represent your best judgment ("If I don't mind heterosexual couples kissing, I shouldn't declare gay people's behavior rude, because it's basically the same thing"). Declaring other people's behavior as rude or uncivil is itself rude, as Miss Manners never tires of pointing out, and unsurprisingly such correction manifests itself as pseudocivility. Taken in aggregate, a process of evolution seems to be at work. Behaviors that used to be impolite—for example, engaging in affectionate behaviors as a gay couple in public—provoke no public notice, whatever people may think privately.

A pervasive anxiety grows out of the critical imaginary about whether the "civility police" or "tone police" (this image comes up remarkably often) will not allow people to say the difficult and challenging things that should bring about change. In truth, we have no doubt pseudocivility happens and happens intentionally; people sometimes use a charge of incivility ("That's rude," "That makes me uncomfortable") as a rejoinder to things they do not want to hear. It can also happen that incivility itself—endless outrage and personal attack—may be a way of avoiding genuine engagement with ideas one does not like. The "debates" over new atheism often include a level of vitriol that makes one wonder whether anyone involved is willing to risk engagement with the other side. Being a civil warrior is probably the trickiest balance of all, and the project of exploring that role (certainly begun by Martin Luther King Jr., among others) is an ongoing one.

The lesson we can draw from exploring roles and public argument is that civility, in its specific function for public argument, cannot be applied only to a kind of idealized argument process. We need to be attentive to the variety of rhetorical roles through which people, in the modern media ecology, engage issues of public concern; a finer-grained account of these roles allows us to better understand the different ways that civility manifests itself as well as the consequences of maintaining civility or choosing incivility. In particular, the association of certain roles with incivility should make us ask questions about that choice, and in the next chapter, we will explore incivility and its consequences.

4

THE STRUCTURE, USES, AND
LIMITATIONS OF INCIVILITY

Mr. President! Fuck you!

—WHITE HOUSE INTERN TO PRESIDENT DONALD TRUMP, 2018

Trolling has become an increasingly common part of our public culture. To troll is to deliberately make controversial (usually rude and outrageous) remarks intended to solicit an emotional response from another person, often masquerading as a member of the community to be offended. Trolls use internet platforms and social media to intentionally agitate or offend people, causing endless arguments and disruption. Terms like *trolling* and *troll* may be relatively new when used in this way; their current ubiquity may seem to have ushered in a new form of public discourse that has accompanied the rise of social media in our daily lives, but as a communication strategy, trolling is not a really radical innovation. Forms of incivility, like trolling, have been a characteristic of life in any democratic system in our collective historical memory—not because we have failed somehow but because verbal conflict is part of life in democratic societies. American history is replete with examples of incivility, especially at times when conflicts seem deeply intractable, like the run-up to the Civil War, which included examples of flipping desks, punches thrown by and at congressmen, and all manner of aggression (Freeman 2018). The prevalence of trolling in our moment is both a sign and a symptom of the depth of the conflicts at the core of the Western democratic project, but the shape and form of trolling is a relatively common and consistent feature of deliberation.

Parallel to an earlier discussion, we begin with an initial distinction between *weak* and *strong incivility*. By "weak incivility," we mean a network of rude behaviors intended to offend or produce discomfort through acts that violate social norms or expectations. Insulting someone by, for example, calling his or her motives for making a policy argument into question is a form of weak incivility. Such public disrespect (whatever one might say privately) is corrosive to productive interchange. We can ask important questions about what happens to public discourse in democratic societies when forms of "weak incivility" like this become common practice. But we can also find forms of "strong incivility" that go further. By "strong incivility," we mean a network of behaviors and communication practices that disrupt, intentionally or not, the regular flow of discourse and thus strengthen and deepen divisions between groups that are understood as morally distinct and opposed. Strong incivility includes attempts to silence, delegitimize, and remove specific voices from public deliberation. As a communication strategy, "strong incivility" employs insults, personal attacks, and interruption for the purposes of neutralizing specific agents within the theater of public discourse because those agents are understood as unworthy of a fair and reasonable hearing in deliberation. Members of both the left and the right have used versions of strong incivility and seen themselves as justified by the context. Specific tactics can be deployed in different ways: one could use trolling as a form of either "weak incivility" (as simply a way to insult a fellow citizen in a crude fashion) or "strong incivility" (as a way of using insults and threats to disrupt, delegitimize, and silence participants in public discourse).

This chapter will consider the rhetorical forms of both strong and weak incivility and track some of the rhetorical effects of the uses of incivility in public discourse. Obviously the values, roles, and practices of the troll (as one example of an uncivil actor) will be distinct from what we described in most of the previous chapter as forms of civil communication practiced by dialogic actors. Some have argued, notably John Durham Peters (2005), that life in democratic societies has long required a kind of thick-skinned tough-mindedness whereby we need to expect and tolerate levels of offense in public life given the kinds of broad commitments to free speech required by democratic culture. Peters has also argued that there will always be those who test, in provocative ways, to see where the edges of acceptability are. We may even argue that uncivil communication practices are necessary, as many who see President Trump as a neofascist have recently claimed. From within the critical imaginary (the argument goes), incivility is the only option when faced with morally bankrupt actors in the public sphere like President Trump and the members of the alt-right. The critical imaginary justifies forms of incivility as legitimate and useful instruments of change because the civil treatment of morally noxious others who hold power seems like a form of capitulation or quietism in the face of deeply wrong and offensive positions. From the perspective of rhetorical studies, four questions about incivility are particularly pressing: What work do uncivil communication practices do in public discourse? How do they do that work? What kind of change is produced or made possible by uncivil communication? And can we rescue or preserve a form of incivility that might constructively and usefully contribute to the action within the theater of public discourse?

Answering these questions can deepen our understanding of rhetorical citizenship by creating a more sophisticated picture of the uncivil communicative agent within the critical imaginary—and the consequences of tactical incivility within the deliberative imaginary. This picture can both provide an awareness of the modes and effects of incivility and create the conditions in which we might make an informed choice about whether, where, or how to engage in practices of incivility (or what is at stake when we do engage in such practices). From the perspective of rhetorical theory, it seems impossible to imagine a world in which we only understood or engaged in civil deliberation. The temptation to use rhetorics of division to delegitimize opposing actors in the public sphere will persist regardless of the democratic culture that we build. But the maintenance, strength, and depth of our democratic culture probably depends—to some extent, at least—on limiting the uses of this kind of rhetoric (or finding a way to practice it such that disruptions to the normal flow of discourse do not endanger the system itself), lest it rip the whole system apart. This ought to become clear as we pursue a rhetorical understanding of incivility. Such analyses will also help us understand if, when, and how incivility might help generate social and political change. Perhaps the best place to begin to develop that kind of understanding is the realization that the social glue that holds democratic societies together is dependent on the twin, related rhetorical functions of division and identification.

The Rhetorical Structure of Incivility

In *A Rhetoric of Motives*, Kenneth Burke argues that "identification" is the key rhetorical concept that helps explain persuasion. To support this view, Burke offers a humanistic philosophy positioning identification as central to being a person because we are all born as biologically separate beings that seek to unite through communication in order to overcome that separateness. We experience a feeling of separateness from others and hence seek a feeling of identifying with others; we are "both joined and separate" (1969b, 21). Or as Burke explains, "Identification is affirmed with earnestness precisely because there is division. Identification is compensatory to division" (22). To overcome our divisions, we look for ways in which our interests, attitudes, values, experiences, and perceptions "overlap" or make us "consubstantial" with others. We seek out an association with others to relieve our sense of separateness, but as soon as we do, we have also reasserted a difference or division from a group of others with whom we do not identify. From Burke's view, the human need to identify is a very rich resource for those interested in persuasion. The goal of rhetorical practice is, in part, to build social cohesion (and thus agreement) through language, but that cohesion always comes at the cost of division as well. In other words, symbolic acts through which identifications are formed are also difference-making. This kind of move is at the core of incivility, as we will show; it rhetorically accelerates the adherence and corrosion of the social glue that binds us together in communities. From Burke, we learn the lesson that rhetorics of division are also always already rhetorics of identification (and vice versa).

Burke's commitment to identification ought to be understood in relationship to his view of language as symbolic action (a view that aligns with pragmatist philosophy). Using language is one of the ways in which we act in the world to affect the world. People act by using language that is both purposeful and expressive of an attitude. This is why Burke explains rhetoric as "the use of words by human agents to form attitudes or induce actions in other human agents" (1969b, 41). Incivility is often an attempt to purposefully express an attitude of derision toward some other person or opponent and intends to induce actions and reactions (thus making it a clear example of symbolic action). These attitudes and actions may be different depending on whether we are working within the deliberative or the critical imaginary. But in either case, we construct an enemy useful for binding a team of likeminded citizens together. Burke argues that identification involves at least three processes (all of which are related to incivility): first, the process of naming something according to specific properties (this is often how insults work); second, the process of associating with and dissociating from others (some people share, or do not share, "our" important qualities); third, the process of feeling consubstantial with others and deeply bonded to those with whom we identify or against those with whom we believe we are opposed. Incivility works in each of these three ways but from a kind of reverse polarity compared to rhetors who begin by looking for points of commonality. A standard example of identification is used when, for example, a car salesman notices, as you drive into the dealership, that you have camping equipment in your car and then begins a conversation with you about a camping trip that he or she was just on a few weeks ago. Camping, in this example, becomes the mechanism for creating an association or identification between the salesperson and the customer (making the two consubstantial for a moment at least). The salesperson seeks out a point of commonality to use rhetorically in conversation. However, if, for example, the president of the United States used Twitter to call someone "stupid" (as President Trump has frequently done; http://www.trumptwitterarchive.com/archive/stupid), then the implication is that the person whom he has identified as stupid is different from him (and others like him) because they do not share any key properties in common. Consubstantiality is generated through an explicit opposition and an act of dissociation (roughly, good guys and bad guys). Nearly all forms of incivility contain this kind of dissociation and division and, in so doing, enact a form of identification in reverse.

As a matter of rhetorical practice, we cannot avoid the twin tasks of associating and dissociating or identifying and dividing inherent in our speech acts. Some forms of rhetorical leadership attempt to weave together large, disparate groups of people through symbolic means of identification, while others use dissociation to create an identification that exists in opposition to some other party, person, or group. Anodyne versions of this process certainly exist, since one politician might declare themselves the friend of people who care *most* about jobs and another may declare themselves the friend of those who care *most* about health care; both care about jobs and health care, and this difference does not entail that anyone is evil. Acts of incivility (from "You're stupid!" to "You're racist!") begin rhetorically with the naming of a specific property of a person and then use that as leverage to dissociate one group from the person or group with that property, thus generating a feeling of identification with the in-group that is dissociated from the target of the incivility. This kind of rhetorical practice is a necessary and strategic component of life in either the deliberative or the critical imaginary. What is particularly interesting about incivility is often the degree or intensity of the dissociation, the disvalue of the out-group. The ancient rhetorician Prodicus taught his students a method of dissociation as well, which he called the "correctness of names." One version of a standard exercise that his students had to do was to make careful distinctions between synonyms. For example, one might be asked to make a distinction between *pliant* and *flexible*. This would require the naming of a property that belonged to the adjective *pliant* but did not belong to the adjective *flexible*. Students skilled in the art of rhetoric are able to make such fine distinctions and use those distinctions to advance careful arguments. This also amounts to a kind of careful division of two closely aligned ideas, concepts, or things. Incivility is a hyperbolic extension of this practice designed to supercharge the division being rhetorically constructed (and to add moral weight to that division, as we will show).

We can use conspiracy theorist Alex Jones's remarks about former director of the Federal Bureau of Investigation (FBI) Robert Mueller as an example of incivility. In July 2018, Jones claimed, during a posted YouTube video, that Robert Mueller was a "demon" and a "monster," and he followed those claims up by suggesting he would shoot Mueller in a cowboy-style showdown. Then Jones claimed that Mueller was also a "pedophile" who has helped cover up a child sex ring operation in Washington, DC. *Demon*, *monster*, and *pedophile* would all, in this case, constitute rough, crude, oversimplistic, and uncivil descriptions of an American war hero and lifelong Republican. At work in Jones's rant is the rhetorical task of dissociating Mueller from other presumably more faithful and committed Republicans as well as the general category of rational civic actors or citizens. This act of dissociation effectively constructs an enemy who might strengthen the bonds among those who oppose what the enemy stands for. In other words, a rhetoric of division and identification that is useful for the purposes of persuasion and framing public conversation underpins Jones's comments.

But there were other, perhaps more civil, ways to express or construct this division. If Jones wanted to undermine the legitimacy of Mueller's work as special counsel, he could have called him, for example, a "RINO" (the acronym for "Republican in Name Only," which is used to make a tendentious distinction among different members of the Republican Party). A catalog of other possibilities for naming properties that might distinguish Mueller from the group watching the video (*elitist, globalist, boy scout,* etc.) could have been used to construct a rational and careful distinction (and thus build a rational and careful argument that had the possibility of dissociating Mueller from others while still maintaining some degree of general identification). But Jones's words were morally tinged and hyperbolic in order to exaggerate the difference. A more civil designation like RINO would have preserved some link between Mueller and the other Republicans and right-wing actors watching Jones's YouTube video, but a crude and outrageous designation makes the division impossible to bridge and magnifies the stakes of the division. The use of incivility here also magnifies the affective sense of identification felt by the in-group that now has a targeted enemy with such an outrageous set of properties that they can no longer see any connection or link among themselves and this civic actor. In other words, this act of incivility can strengthen the glue that binds Jones's audience to one another. (Mueller, having now been constructed as a morally noxious enemy, becomes a rhetorical vehicle for exaggerating the feelings of Alex Jones fans who see themselves as an in-group.)

Notice that in the previous paragraph, we used the term *conspiracy theorist* to name Jones's role and, in so doing, constructed a division between ourselves and some other members of the public sphere who believe in the veracity of Jones's claims. (We have also likely constructed an identification with our readers who, we can assume, also think of Jones in our way of describing him.) But the division we chose to construct does not hinge on the use of hyperbole—or at least, we would argue that it does not, but we are aware that some others might disagree. We cannot, in other words, avoid the rhetorical work of identification and division that we are always already doing, but we can choose to magnify or intensify that work through hyperbole or mitigate it through civility. By this we mean that civility demonstrates a kind of care that attempts to preserve even thin bonds of association, while incivility, through hyperbole, attempts to strengthen division. The rhetorical effect of hyperbolic division is the framing or construction of a world in which opposing civic actors are unable to compromise or cooperate. The rhetorical structure of incivility, in other words, is intended to make cooperation, compromise, and coordination impossible. This is, in part, why incivility is dangerous for democratic culture. We make cooperation, compromise, and coordination impossible by creating such a strong division that the possibility of any remaining identification with the other civic actors we have treated with incivility would be disgusting. If Mueller is a "demon" and "monster," then we cannot work with him in any way (and our only option might be the kind of violence for which Jones ultimately advocates).

Hyperbole is derived from the Greek word for "overthrown" (as in a ball launched too far to be caught) and serves to affect an audience, not to represent the world in a truthful or accurate manner. In other words, hyperbole as a literary trope is a kind of creative inaccuracy meant to exaggerate or highlight a property of an event or person so as to intensify some feeling. The technique of the internet troll is to almost always use some form of hyperbole in order to gain attention and produce a reaction with a high degree of intensity. That, of course, is also a generic description of Alex Jones's entire communication strategy as a right-wing conspiracy theorist. Not all forms of disagreement or discomfort are the result of hyperbole, but many forms of incivility tap into hyperbole as a rhetorical resource regardless of the political orientation of the uncivil actor. In 2018, a Georgia high school teacher compared a student's Trump T-shirt to a swastika, and shortly thereafter, the *Daily Caller* sent reporters out in Washington, DC, to ask if the "MAGA" symbol was like a swastika. Here again, we see intentional division tinged with moral language and supercharged by hyperbole. Many on the political left in the United States believe that Donald Trump's politics have authoritarian tendencies and implications, and maybe the use of the comparison between MAGA hats and swastikas is meant to highlight and exaggerate that connection, but not in a reasonable way. The rhetorical benefits of using incivility in either the Alex Jones case or the case of comparing MAGA hats to swastikas is the stronger sense of identification and division between an in-group and an out-group. In the case of the MAGA hat as a swastika, we have a form of strong incivility that attempts to remove a faction of civic actors from the public sphere by virtue of their association with the Nazis. As rhetoricians, our interest here is not in the factual accuracy of whether Trump and his followers really do have an association with the Nazis (or whether Robert Mueller really is a "demon" or "monster"). Instead, our interest is in the work done by framing the public conversation in such a manner: What is gained and what is lost? In both cases, the combination of division and hyperbole is designed to make cooperation, coordination, and compromise impossible and to strengthen the bonds between a morally righteous group divided and separated from a morally noxious group.

Hyperbole is not the only rhetorical feature of incivility. Often incivility also includes the rhetorical practice of reification or objectification. Reification, in the way we are using it here, is the process of making a person into a thing or object. We could also understand reification as a form of metonymy whereby we use an attribute of a thing or person to stand for the whole of that thing or person. Both reification and metonymy are forms of reduction that work by simplifying whatever is being described. Let us consider a popular alt-right insult used on Reddit (an internet discussion forum): *femoid*. *Femoid* is a portmanteau of the words *female* and *android* used by those on the alt-right to describe women as subhuman or nonhuman. The use of this kind of insult is meant to reduce and objectify women so as to render any kind of identification with women impossible. The left also has a vocabulary of insults like *femoid* that it uses to describe those on the far right. For example, *neckbeard* is designed to signify a portly, unkempt, and lazy male person who spends all his time online and usually gaming. We see here the use of reification and reduction again through the identification of a crude characteristic of a person (his facial hair). *Snowflake* is perhaps the most popular and widely recognized insult that works through reification. For those on the right, *snowflake* signifies the entitlement and emotional fragility of liberals, but it is being reclaimed by the left as a badge of honor. Regardless, the word works by reification and objectification. What we mean here is that we struggle to feel a sense of an identification with women if we see them as "femoids," with men if we see them as "neckbeards," or with those generally that we see as "snowflakes" because each of these descriptors (designed and used to insult) objectifies the person or group being described in order to construct a more forceful division between us and them.

The use of reification or objectification, often in conjunction with hyperbole, accelerates the kind of rhetorical division/identification that happens within public culture. One further example that can help us make sense of how these insults work: the term *soy boy* has become a very popular insult used by the alt-right. A *soy boy* is a man who drinks a lot of soymilk. The connotation trades on the urban legend that drinking soy products increases the production of estrogen in men, and the purpose of this kind of insult is to reduce and objectify the target of the insult. A *soy boy* is effeminate and weak. Collectively, all these insults operate as forms of weak incivility—they are crude insults meant to elicit a reaction from their target. Rhetorics of division that rely on hyperbole and objectification are particularly effective ways to render any degree of cooperation, compromise, or coordination impossible. In other words, the goal of a phrase like *soy boy* is to render identification with the target of the uncivil insult impossible, which thus strengthens the identification of those who feel morally righteous when using the word. In addition, the rhetorical practices of hyperbole and objectification at work in these examples rely on moral values that are symbolically tied to the insults. The uncivil actor only chooses insults that are charged with an existing set of assumptions about good and evil. The earlier swastika example is perhaps the clearest case of how to symbolically forge an identification/division that rests on a morally charged hyperbole. Thus we have a kind of calculus for both forms of strong and weak incivility: morally charged modes of using division/identification, hyperbole, and/or objectification to create the strongest possible reaction. This calculus leaves us with two critical questions: As a communication strategy, what work does this do in public culture? How do some civic actors use this form of communication to pursue or generate sociopolitical change?

An Uncivil President and a Divided Public

On October 27, 2018, eleven people were murdered and seven injured in a shooting at a synagogue in Pittsburgh. The shooter had engaged in a number of anti-Semitic rants through social media (similar to Alex Jones's rants). Following the event, a poll conducted by National Public Radio (NPR), Public Broadcasting Service (PBS), and Maris College showed that 80 percent of Americans believed that incivility would lead to further violence in the United States. The cover of the October 2018 issue of the *American Conservative* read, "The Civil War on America's Horizon." Violent events like the Pittsburgh shooting are not uncommon in the current political moment, and thus polarization, incivility, and political violence all seem to be intertwined. A growing public narrative that our political differences cannot be overcome has led to the sense that the threat of violence, civil war, or the breaking up of the United States is ever more likely. Given that the rhetorical function of a simple uncivil insult is to construct a hyperbolic division that makes it difficult for an "us" to identify with a "them," it should not come as a surprise when weak incivility becomes strong incivility and public culture becomes a matter of who is included or excluded in deliberation. Donald Trump's Twitter feed is perhaps the best illustration of what happens when weak forms of incivility become strong forms of incivility, and nearly every metric seems to confirm that the American public in 2018 was as deeply divided as ever.

Incivility seems, at nearly every turn, to be the central rhetorical strategy behind President Trump's messages, most prominently on Twitter and at his regular campaign rallies (which have been ongoing after his inauguration in 2017). As rhetorical artifacts, his Twitter feed and campaign rallies enact—over and over again, on an almost daily basis—division/identification, hyperbole, and objectification. Unlike the Pittsburgh shooter's, however, Trump's social media presence engages millions of civic actors, and his rallies are attended by large crowds and broadcast on television. At times, his tweets amount to simple cases of weak incivility ("loser!") for one particular person. At other times, however, the potent rhetorical structure of incivility is magnified with false analogies, false choices, ad hominem attacks, and perhaps most importantly, hasty generalizations or overgeneralizations (i.e., drawing a conclusion based on an insufficient sample size). Overgeneralization uses one experience to draw a general conclusion about all experiences. Interestingly, overgeneralization tends to be a common concern for those with mental health issues like anxiety and depression. When overgeneralization becomes commonplace in political discourse, then it becomes easier to treat others with incivility, and when overgeneralization and hyperbole mix together, then we have potent circumstances for violent conflict within the critical imaginary.

President Trump tried to feature a group of migrants from Honduras seeking asylum in America as a campaign issue in the 2018 midterm elections. This resulted in a series of tweets about what he called the "caravan" of dangerous criminals trying to illegally gain entry to the United States. He repeated, over Twitter and at rallies, various lies about the defining features of the group of asylum seekers. At different points, he claimed the group was made up of terrorists, hardened criminals, dangerous young men, and gang members. All these claims were argumentative overgeneralizations and rhetorical hyperboles at the same time. Alone, they do not seem quite as uncivil as insults like "femoid" or "soy boy," though they do the same rhetorical work. They are intentionally hyperbolic uses of division, in this case, relying on the practice of overgeneralization as applied to a whole group. A false, simplified treatment of a group like this is not meant to simply offend the group in question. Instead, by design, it offends those who might identify with the group of asylum seekers and to remove from public discourse any rational conversation about the virtues of immigration. No one willingly identifies with hardened criminals, terrorists, or gang members, which means that once the "caravan" is defined in this way, careful arguments used to support practices of asylum are silenced within the public sphere. In addition, those who would align with rational arguments in favor of immigration can be openly labeled "libtards" or any other derogatory form of incivility. To peruse the threads on a site like Reddit is to witness an endless barrage of both weak and strong incivility as one group hurls insults at another around interpretations of the meaning of the caravan. The use of hyperbole and overgeneralization is also meant to strengthen the identification Republicans feel for one another and their cause through the clarity of a morally noxious enemy (the supposed "tough people" from the caravan) looking to "invade our country," to use Trump's words. The moral division acquires a kind of deep certainty from the overgeneralization and legitimizes name-calling and insults from either side of the divided public.

The treatment of the caravan is similar to Trump's initial announcement that he intended to run for president. During the speech he delivered to announce his candidacy, he called Mexicans "rapists"—a crude, simplified, hyperbolic overgeneralization. This clearly did the rhetorical work of division/ identification and included morally charged language designed to produce a powerful effect on the audience. Viewed as strong incivility, all Trump's racist remarks about nonwhites are a mechanism for dividing the public sphere and delegitimizing voices that might through regular discourse participate in public deliberation. But why? Because incivility is, at its core, a profound kind of critique that seeks to produce powerful feelings of discomfort. Once those feelings of discomfort are present and a rationale for defeating a morally noxious other is in place, then, so the argument goes, political change becomes possible. This is why President Trump continues to demonize and insult immigrants looking for asylum in the United States—he wants to politically transform the immigration system. Discomfort with the threat of immigrants and clarifying the set of identifications that specific constituents may feel makes political change possible.

The same can be said about antifa and the far left. Antifa is a loose political movement of antifascist militants who engage in "direct action" against white supremacists and others. "Direct action" includes harassing those who are deemed fascists, which can include property damage and violence designed to silence public hate speech. For the antifa movement, civility in the face of fascism is unthinkable and tantamount to a morally objectionable complicity. Just like Trump wants us to feel uncomfortable at the prospect of a migrant caravan or Mexican immigrants, antifa wants to produce an agitated sense of discomfort in white supremacists and neofascists, and harassment and threats are their tools. The rhetorical styles of the Trump movement (and the alt-right more broadly) and antifa are similar in that both use hyperbole, overgeneralization, division/identification, and reification to make cooperation or compromise impossible with a morally bankrupt other. Change becomes a matter of defeating the morally noxious other and advancing the core interest of the winning side. Little to no thought is given to how we might continue to live with the others whom we have insulted and defeated because the process of hyperbole and reification have ensured that we no longer think of those others as viable members of "our" democratic culture. Only when we have rhetorically constructed and framed others through incivility can we conceptualize change as a kind of victory over competing forces. In this way, incivility feeds a kind of narrative, values-based worldview in which heroes and enemies play central roles, and change is just a matter of the heroes beating the enemies (regardless of whether you view the world from the perspective of Trump or antifa).

The kind of narrative view of the world made possible by strong incivility allows for the repeated use of false analogy, false choices, and ad hominem attacks as central features of public discourse. These rhetorical acts are, in and of themselves, forms of incivility given that they are crude oversimplifications, and they magnify the process of identification and division at work in our treatment of others. Trump's penchant for assigning insulting nicknames to his political opponents is a clear example of an ad hominem attack (just as the use of "femoid" and "soy boy" is as well). His repeated use of the descriptor "crooked Hilary" to identify Hilary Clinton is an obvious case of an incivility constructing a division with a morally bankrupt other. With each character insult and each ad hominem attack, Trump solidifies identification of those who oppose, for example, crookedness; exaggerates the differences between an "us" and "them"; and overgeneralizes with the intent of objectifying the others he insults. Ad hominem attacks become commonplace in a democratic culture marked by division and by both weak and strong forms of incivility. They reduce communicative interactions in the public sphere to discussions of the character of civic actors instead of the substance of policy decisions or inquiry into the deep problems that collectively demand our attention. This is why ad hominem attacks are fallacious: the character of the person does not typically determine the utility or soundness of the arguments that they advance, though it does undermine trust in that person and make it harder to hear their arguments. But in the critical imaginary when civic actors engage in ad hominem attacks, they do so because they have already defined the opposition in morally bankrupt, hyperbolic terms.

President Trump also frequently uses false analogies and false choices, and these practices are legitimized by incivility and accelerate or deepen the divisions among civic actors. One of his favorite bogeymen is the criminal gang "MS-13." During an immigration round table with California sheriffs on May 16, 2018, Trump referred to the members of MS-13 as "animals." The White House Press Office followed up this comment with a press release on what we all needed to know about "The Animals of MS-13." This analogy fails because Trump assumes that the same properties that animals possess are also the properties that MS-13 gang members possess. He means, of course, properties like viciousness or danger, but surely not all animals are vicious and dangerous (in fact, the vast majority are not). Sean Spicer, Trump's first press secretary, infamously compared Bashar al-Assad to Adolf Hitler and was roundly criticized for the false analogy. Civic actors in the critical imaginary who become habituated to uncivil discourse rely on false analogies like this to engage in increasingly hyperbolic discourse. The more extreme the analogy, the more work it can do to demonize and silence civic actors. The president's son Donald Trump Jr. compared the platform of the Democratic Party to the Nazi Party in Germany in the 1930s; he made these comments at a movie premiere for Dinesh D'Souza, a controversial right-wing personality who pleaded guilty in 2014 to violating campaign finance laws. They were, no doubt, designed to provoke a response and not to carefully represent a position. And civic actors in uncivil times will continue to look for more hyperbolic forms of false analogy because that is the only way to continue to get attention and provoke reactions. The more extreme the analogy, the more it can rhetorically work to enact division/identification.

False dilemmas or choices arise when two options are presented as if they are the only two options. Take, for example, President Trump's repeated claim that the Democrats favor "open borders" while the Republicans prefer "closed borders." (He often emphasizes the difference with the phrase "totally open borders.") This, of course, is a false choice because many policy options exist in between these two; this move is an oversimplification just like practices of incivility. We do not interrogate the choices if we assume that one of the sides in the choice is offered by a morally bankrupt actor with whom we do not identify; then the false choice can do the rhetorical work of preserving the division built into democratic culture. Whenever Trump suggests that there "really" are only two choices, he relies on the divided public to not bother interrogating the claim because the choices fit into the narrative that includes enemies who have been denigrated and delegitimized. The catalog of false dilemmas that Trump offers us is extensive: vote for Trump or the Democrats will "destroy" the Second Amendment; you are either tough on crime or for anarchy and lawlessness; you either know that we need a wall built between Mexico and the United States or you are for unlimited immigration. All these simplified choices are irrational, but they work given the rampant incivility that has demonized, simplified, and objectified some civic actors. These false choices then further remove arguments from public deliberation because we see the denigrated and morally bankrupt others as incapable of productively contributing to public discourse. They rely on the righteousness of one side of the debate (along with the certainty of the positions advanced by the righteous) and the evil of the other side (along with the certainty of the emptiness of the positions advanced by the other side).

We can be easily preoccupied with our own historical moment, especially given the startling evidence of incivility and even violence we are experiencing. But Trump's rhetorical practices are not new, just as the structure of incivility is not new. Incivility, unfortunately, produces a sense of certainty along with the sense of identification that comes as a byproduct of division. This certainly is a result of the degree to which some civic actors think their positions are the only right positions and the only morally virtuous options. In other words, with fewer and fewer civic actors taking on the role of inquirer and more and more taking on the role of troll, then the plot driving the theater of public discourse begins to assume more and more of the characteristics of violent conflict. When in such a performance, civic actors will feel justified in treating others in our democratic culture with incivility. When they do treat "others" with an incivility that supercharges or accelerates the feelings of division, they amplify the sense of certainty with which each side holds their positions and additionally the degree of hyperbole with which positions get articulated.

This cycle has plagued democratic cultures across the world. Difference or debate or disagreement can seem so pressing that we believe the only route to change is through victory over opposing forces. And no doubt such a route is available to us. The U.S. Civil War was fought and won, which led to specific, material changes. But when change perpetuates a morally noxious other who does not become part of a new national identity, then that change is purchased at a terrible price. African Americans may have been freed from slavery after the Civil War, but Jim Crow laws and countless other forms of racism and abuse persisted in the attitudes and beliefs of those who lost the war. The divisions, in other words, persist after the victory. The forces of the alt-right or alt-left may ultimately provoke and win another civil war in the United States, which might lead to specific, material changes in American policies and government actions. But if we have treated those others in our democratic culture with incivility and derision the way that Trump and his followers do, then how will we learn to work with and identify with those others? What happens after the war? Will some characteristics of our world remain unchanged even if one side wins?

The Desire for, and Limitations of, Critique

At the core of all acts of incivility is the desire for, and commitment to, critique and change; this is the driving force in the critical imaginary. We critique positions that we find objectionable, and we do so with the intention or interest in making our worlds better. We act with incivility in order to cause discomfort in others, and that discomfort seems necessary in order to transform or change the circumstances that we wish were different. We want those with whom we disagree to feel discomfort so that they know their positions are being challenged. But when critique is practiced with the kind of hyperbole, objectification, and divisiveness that are characteristic of

incivility, then we need to ask how our treatment of others, and our obligations to others, may short-circuit or prevent the very change that we seek.
When living in a democracy, we must disagree one day and then still manage to live with those with whom we disagree the next. Incivility can make
living together with those with whom we disagree more difficult given that
we have rhetorically constructed them so as to prevent any sense of identification. This is the limitation of the style of critique that positions others as
morally noxious beings: its reliance on hyperbole, along with the act of dif-
ferentiation, makes the strategic and effective use of incivility in the critical
imaginary difficult and dangerous. Despite these constraints, our desire for
critique will persist and drive questions of whether or how we may productively engage incivility. The question, therefore, is whether we can imagine
and articulate forms of incivility that might still constructively promote
change through discomfort. Many on both the left and the right clearly
desire some form of vigorous, uncomfortable, tense disagreement as an avenue to altering our sociopolitical circumstances. Can we do that without being
so insulting and harmful to others that we tear the very fabric of democratic culture?

In the early 1980s, the Denominational Ministry Strategy (DMS), an alli-
ance of militant union members and Protestant priests in Pittsburgh, Pennsylvania, targeted banking and manufacturing corporations in Pittsburgh
as the primary reason behind the region's deindustrialization and growing unemployment. As part of their protest tactics, members of the DMS
rented out safety deposit boxes at Mellon Banks throughout Pittsburgh on
Friday afternoons. Then they placed frozen fish inside those boxes (sometimes using skunk oil). This meant that by Monday morning, the banks had
a horrendous odor, which led to the label "smellin' Mellon" as an insult. The
"smellin' Mellon" campaign forced bank branches to close, sometimes for
days, while bank staffers and professional cleaners located and eradicated
the source of the smell. DMS did not have much success altering the banks'
investment decisions, but they were able to disrupt the normal flow of civic
life in Pittsburgh through what we take to be acts of incivility. The crudeness
and simplicity of the rotten fish (with all their metaphorical baggage), clearly
used to provoke a reaction, align with the general definition of incivility we
offered at the beginning of this chapter, but somehow this example feels different from Trump's use of Twitter.

The DMS tactics were inspired by Saul Alinsky, author of *Rules for Radicals* and political organizer from the 1930s to the 1970s. Alinsky advocated
for the use of polarization in campaigns designed to generate change and

also recommended the use of ridicule and disruption, which we can see in the "smellin' Mellon" example. These tactics were undoubtedly uncivil and used rhetorics of division (along with the identification of enemies and the strengthening of bonds of identification among specific groups). Alinsky was also notorious for the crudeness and simplicity of some of his techniques and believed that those seeking change ought to enjoy (take pleasure from) the practices that they used to ridicule, challenge, and disrupt the others standing in the way of the change they demanded. But they were part of a dialectic. We often forget that at the same time, Alinsky always advocated for depolarization sessions with the opposition and always emphasized the importance of maintaining relationships—albeit somewhat tense and strained—with his targets. His depolarization sessions were critical because Alinsky believed that he never knew when an enemy would become a friend or when an oppositional force would suddenly align with him on a new issue. He knew that, after the moment of confrontation, he would need to live with those he ridiculed in the moment and thus needed communicative practices to help move beyond the initial provocation. One difference between the kinds of ridicule practiced by DMS and other organizations inspired by Alinsky and President Trump's stream of vituperation is the presence of contempt or resentment. Alinsky just might offer us a view of incivility that allows for critique and disruption but stops short of the kind of contempt or resentment that would make future civil relationships impossible. In addition, Alinsky sought tactics that were specific, local, and direct without the overgeneralization of hyperbole. How did he do this?

During Alinsky's earliest years of organizing, his approach depended on uniting ordinary citizens around immediate grievances in their neighborhoods and protesting vigorously (with varying degrees of incivility) against all kinds of injustices in ways that were often outside of the established modes of expressing dissent. In other words, he worked at the fringes of the deliberative imaginary where it shades into the critical imaginary. For Alinsky, political action must be rooted in the practical concerns of local people but not necessarily inside the "normal" rules of discourse because it was those norms that had excluded many ordinary people. However, this did not mean disregarding those norms but rather cultivating a more nuanced sense of how and why communicative norms work as they do. Alinsky lamented many young radicals' lack of communication skills, along with the alienation that resulted from their inability to connect with allies, with people who might otherwise have been supportive of their causes. For example, the trend for burning the American flag to protest the Vietnam War was a spectacle that Alinsky saw as going outside of (and alienating) the norms and values of many people who might otherwise be sympathetic with the movement for peace, and so in that specific moment, he saw this incivility as going too far. Alinsky claimed that "the responsible organizer would have known that it is the establishment that has betrayed the flag while the flag, itself, remains the symbol of America's hopes and aspirations" (1989, xvii). By this, he means the flag could serve as a resource for identification, a necessary communicative practice to generate change even if uncomfortable confrontation needed to happen. By contrast, recent outrage about kneeling during the anthem seems disingenuous; the anthem is not the symbol of the country, there are no rules about how we have to listen to it, and a Supreme Court decision (West Virginia State Board of Education v. Barnette, 319 U.S. 624 [1943]) prohibits mandatory patriotic rituals. This is not to say we should give no thought to the feelings of those for whom professional football games are important moments of militaristic patriotism, just that the weighing of that obligation seems very different when the response seems to grow more out of pseudocivility than anything else.

As a community organizer, Alinsky tried to develop a handbook for generating political change, and driving change was always a matter of connecting with people first and critiquing them second (or identification before division, to put it in rhetorical terms). To develop his rules for radicals, Alinsky argued that the radical, at least in the first instance, should work within the system even while challenging and critiquing the norms of the system, consistent with how social change works in the deliberative imaginary. Many radical groups separated themselves from the system intentionally, but this only marginalized their position and limited their abilities to act. We can take this to mean that incivility could only generate change when practiced inside an ongoing deliberative ecology. For radical change to happen, the majority of people must be in favor, even if only passively, of change. However, Alinsky also believed people to be naturally fearful of change and that unless they feel "so frustrated, so defeated, so lost, so futureless in the prevailing system that they are willing to let go of the past and chance the future," revolution will not happen (1989, xix). Incivility, then, challenges the norms of a system but works within those norms by disrupting them to just the right degree and with just the right form.

Alinsky's *Rules for Radicals* touches on several key themes for community organizers critical to our understanding of rhetorics of division and identification: symbolic construction to strengthen the unity within an organization, nonviolent conflict as a uniting element in communities, and direct action to bring issues to the community. Alinsky used symbolic constructions and nonviolent conflict to create a structured organization with a clearly defined goal in order to take direct action against a common oppressor; he taught organizations to do the same, empowering them to create change for whatever issue they were battling. This was essentially a matter of effective communication: "My 'thing,' if I want to organize, is solid communication with the people in the community. Lacking communication I am in reality silent; throughout history silence has been regarded as assent—in this case assent to the system" (1989, xix). This requires that the organizer communicate "within the experiences of his audience" (xviii). One starts where one's audience is because "believing in people, the radical has the job of organizing them so that they will have the power and opportunity to best meet each foreseeable future crisis" (xviii). Such a perspective is deeply other-centered and does not seek to lead by persuading a group of people to follow an already-decided-upon course of action. An organizer does not have an agenda other than to organize and communicate with the people in the community to help give expression to the ideas, problems, and relationships within that community. Alinsky, to use the terms from the previous chapter, is clearly arguing that the organizer begins as an inquirer only; enacting the role of warrior comes later, and that context clarifies incivility and direct confrontation in the critical imaginary. Effective communication is always already also a matter of experience: "An organizer can communicate only within the areas of experience of his audience; otherwise there is no communication. The organizer, in his constant hunt for patterns, universality, and meaning, is always building up a body of experience" (69–70). Alinsky imagines an artful process: "Through his imagination he is constantly moving in on the happenings of others, identifying with them and extracting their happenings into his own mental digestive system and thereby accumulating more experience. It is essential for communication that he knows of their experiences. Since one can communicate only through the experiences of the other, it becomes clear that the organizer begins to develop an abnormally large body of experience" (70). This means that an organizer "listens to small talk"; learns "local legends, anecdotes, values, idioms"; and "refrains from rhetoric foreign to the local culture" (70).

But the organizer cannot fake this sort of empathetic communication. Alinsky tells a story of some work that he did with Mexican immigrants in California with whom he shared a special dinner. Midway through the dinner, he made an uncivil joke about how horrible he thought the food was, and this joke managed to break down barriers and get many to laugh with him. This anecdote showed how organizers might meet the members of a community on the terms of their own experiences while simultaneously showing themselves to be authentic. Incivility worked to enhance relationality in this example, and it did so upon an already existing layer of identification. Communication is a matter of mutual understanding for Alinsky: "Communication with others takes place when they understand what you are trying to get across to them. If they do not understand, then you are not communicating. . . . People only understand things in terms of their own experience, which means that you must get within their experience" (1989, 81). Alinsky packs a lot into "understanding" here, where he seems to mean a view of a system (economic, political, social), not just specific facts about the behavior of city officials or factory owners. So understanding another in terms of the other's experience is a matter of "personal identification of the organizer with the others" (84). Again, Burke's conception of rhetoric as identification returns. What Alinsky has identified as a central feature of a leader is the ability to symbolically produce a sense of consubstantiality. This all unfolds within the context of already existing relationships that condition what can and cannot be said. According to Alinsky, "One of the factors that changes what you can and can't communicate is relationships. There are sensitive areas that one does not touch until there is a strong personal relationship based on common involvements" (93). Otherwise, the other party will be "turned off" or will simply not hear what is said. And finally, communication is also a matter of sticking to particulars, specifics, and/or concrete objects or circumstances. For Alinsky, an organizer always needs to remember that he or she is communicating with "one specific person and not a general mass" and about specific issues that "are small enough to be grasped by the hands of experience" (96).

Much of *Rules for Radicals* is devoted to specific tactics for organizing. We are less interested in these specific tactics and more interested in the strategic commitment to communication and community that precedes and contextualizes the use of some pretty aggressive forms of incivility. What we think is most telling about Alinsky's position is that persuasion, or rhetorical practice, is never a matter of deciding on a course of action or belief and then convincing a group to take that course of action or adopt that specific belief. Instead, persuasion is a matter of forming relationships within a social scene of experience and then, afterward, deciding on what beliefs or courses of action ought to be followed. Incivility within that scene of relationships can work differently. The political purpose of an organization, for Alinsky, grew out of the kinds of relationships that were formed by virtue of the work of the organizer. The issues never come before the relationships. This we take to be an essential feature of democratic culture—we act as inquirers before we act as warriors, and doing so may create spaces for incivility to actually generate change. A leader is able to organize a community by creating relationships that can be leveraged for political change later on. When Alinsky celebrates the communication skills of the organizer, he is celebrating the ability to forge these relationships, not imposing a vision on a group of people but forging bonds and so making possible the collaborative and cooperative process of deciding on a course of action that improves the well-being of the community.

Within such a context, we can read incivility as a different kind of tool than the tool used by President Trump (a person who has spent no time whatsoever concerned with learning about the experiences of his constituents or forming robust relationships within which incivility may be practiced as critique more effectively). In this context, incivility can generate change only when practiced in light of already existing social bonds and only when targeted, concrete, specific, or particular (just like the "smellin' Mellon" example). Alinsky's practices manifest some humor and joy because he knows the importance of relationality and seeks to test the limits of relationships with his acts of ridicule and interruption. Nowhere does he communicate resentment and contempt for those who hold opposing views because he knows that those whom he ridicules one day may be his allies the next. The particularity and concreteness of the acts of incivility are also designed to mitigate the possibility of communicating resentment and contempt for a person or group by avoiding the fallacies so readily committed by Trump. Alinsky teaches us that we must balance our uses of incivility with our commitments to relationality. This insight remains at the core of our argument in this book. Incivility unchecked by relationality risks destroying the system.

Microaggressions and Interpersonal Conflict

The claims we have just made about incivility in public discourse are echoed by research on interpersonal communication as well. John Gottman, preeminent marriage and relationship expert, has spent decades showing how criticism and resentment corrode interpersonal relationships and lead to failed marriages. Gottman's work reminds us, however, that relationships are broken not by single acts of incivility that communicate resentment but by a repeated pattern over time that makes it impossible for couples to feel connected to one another. Much research on interpersonal communication practices points to the ways in which name-calling, ad hominem attacks, overgeneralizations, hyperbole, false analogies, false choices, and general forms of expressing disdain for our partners, friends, and family are the surest ways to undo and destroy those relationships, while myriad other forms of interpersonal communication, like active listening and expressing support, build constructive relationships in which cooperation and compromise are possible. When we move from considerations of interpersonal communication among those who are already close to consider interpersonal interactions among strangers in the theater of public discourse, then we can begin to see the ways in which incivility might accelerate and deepen the damage to relationality done by expressions of resentment. If we know that crude insults can ruin a marriage—a relationship built on intimacy, history, trust, and so on—then we cannot ignore what work those insults do on the strangers whom we meet as civic actors. Our reactions to incivility are stronger, deeper, and faster when the person making the comment is a stranger to us. We also know that in interpersonal communication, mirroring is one of the central and unavoidable ways we relate to others. This means that one act of interpersonal aggression has a good chance of leading to a return aggression. In other words, one insult leads the insulted party to insult a person in return, thus forming an interpersonal cycle of communication that prohibits relationship formation.

We see escalation work for President Trump. Countless targets of his hostile and uncivil comments return insults back to him with similar form and structure (albeit different content). Trump's instances of incivility are almost always performed publicly through social media or traditional media (he seems charming and conciliatory in personal meetings)—he insults people over Twitter or while speaking at a rally. But that does not mean people will not mirror these forms of discourse in their own interpersonal encounters. Our everyday interactions are just as likely to become sites of incivility given the examples being set by political leaders, and given our description of democracy as a way of life, those interactions are essential for the maintenance and development of democratic cultures. We see countless mediated representations of interpersonal conflicts now, particularly but not exclusively related to protest movements. These can extend from YouTube videos of road rage or national news networks showing violent clashes among protestors. To spend time reading the comments section from Trump's Twitter feed is to get an immediate sense of the ways in which incivility in public discourse trickles down to our interpersonal interactions. We have all experienced Facebook fights that easily and quickly devolve into the kind of hostile, uncivil name-calling that Trump exemplifies. Recently on our Facebook feed, a prominent scholar called Tucker Carlson, of *Fox News*, a "pig fornicator." This is unfortunate; Carlson is frequently annoying, snide, and offensive, yet we struggle to see how this is helpful incivility rather than self-indulgent. When these instances of incivility are targeted at our fellow citizens and we do not have already existing relationships with those other citizens who might withstand or weather the insults, then cooperation and compromise become too difficult to manage. (Just as divorce is the outcome of the presence of these acts in marriages, so might civil war be the outcome when we consider these acts on a more public scale.)

Microaggressions are the everyday verbal, nonverbal, and environmental slights, snubs, or insults, whether intentional or unintentional, that communicate hostile, derogatory, or negative messages to target persons based on their marginalized group membership. They seem especially noxious to the extent that the stereotypes that fund them are implicated in large structures of oppression (the "angry black man" is a stereotype with serious consequences when connected to already violent policing). In many cases, these subliminal messages serve to invalidate a group's identity or their experience of reality; these actions demean people on a personal or group level, communicate they are lesser human beings, suggest they do not belong with the majority group, threaten and intimidate, or relegate them to inferior status and treatment. We might ask, from what we know of Saul Alinsky, why would an organizer be obligated to avoid these microaggressions? Because the organizer must gain some access to the experiences of the people with whom he or she works, microaggressions are a sure sign of the failure to achieve that kind of relationality. Avoiding a faux pas is less about political correctness and more about the good communication practices that help drive change. We can understand microaggressions (like failing to use someone's correct pronouns after being told what they are or assuming that a person with a Hispanic surname is Mexican and likes Mexican food) as forms of incivility that fail to work within a framework that recognizes and appreciates relationality. "Hey, don't be so sensitive" is an odd response for anyone who wants to maintain relationships; that response is appropriate when we want people to know we do not care. We are not arguing here that we should never insult another person or never cause another person discomfort, but if we do engage in such practices, then we ought to do so with an awareness of the priority of relationality. This is what John Gottman and Saul Alinsky realize and Donald Trump does not.

5

STRONG CIVILITY FOR SOCIAL JUSTICE

Some eighteenth-century proponents of civility speak of polish and refinement, and so sound a little prissy. Montesquieu is harder: civility is a necessary virtue to help us negotiate a world of pain. That is why he places so much emphasis on knowledge and, above all, on toleration, itself almost a synonym for civility.

—JOHN A. HALL, *THE IMPORTANCE OF BEING CIVIL*

The gist of our argument so far is that we reject casting civility as the friend of oppression and enemy of change. We believe that civility, in practice, is the enemy of oppression in its requirements for respecting others' dignity and equality of treatment. Many of the objections to our arguments could be summed up in a challenge: Why be civil to a racist or a sexist? Or to take up the epigraph to this chapter, on whom does the burden of toleration rest? Answering this question will tie together several strands of the arguments we have been making throughout and show how we might develop a more positive program for endorsing civil communication practices in the service of social change and justice. It might also provide some insight into why those who have experienced oppression might still find civility a useful resource for social change. In other words, if we are persuasive, this chapter will also provide an effective rejoinder to those who might question the utility or efficacy of democracy itself or those on the margins who are justifiably cynical of civility as a force for social change. Strong civility, in balance with careful critique, can drive change while still holding the social fabric of democratic life together.

In the critical imaginary, civility is considered (rightly) a kind of mutual respect, and to respect someone, even minimally, with racist, sexist, or homophobic beliefs is to extend respect to his or her racism or sexism (or homophobia) as well. Basically, this is the question of whether we can oppose—and mitigate or eliminate—racism or sexism if we maintain any kind of civil relationship with a racist or sexist. Why, in other words, try to at least balance a commitment to civility with our desire to reject those we morally oppose? The answer to this question relies on understanding the trade-offs it poses in at least two dimensions: personhood and social democracy. We could ask the same question from the perspective of those on the margins: Why try to balance a commitment to civility with our desire to reject those who have oppressed us? In this latter case, civility simply preserves the status quo of oppression. Can balancing civility with our desire to critique or resist others' positions (whatever they may be) help drive change?

People are multidimensional creatures despite their inevitable failings, their sometimes morally noxious positions, or the disagreements that divide us from one another. A common way of putting this point is that even if we disagree on some values, there will be others on which we do agree, which could be a basis for navigating our differences. That formulation, however useful and successful in some cases, is not completely satisfactory because it seems to presume a neutral background in which your racism is on equal ground with my antiracism, as if racism was a negotiable value. Civility does not assume or require such a neutral ground, since it presumes equality and constitutes part of the movement (as documented by Taylor) toward the leveling of differences that make a difference. One function of civility (mentioned in chapter 2) is that it allows us to live together *without* achieving consensus, without having to believe or to like the same things—your taste in movies, food, or religion is none of my business. We mean here to push back on the view that we need to get consensus on basic values before we can talk to one another when that consensus, if it happens at all, is an outcome of talking. And we acknowledge that in every context, people "speak" from different locations or positions within social and political hierarchies (this is also a feature of our democratic lives for better or worse), but again they must find ways to talk regardless of those different positions (marginal, dominant, etc.). If nothing else, politics shows that people who disagree "philosophically" can agree on the best course of action in a specific setting. This equanimity about disagreement should extend to equal treatment in most contexts. Considering someone's race, gender, or sexuality in hiring is not just illegal—it is also uncivil. A fundamentally civil society would be one in which people try to treat one another as equally as possible. Notice that this is a behavioral requirement; I do not have to approve of atheism to try to consciously bracket my disagreement and treat atheists (or Catholics or Wiccans) as fairly and considerately as possible. No society has yet approached the perfection of this ideal, yet it remains a compelling and functional ideal, not least for how often we come close.

The deliberative imaginary encourages us to see others in multidimensional ways or at least encourages us not to reduce them to single positions or make caricatures of them out of their most extreme beliefs (like uncivil actors do so often in their practices of reification). Sometimes those positions may be so noxious that reduction and defeat are the only options (defending slavery—philosophically or militarily—as an institution, it turns out, proved to be impossible), but surely every instance of racism is not the same as institutional slavery. We tend, unfortunately, to take principles, like those underlying civility, and test them against extreme examples and limit cases even though they are least useful in those contexts. We can easily see why, because of the problem discussed in chapter 1 as "the line." A line (beyond which civility does not apply) must surely exist, though different people draw that line differently, and its location is vague. We can in practice discover where someone's line is by bringing up test cases. This is not intrinsically wrong-headed, unless someone thinks either that there is "really" an objective line or—more important—that looking for the line invalidates principles of civility altogether (if racism is wrong, it is completely wrong and wrong in every guise). The latter inference does not seem useful, and in practice (as opposed to punditry) few seem to make it.

The long-running controversy over the use of Native American mascots by college and professional sports teams exemplifies a case with broad disagreement, even (to an extent) within the Native American community, about whether such mascots are racist. Let us stipulate that they are an expression of systemic racism in a way that mascots such as Vikings, Spartans, or Fighting Irish could not be (since they represent groups that did not suffer systemic, long-term, legalized oppression). Suppose you have a friend who celebrates such a mascot even though he is aware of the objections to it. We could reasonably see the use and endorsement of these logos as a kind of acceptance of the material/historical conditions that enabled the theft of Native lands and the murder of Native Americans. Given this, you may be forced to conclude your friend is, in this regard at least, racist. So what should your response be? Notice that probably not just a single incident but a series of interactions convince you he is aware of objections but discounts them. You have some choices. You could decide to be uncivil, which might include telling him directly what a terrible person he is, cutting off your friendship, severing all contact, and publicly chastising him when possible. What would be accomplished by these actions in this case? Probably not a lot; U.S. history with indigenous people will not be undone, the structures that perpetuate racism will not be affected, and the team and your friend will continue using the logo. There might be strength in numbers ("If *everybody* boycotted, maybe the owners would see . . ."), but that would require your friend, the fan, to be part of the boycott. Imagine another scenario in which you are an indigenous person whose ancestors were murdered and whose land was stolen by colonists. In such a scenario, you likely have lots of experience acting with civility toward those in power as a way of self-preservation and safety despite your desire to reject or critique others for their history of oppression and their present disrespect. You have similar choices to the first imagined friend despite your different positionality. Incivility seems limited from both perspectives, and we would suggest that something can be gained from civility in either case.

Even though this friend is on the wrong side of history, you might decide that the offense does not quite justify this treatment, and you might take into account that your friend is also explicitly antiracist on a number of issues, is careful about sexist language, and in other ways is kind and generous. So civilly, you could do some or all of the following: Tell him he is wrong and explain why. Let him know you cannot share in his joy over this particular team and explain why. Ask him (though you cannot compel him) not to wear clothing with team mascot logos around you. Keep checking in to see if he becomes any more conscious of the problematic character of the mascot. Here you have taken into account a total person and chosen to keep a relationship, both for its own sake and for the possibility of influence. Now your friend may or may not find your haranguing (once or ongoing) to be "rude." Can he be right about that? It depends on how you do it, since stating your case clearly and without insult or accusation is not necessarily rude. Very likely, having decided to try to preserve the relationship, you two will engage in a delicate dance between your need to acknowledge racism and his discomfort with being confronted with it.

While any action that does not attack symbolic and structural oppression is in some sense complicit in propping it up, all complicity is not created equal; it can be arguably more or less direct and significant. Will persuading your friend to be woke about mascots change either the behavior of sports teams or the material structural conditions that constrain the lives of Native Americans? Probably not. (Boycotting advertisers or activism with fan or alumni groups would probably produce more change.) Does it still matter that this is important to you and that your friend should share your values? Sure, though that may not require your friend to share your judgment about what action is needed on such a value. Because you have decided in this case to keep the relationship, does that mean you would decide *every* case this way? Of course not. If you found out this same friend had joined, and defended having joined, a paramilitary group organized for the purpose of harassing people of color, you should make a different decision, cutting him off and notifying the authorities (since the actions of such a group are illegal as well as uncivil).

In the deliberative imaginary, change is much slower and does not come from victory, leaving a defeated enemy behind, but from a civil consideration for other's multidimensionality that allows us to leverage connections (both intellectual and relational) for the purposes of more modest or gradual changes that have the potential to endure over longer periods of time. This is the central lesson of liberalism that we referenced in the introduction through Adam Gopnik's *A Thousand Small Sanities*. We also see this as a central avenue of change whether one is marginalized within our current cultural scene or not. We treat others with civility because we see them not simply as articulations of oppression to be defeated but as complex persons with the potential to change and evolve (this is an obligation all of us have regardless of our positionality). We also do not see civility as a position of political moderation or quietism per se. In other words, by understanding civility as a set of communication practices, we have untethered the concept from preexisting ideological belief systems. This means that it becomes incumbent on citizens to treat others, as far as possible, with civility regardless of the views of the multidimensional others whom we encounter and regardless of our own views. I might, in other words, hold very radical views about racism and its influence on the sociopolitical culture of the United States, but those radical views do not legitimate my uncivil treatment of others. My obligations to others mean that I must be strategic in how I choose to communicate with those who hold radically different positions than mine.

Tests for Balancing Civility, Social Justice, and Social Change

To understand the role of civility in social change and for helping move us toward social justice, we have to carefully track its double role as both supporter and solvent of the status quo. As we have seen, in the critical social imaginary, the status quo is a totalizing and systemic set of economic, social, and cultural forces that are strengthened at every moment they are not challenged, and the challenge itself must take very specific forms. Here we want to tackle head-on the claim that advocacy for social justice requires a rejection of civility. We challenge this partly because we should not cede civility to racists, sexists, and other oppressors and partly because it will illuminate how civility can, and should, help create social change.

We propose that we use three tests, similar to "balancing tests" in legal reasoning, to make determinations about whether and how civility can be helpful. These tests can be used in specific cases ("What should I say to this person right now?") or to cover classes of cases ("Is it ever OK to curse in a public argument?"), and we propose that with refinement these tests can cover both uses. To make these tests useable, we need to clarify some assumptions. First, what is the relationship between civility and the status quo? The status quo itself is complex and multidimensional. In the early twenty-first-century United States, for example, literacy and education are at an all-time high, yet life expectancy and infant mortality are higher than in comparably well-off and educated countries. More seats in college are available, yet college debt paralyzes graduate and nongraduates alike. Income inequality has regressed from the gains of the mid-twentieth century to levels closer to the Gilded Age. The United States is more inclusive and diverse than it has been before, yet many striking gaps remain, some of them at the level of personal and group respect (transgender visibility and acceptance are increasing, though we have not collectively fully accepted them or figured out how to talk about this community), but in other ways, we still have not come to grips with the physical violence that plagues women, gay people, trans people, and people of color, among others. The need for a Black Lives Matter (BLM) movement testifies to that: the social democracy that underlies our institutions is incomplete. While there has been demonstrable progress, civil society is still very imperfectly civil.

Do calls for civility, even the nuanced kind we are urging, endorse the imperfections as much as the progress? While respecting those who disagree, we believe the answer is no. We have tried to show that civility is not a static tool of a power structure but dynamic and flexible enough that it can challenge defective parts of the status quo while preserving relationships and communities needed to maintain democratic functioning. The complexity of civility across multiple intersecting systems can make some perverse outcomes seem normal or normative when they are not. Oppression and violence are inherently uncivil and cannot be defended by appeals to civility, even if a weak sense of civility makes people feel keeping silent about them is acceptable.

A second confounding factor for the balance tests is what might be called the "heroic narrative of incivility." Rejecting the pacifist heroism of MLK (as, indeed, others did in the 1960s), this story highlights the need to "fight fire with fire" and claims that outrage and transgression are the only efficacious tools for social justice. We saw this story with many of the incidents discussed in chapter 1 and in the commentary on them: only those with the courage to transgress social norms will be able to resist oppression. This story is rooted in a critical imaginary, in the faith that opening people's eyes through righteous wrath will result in dismantling structures of oppression. While collective outrage may be an important component of social change, is endless transgression guaranteed to produce this result—may it not, itself, lead to perverse outcomes? And even in the heroic narrative, civility is necessary, of course, if only so that transgression is possible—without civility, there is only rage, not outrage.

To be uncivil is to reject community (that is, someone or some group), perhaps for principled reasons. The deliberative imaginary includes, but does not valorize, incivility, while the critical imaginary acknowledges, but does not valorize, the uses of civility in conflicts over systemic injustice. We want to argue that even if one holds these imaginaries in a kind of balance, both necessary ways of thinking about social change, we may still want a sort of asymmetry in favor of civility. Since both imaginaries emphasize the creation and maintenance of communities, in a sense, both value civility more than incivility, just (for the critical imaginary) in a roundabout way. In practice, this points to a dilemma of choice: Ethically, shouldn't we weigh the trade-offs of breaking community? Certainly moments when that is the right choice will happen, but it cannot *always* be that moment in the endless struggle and disruption that attend our attempts to improve things. Community happens on many levels, and we have to get along with our fellow travelers in the project of resisting the structural status quo. We know that this is difficult; the oft-observed phenomenon of the "political left eating its own" is proof of the difficulty.

How should we understand the trade-off nature of civility? Most of the public rhetorical roles outlined in chapter 3 are compatible with civility. Bigotry is a form of rudeness, but reacting to acts of bigotry rudely is also uncivil. When we react against bigotry without disrespect, then we have acted with more civility than if we ignore bigotry (which may appear to be polite but does not meet the standards of strong civility that we have laid out). To use an example, this boils down to the question of professional football player Chris Kluwe and his strategy to challenge homophobia: Does the satisfaction of a good dressing-down excuse the overall damage it causes, especially if

writ large? In 2013, a Baltimore Ravens player, Brendon Ayanbadejo, publicly endorsed same-sex marriage, and in response, a state senator, Emmett
Burns, declared that the Ravens should prohibit him from making public
statements of this type. Minnesota Vikings kicker Chris Kluwe responded
in a widely circulated letter (http://big.assets.huffingtonpost.com/Emmett
-Burns-letter-over-Brendon-Ayanbadejo.pdf):

> Dear Emmett C. Burns, Jr.,
>
> I find it inconceivable that you are an elected official of the United
> States government. Your vitriolic hatred and bigotry make me
> ashamed and disgusted to think that you are in any way respon-
> sible for shaping policy at any level. The views you espouse neglect
> to consider several fundamental key points, which I will outline in
> great detail:
>
> 1. As I suspect you have not read the Constitution, I would
> like to remind you that the *very first* amendment in this found-
> ing document deals with the freedom of speech, particularly the
> abridgment of said freedom. By using your position as an elected
> official (when referring to your constituents in order to implic-
> itly threaten the Ravens organization) to argue that the Ravens
> should silence Brendon Ayanbadejo from voicing his support for
> same-sex marriage, not only are you clearly violating the First
> Amendment, but you come across as a narcissistic fromunda
> stain. What on Earth would possess you to say something so
> mind-bogglingly stupid? It baffles me that a man such as your-
> self, a man who relies on that same First Amendment to pursue
> your own religious studies without fear of persecution from the
> state, could somehow justify stifling another person's right to
> free speech. To call that "hypocritical" would be to do a disser-
> vice to the word. "Mindfuckingly, obscenely hypocritical" starts
> to approach it a little bit.
>
> 2. You wrote, "Many of your fans are opposed to such a view
> and feel it has no place in a sport that is strictly for pride, enter-
> tainment and excitement." Holy fucking shitballs. Did you
> seriously just say that, as someone who is, according to your
> Wikipedia page, "deeply involved in government task forces on
> the legacy of slavery in Maryland"? Have you not heard of Kenny

Washington? Jackie Robinson? As recently as 1962 the NFL still had segregation, which was only done away with by brave athletes and coaches daring to speak their mind and do the right thing, and you're going to say that political views have "no place in a sport"? I can't even begin to fathom the cognitive dissonance that must be coursing through your rapidly addled mind right now; the mental gymnastics your brain has to tortuously contort itself through to make such a preposterous statement are surely worthy of an Olympic gold medal (the Russian judge gives you a 10 for "beautiful oppressionism").

3. This is more a personal quibble of mine, but why do you hate freedom? Why do you hate the fact that other people want a chance to live their lives and be happy, even though they may believe in something different from what you believe, or act differently from you? How does gay marriage affect your life in any way, shape, or form? Are you worried that if gay marriage became legal, all of a sudden you'd start thinking about penis? ("Oh shit. Gay marriage just passed. Gotta get me some of that hot dong action!") Will all your friends suddenly turn gay and refuse to come to your Sunday Ticket grill-outs? (Unlikely. Gay people enjoy watching football, too.)

I can assure you that gay people getting married will have zero effect on your life. They won't come into your house and steal your children. They won't magically turn you into a lustful cockmonster. They won't even overthrow the government in an orgy of hedonistic debauchery because all of a sudden they have the same legal rights as the other 90 percent of our population, rights like Social Security benefits, childcare tax credits, family and medical leave to take care of loved ones, and COBRA [Consolidated Omnibus Budget Reconciliation Act] health care for spouses and children. You know what having these rights will make gay Americans? Full-fledged citizens, just like everyone else, with the freedom to pursue happiness and all that that entails. Do the civil-rights struggles of the past 200 years mean absolutely nothing to you?

In closing, I would like to say that I hope this letter in some small way causes you to reflect upon the magnitude of the colossal foot-in-mouth clusterfuck you so brazenly unleashed on a man whose only crime was speaking out for something he believed in. Best of luck in the next election; I'm fairly certain you might need it.

Sincerely,

Chris Kluwe

P.S. I've also been vocal as hell about the issue of gay marriage, so you can take your "I know of no other NFL [National Football League] player who has done what Mr. Ayanbadejo is doing" and shove it in your closed-minded, totally-lacking-in-empathy pie hole.

As satisfying as one may find his clever and nearly unprintable takedown, was Senator Burns—or anyone sympathetic to his view—persuaded by it? Could they even grasp some of the (very good) underlying arguments that should have gotten their attention? One can understand that Kluwe here is trying to muster rhetorical firepower to equal the oppressive assumptions that make Senator Burns feel justified in making such a request. Yet we have to question what is accomplished by this strategic incivility.

Here is the paradox: We can all agree that bigotry is rude, but answering rudeness with rudeness may make things worse and change difficult. So are there polite means to mount a challenge to bigotry? Perhaps yes:

Dear Miss Manners,

You're a rising star, black, Ivy League, at a private corporate party at the president's home, cocktail attire, with senior executives. The chief financial officer has everyone one gather around and tells an off-color racial joke. After it's told, everyone turns to you and your wife standing by . . .

Gentle Reader,

. . . and you look unsmilingly around the room, finally allowing your eyes to rest on the person who told the joke. The room goes silent. Slowly, and in a conversational tone, you ask, "Do you find that amusing?" Then you allow your eyes to travel back around the room.

Here's what Miss Manners promises you will happen: One person will become unfrozen and declare, "No, I don't, as a

matter of fact." Immediately, the rest of the guests will fall all
over themselves to show that they didn't like it, either. Before
the teller of the joke can recover enough to attempt self-defense,
you say, "But I'm sure Brian didn't mean any harm by it." Then
you turn to him and engage him in innocent social conversation
that has nothing to do with what just happened. Against his will,
he will feel grateful to you for having rescued him. The senior
executives will register that you are not to be trifled with. The
president will observe that you know how to be simultaneously
smooth and firmly in charge.

Of course, responding to racist jokes should not be the burden of people of
color in the workplace, and of course, that person's coworkers should have
spoken up immediately. But in the situation described, communicating
with civility is difficult, takes discipline (no one could condemn an urge to
respond in anger), and changes the frame and the context, and thus ensuing
interactions. (Of course, the example assumes that the executive does realize that his joke is inappropriate and he was wrong, which might not always
be the case.)

In order to more fully flesh out a substantive form of civil communication, useful in the kind of example we just described, we offer the following three tests for use as rules of thumb in a variety of communication
situations. While we describe three tests here, we do not claim they are
mutually exclusive, since they appeal to many of the same values and exigencies. They simply seem like a useful set, and other valid ones could certainly
be proposed. These tests apply equally to each of the roles that we identified in chapter 3, but perhaps each test is easier to enact depending on your
role. Inquirers and discussants, in other words, might have an easier time
meeting the corrosion test than trolls.

The Corrosion Test

One of the underlying assumptions of civility (and politeness) is that you
should interact as if you will interact again. Many times people do not burn
bridges so much as chip away at them, as rust slowly eats a metal bridge.
With respect to interpersonal relationships, rudeness can have obvious
consequences. But even in public communication, incivility, justifiable or
not, can corrode the possibility of deliberative or democratic engagement,
because as we saw in chapter 3, the networked relationships among publics

are still relationships. So before choosing incivility, you have to ask whether it is worth weakening a relationship that, as one of many in your life, makes social life possible. One of the themes in Robert Putnam's *Bowling Alone* is that the unwillingness of people to put the work (sometimes just showing up) into maintaining relationships beyond their families undermines democratic institutions by undermining the social democracy that supports them.

Sometimes, as we have seen, incivility is not just tempting but satisfying—the sarcastic comeback, the email riposte, and the cutting blog comment can satisfy a deep need to set things right. Yet this satisfaction must be balanced, even in public discourse with strangers, against the potentially corrosive effect. While trolls are common enough in web page comments, even without them, most people have seen comment sections slide from commentary and dialogue to insults and flame wars to the point where many blogs and online publications have turned off comments. Sometimes the price of corrosion is worth paying, but if everyone indulges all the time, then public discourse becomes impossible. Breakdown may be the goal for trolls, but most people would like to have discussions, even vigorous discussions.

The Degradation Test

Even if a given behavior passes the corrosion test, and perhaps is likely to produce a desired effect (shocking people into consciousness of a moral wrong), does it risk demeaning or debasing one's own character or moral standing? That is, both civility and incivility, in particular settings, may entail a kind of moral cost (which is, of course, another kind of outcome). The more often one practices incivility, the less standing one has to expect or demand civility from others and the less sensitive one will be to standards for one's own behavior. Many commentators have noted a "race to the bottom" pattern to engaging with President Trump: his rudeness seems to justify returning with similar rudeness that he takes as justifying his original name-calling or insults, and the cycle continues. Because we are so mortified by a president who betrays the norms and expectations of his office, we may feel the situation is sufficiently dire to allow for returning his rhetoric in kind. Yet each of us has to question whether the personal cost is worth the effect they may (not) be having.

The Comfort Test

Both civil and uncivil actions make many people uncomfortable. As we noted in the introduction and in chapter 1, pseudocivility is the equation of discomfort with incivility ("I am uncomfortable, so you must have been uncivil"). This equation does not hold for a number of reasons. If you cannot stand someone or hold a grudge against them, you may be uncomfortable if they are polite to you, yet they are still being polite. An editorial with a good argument you disagree with can be uncomfortable, but the argument is not uncivil. If someone objects, politely, to your use of a particular word, it may make you uncomfortable, but their request can be polite as can be your response; the awkwardness of the situation does not remove it from the realm of civility. On the other hand, in the context of a friendship, you may be amused rather than uncomfortable with a friend's habitual but minor rudeness.

Consider the case where you are deliberately making someone uncomfortable, as in the situation of challenging an expression you consider racist or sexist. For one example, in the Thanksgiving dinner scenario covered in chapter 1, a fairly complex calculus is necessary to balance the need to speak up with its outcomes, especially the possibility of a perverse outcome; the offender can become angry and obstinate, which might not have been the case had you taken them aside privately (yet not speaking up at the table risks a negative judgment from others). The line between assertive and aggressive can correspond to the line between civility and incivility. In the case of public rhetoric, the calculus may be very different. Journalists sometimes think their job is to "afflict the comfortable and comfort the afflicted," which is to say redress power differentials through reporting. Sometimes this point is put as "Do not punch down." This suggests that through journalism or humor or activism, we are justified in making those with more power or privilege uncomfortable but not those who are already in a one-down position.

Consider two test cases. The first case concerns Rashida Tlaib, a congresswoman from Detroit elected in November 2018. On January 3, 2019, at a rally just after her swearing in, her speech rose to a climax with the cry "We're going to impeach this motherfucker!" and was cheered by the crowd (Rupar 2019). Setting aside political questions of strategy and impeachment, a great deal of attention was centered on the use of an expletive, especially in the context of a president who regularly employs such language. In terms of the immediate effect, cursing was certainly approved by the crowd and therefore effective on that level, and certainly Representative Tlaib may have been carried away by the passion of the moment.

In terms of the comfort test, complaints by conservative pundits and the president seem pseudocivil to the point of hypocrisy (Pitts 2019). Hence we have no apparent evidence that anyone was uncomfortable with the remark.

In terms of the corrosion test, the case for this word is shakier. With all due credit to the validity of the sentiment, name-calling tends to beget name-calling; whether Donald Trump personally deserves respect leaves open the question of what is owed to the maintenance of public discourse, even if President Trump is prepared to degrade it. Of course, Representative Tlaib cannot sink the level of public discourse all by herself, but in her visible public position, her words matter. The question is whether the immediate or short-term effect was worth rounds of "They do it too" and the perception that politics has been fully degraded. A useful test would be a Kantian one: Could this choice be generalized? In this case, we are inclined to say no. While the damage is not great in the moment, anger and cursing to register disagreement is not a desirable standard. A similar analysis would accompany the moral degradation test. Representative Tlaib was not sorry for her manner of expression, and it is understandable that she might think it justified. But she probably would not want to be the person who can *only* express herself this way and would want to be the person who at some point is able to reach across the aisle and/or connect with people who voted for President Trump.

A second example concerns some remarks President Obama made about BLM in April 2016 in which he seems to question their civility in a manner reminiscent of Alinsky:

> As a general rule, I think that what, for example, Black Lives Matter is doing now to bring attention to the problem of a criminal justice system that sometimes is not treating people fairly based on race or reacting to shootings of individuals by police officers has been really effective in bringing attention to problems.
>
> One of the things I caution young people about, though, that I don't think is effective is, once you've highlighted an issue and brought it to people's attention and shined a spotlight, and elected officials or people who are in a position to start bringing about change are ready to sit down with you, then you can't just keep on yelling at them. And you can't refuse to meet because that might compromise the purity of your position.
>
> The value of social movements and activism is to get you at the table, get you in the room, and then to start trying to figure out how is this problem going to be solved. You, then, have a responsibility to prepare an agenda that is achievable, that can institutionalize the changes you seek, and to engage the other side and occasionally to take half a loaf that will advance the gains that you seek, understanding that

there's going to be more work to do, but this is what is achievable at this moment.

And too often, what I see is wonderful activism that highlights a problem, but then people feel so passionately and are so invested in the purity of their position that they never take that next step and say, okay, well, now I got to sit down and try to actually get something done.[1]

We have already discussed the BLM movement in chapter 3 and why it in general seems civil. But here Obama seems to be giving a mild rebuke to the BLM activists—is it justified? In terms of the corrosion test, the BLM motto or protests do not seem corrosive; asserting the value of the lives of a historically marginalized group should be uncontroversial. Specific incidents (such as BLM activists grabbing the microphone at a Bernie Sanders rally) might get a different judgment, but the circulation of the BLM motto and the demands for police reform, in light of the evidence, are within the bounds. In the same way, we could argue that BLM protesters could easily assent to generalize this practice—other groups can and should declare their lives to be of value in the face of oppressive governmental and police systems. Obama seems to be calling them out relative to the comfort test. The bluntest way of understanding his critique is that creating discomfort for the police and their allies undermines the possibility of moving forward—more or less, "honey is better than vinegar." Yet there may be, as Kirt Wilson has suggested, more nuance here. Certainly some of the reaction to BLM can be chalked up to pseudocivility and outrage manufactured in the familiar mode of the culture wars, combined with the (seemingly) obligatory veneration of "first responders" as well as those in the military and the police since 9/11. Pseudocivility takes umbrage with the objection to racism rather than with the racism itself. We doubt that those in the BLM movement have refused to take half a loaf and have insisted on the purity of their position. In terms of Black Lives Matter, they are of course right to insist on purity—unequivocally, black lives should matter as much as everyone else's; no compromise on that makes any sense.

But beyond "Black Lives Matter" versus "Blue Lives Matter," the actual demands are for reform of policing—which is a policy argument and therefore subject to the practical demands of coalition building, incrementalism, half loaves, and all the familiar issues that attend making improvements on wicked problems and life in a liberal society. Will that reform effort have more momentum and energy if we have public consensus about the need and rightness of it? Absolutely. Will uncomfortable but civil protest contribute to this consensus? Probably so, and so President Obama, in our view, made a bad call on this case. This protest and resistance may well take place at many different levels, from interpersonal to institutional to public and mediated, and of course, it would include viral campaigns and social media as well as popular music and movies.

Wilson's complaint is that Obama conjures a flawed picture of social change here; he thinks the picture derives from Obama's retrospective (and maybe retrograde) understanding of the civil rights movement, which is roughly "Get attention through protest and demonstration; based on that, get a seat at the table and, based on that seat, engage in the politicking necessary to make change." While unquestionably this model has worked to a degree in the United States (before and during the civil rights movement), it certainly has its limitations (as does interest group democracy in general), especially with regard to the most deep-seated American pathologies of racism, sexism, and homophobia. Our question here is whether the unwillingness of some BLM leaders to engage existing democratic state and local institutions, believing them to be corrupted by a racism that ignores violence to black bodies, is per se uncivil. The accusation of racism against the policing and justice system is itself an uncomfortable one, yet the gravity of the death toll seems to justify it. The actual incivility inheres in a system in which an African American man's chance of being shot by the police is more than three times greater than a Euro-American man (Edwards and Esposito 2018). In a deeper sense, the incivility lies in breaking the relationship between the public and police, demonstrating to their communities that the police are systemically unworthy of trust. But in a sense, this trust has always wavered between fragile and nonexistent, and BLM is doing little more than calling attention to a long-term dysfunctional and inequitable relationship; it is hardly, by itself, breaking public discourse or trust in policing. In this context, we find President Obama's rebuke to be ill-advised and unfair. While the best model of social change is an arguable topic, and President Obama and the BLM might respectfully disagree about it, the refusal to engage deeply uncivil institutions but instead seek a larger public consensus seems reasonable and civil to us.

Can Civility Save Democracy?

Rising forms of populism and authoritarianism across the world characterize our historical moment, in addition to systemic and persistent racism, sexism, and homophobia. The history of civility is bound to the histories of racism, sexism, and homophobia. Leaders who win elections (on explicitly racist and sexist messages) and then undermine democratic forms of government without becoming outright dictators have gained control of Brazil, the Philippines, Turkey, Hungary, Venezuela, Poland, and the United States. Political leaders in these places have chosen to pit "the people" against allegedly corrupt elites and have used that framing of events to attack and unmake the institutions of governance central to fully functioning democracies. This trend has caused some to ask questions about "how democracies die" (Levitsky and Ziblatt 2018) or "how democracy ends" (Runciman 2018). Within such a bleak context, civility may seem like a noble but less valuable cause to champion, especially if calls for civility are seen as complicit in histories of racism and sexism. Sober-minded political scientists like Steven Levitsky and Daniel Ziblatt have done essential work to show how important democratic institutions are actively undermined by authoritarians and how those institutions might be saved. And we certainly agree with the calls to protect and strengthen the institutions of governance that make democracies function. But we are also reminded of John Dewey's claim that democracy is not just a system of government. It is also a way of life. Levitsky and Ziblatt hint at the importance of what they call "social norms" in regulating behavior in democratic societies, but these norms are often thought of in relationship to questions about how one behaves inside the institutions of governance that make democracy a functional system of decision-making. What political scientists miss about the rising tide of authoritarianism, and what critics of civility may miss as well, is the importance of the social fabric that underpins our democratic institutions, the fabric emphasized from Tocqueville to Robert Putnam. Trump and other figures like him do rend that social fabric, and it can only be repaired through commitments to a form of communication ethics that takes strong civility as a starting point. We would argue that we cannot save democracy simply by shoring up the institutional forms of governance identified by Levitsky and Ziblatt. We need to also repair the social infrastructure that underpins our deliberative imaginary so that democracy as a way of life can be practiced by all citizens. This involves attending to the three tests we have just outlined in order to help enact civility while driving change.

We have argued throughout that the idea of civility brings with it a complex set of considerations about how we treat others, and we have shown how central such considerations are to the argument that we ought to think of democracy as a way of life and not just a system of government. In order to save the institutions of democracy from the current threats of nationalism, authoritarianism, sexism, and racism, we ought to realize that democracy entails a set of questions about how we can live well with others, particularly when we may have different beliefs or values from those others. Civility, understood as a communication practice, is not just a matter of being nice for the sake of preserving social harmony. Instead, we see it as a commitment to the hard work of connecting with strangers under the conditions of (often deep) moral disagreement. Thus we have not offered a kind of political philosophy that describes an ideal framework for democratic governance, nor have we offered a kind of institutional analysis with policy proposals that might be more typical of political scientists. Instead, we offer both an argument for why we ought to consider civility as an essential communicative value for citizens living democratic lives and a description of what strong civility might look like when enacted as a set of communication practices that would allow us to live well together. This, in our view, turns questions about civility into questions about communication ethics. If we attend to the ways in which our everyday communication practices either embody or fail to embody strong civility, then we can get a better handle on how and why the social fabric that underpins our democratic system of government is both fragile and necessary for building and maintaining a democratic culture. The three tests above are an important way to begin that project, but we need more than just those tests.

We already know the communication practices of dictators, authoritarians, and demagogues—they treat others (especially women and people of color) with contempt, disdain, and suspicion. A quick look at President Trump's Twitter feed will reveal a steady stream of accusations against the others with whom Mr. Trump must share public discourse (the media, immigrants, Democrats, women, etc.). This is more than simply a matter of incivility; it creates a difficult climate within which to build or maintain a democratic culture because it defaults on the hard, necessary work of cooperating and living well with others with whom we may disagree or whom we simply dislike. To relentlessly demonize citizens of one's own country is to create social discord and disharmony, making it ever more difficult to engage in effective public deliberation or decision-making. When public discourse is dominated by trolls alone (and the other roles like inquirers or discussants seem to vanish), how might we preserve our fragile social democracy? In chapter 4, we tried to offer a more detailed explanation of how that decline happens rhetorically. Rending the social fabric through these communication practices ensures that democracies cannot use the advantages of diverse forms of knowledge to make good decisions and promotes a social climate filled with tension and antagonism that threatens to pull the whole system apart at any moment. We each have obligations to ourselves to articulate our own beliefs and advance an agenda that we think is right, good, and useful. But we also have obligations to treat others with civility if we wish to live well together in the face of difference. This is undoubtedly a balancing act that each citizen faces in a democratic culture. And we will forever argue about where lines ought to be drawn to protect some beliefs and outlaw others. Freedom is, in some sense, an endless meeting in which we deliberate where those lines might be. Our sense of our obligations to others ought to bring us to recognize how our communication practices are always already ethical matters.

One objection to civility is that the enormous, systemic power differences between sociopolitical actors within our democratic culture make civility at best a tool only available to the already privileged or at worst a mechanism for preserving the status quo. We certainly acknowledge the fact that actors within our democratic culture do not occupy equal social or political places and that forms of communicative agency are always contingent on the unequal positionality of the diverse citizenry that make up our democratic culture. We have not offered strong civility as a cure-all for the inequalities that plague our deliberative and critical imaginaries. We do claim, however, that the rhetorical values behind strong civility cannot be overlooked if we are seeking social and political change. In other words, relationality ought to be a consideration for our communicative acts regardless of our situated conditions because persuasion depends, to some extent at least, on relationality. Civility will not radically remake the structures of inequality that condition actions within our democratic culture in an instant, but communicative actions that take strong civility as a starting point do open us up to the possibility for sociopolitical change that might otherwise be precluded or made more difficult by incivility. Deep listening, respect, and relationality that transcend disagreement are robust avenues for change; they might not be all that we need, but they are, at least, an essential component of life in a democratic culture. When we supplement strong civility with legal and institutional actions, we have fertile ground for imagining how we might make a more just world without simply defeating and marginalizing the noxious others with whom we disagree. No democratic culture can lose sight of the necessity of relationality that makes collective decision-making possible and that allows us to live well with others regardless of our differences.

Why, then, do large-scale, multicultural, complex democracies require civility going forward? Or more precisely, what do they require *of* civility?

What would be lost if we lost our tradition of civility? Our answer is, on the surface, fairly straightforward: our large-scale, complex, multicultural democracies require civility because that is one of the central communicative means of practicing democracy as a way of life in such a manner that we are able to cooperate and collaborate with strangers who hold opposing views. The more diversity and difference that characterizes our democratic culture, the more pressing it is that we learn to live well with those differences so that the social fabric that makes the institutions of democratic governance possible is not torn asunder. It is at this point when questions of ethics are drawn closely to questions of communication: how we choose to communicate with others reflects and enacts a set of beliefs about right and wrong, good and bad that are essential features of a democratic way of life. If we were to lose our tradition of civility, then we run the risk of losing a set of communication practices that make cooperation and collaboration in the face of difference and disagreement possible. This goes beyond the erosion of the institutions of governance that preoccupy political scientists like Levitsky and Ziblatt because it highlights the grinding down of—and ultimately, the dissolution of—some necessary features of rhetorical citizenship. By this, we mean that our ability to form relationships with strangers for the purposes of persuasion and social/political change hinges on our treatment of those strangers. To foreclose the tradition of civility at the moment when we see increasing degrees of diversity in the public sphere would be to give up on a set of communication practices necessary for sustaining democracy as a way of life.

What do these communication practices look like, and why do they form the foundation for a communication ethics? Answering these questions requires us to recognize the centrality of persuasion in democratic culture and how deeply related questions of relationality are to persuasion. Persuasion, within the very long tradition of rhetorical studies, is not simply a nefarious form of manipulation. Persuasion can replace violence as the means for generating forms of coordinated action, consensus, and shared understandings when trying to live well with others. How can we persuade others that we demonize through acts of incivility? Persuasion also speaks directly to the challenges of social and political change: How do we change others' beliefs or values? How do we convince enough of a population to enact a law or policy? Might civility be helpful for the purposes of persuasion? Elizabeth McKenna's (2014) description of the practices used by the Obama campaign in his first and second presidential election underscores the importance of relationality to persuasion. McKenna calls those practices a form of "relational organizing" that prioritized the social connections being made between campaign volunteers and other citizens instead of the process of delivering a functional message about Obama's policies. The Obama campaign's success turned on this commitment to building a network of relationships *before* attempting to persuade people of policy positions. Pragmatists like William James and John Dewey argued that we ought to think about ideas like tools that could do some work in the world. In our view, both civility and incivility do the work of enacting forms of relationality in our democratic culture, and both hold the potential to enact forms of relationality capable of generating social or political change. If communication is not a matter of transmitting information but is instead forming relationships and creating shared meanings, then civility and incivility become valuable tools in the communication practices of citizens. In some sense, communication practices that value civility foreground cooperation, compromise, collaboration, and identification, while communication practices that enact forms of incivility foreground division, hyperbole, overgeneralization, and objectification. One set of practices asks that we find ways to live well with others not like us and that we approach those others with the hopes of persuading them while acknowledging that we too might be persuaded in and through our interactions. The other set of practices asks that we find ways to defeat other views and the people who hold them so that change is an outcome of victory and not collaboration or cooperation. At stake in the distinction between civil and uncivil modes of communication, therefore, is an ethics of persuasion.

Our democratic future requires thicker, more substantive practices for making connections with strangers who are different from us and then using those connections as the grounds for persuasion and change. We believe that our actions as rhetorical citizens (i.e., citizens who communicate through various modes and media with others in our democratic culture) are best guided by values of civility, and in cases when we are driven by values of incivility, the practices we use would still seek to foreground relationality and persuasion over demonization for the purposes of defeat. Jeffrey Stout's work on grassroots democracy in *Blessed Are the Organized* illustrates the importance of social democracy and its preservation through communicative acts oriented toward building relationships based on cooperation and collaboration: "Grassroots democracy is an evolving collection of practices intended to perfect the exercise of political responsibility by citizens in a republic that officially aspires to be democratic. As such, grassroots democracy is essentially social" (2012, 13). Stout lacks, however, a thick description of how citizens within such a social situation might act as communicative agents to best weave together the kinds of organizations he sees as essential. That is one of the contributions we have tried to make in this book—a deeper description of civility as the enactment of communicative agency for the purposes of building a social democracy. Civic engagement, according to Stout, is vital not just for political ends but for democratic culture as a way of living well with others.

What, then, does strong civility as a form of rhetorical citizenship require? And how would strong civility promote social democracy? We have tried to show that strong civility requires the refusal of reductionism, essentialism, and overgeneralization. One of the most troubling features of our current deliberative and critical imaginaries is the extent to which we speak and write in ways that reduce, essentialize, and overgeneralize both problems and people. These are dangerous habits that quickly devolve into forms of incivility that target and demonize members of our democratic culture. The rhetorical habits of reductionism, essentialism, and overgeneralization are like gateway drugs to incivility and, as habits of rhetorical citizenship, remain dangerous threats to the social fabric. Instead, strong civility requires care. We use the word *care* here to refer to a number of different ways of proceeding as a communicative agent: First, rhetorical citizens ought to care about the strangers whom they meet within the scene of democratic culture even if they disagree with those strangers vehemently about a particular value or course of action. This is because the greatest threat to democracy is in the way in which we treat those with whom we disagree. How can we express, articulate, or communicate care for strangers within either the deliberative imaginary or the critical imaginary? It seems to us that civility is one mechanism for that end. Second, rhetorical citizens ought to also engage social/political problems with care through careful attention to the particularity of the situation. In this way, care is the opposite of the spirit of reductionism, essentialism, and overgeneralization. We ought to resist the temptation to engage with problems from perspectives informed by those values and instead recognize complexity, uncertainty, and particularity. We do this best when we act with strong civility, which is a form of openly acknowledging that we do not have all the answers, that we may be changed in the course of our communicative interactions, and that nothing is gained by hysterical overreactions to the problems that emerge in our democratic lives. Careful thinkers are more likely to act as rhetorical citizens in ways characterized by strong civility. Third, rhetorical citizens take care to recognize that the strangers we meet and the situations we encounter are always already multidimensional and that democracy functions best when we acknowledge or live with that multidimensionality instead of ignoring it or erasing it. This means that when we meet strangers, we take care to recognize that we are likely to find both points of identification and difference in our encounters, and to focus on one point at the expense of another would foreclose forms of communication that might be helpful for persuasion or social/political change. Strong civility is premised on a predisposition to care in all of these ways. We ought to, as rhetorical citizens, enact such modes of caring even when we meet those others whom we find morally noxious.

Our deliberative culture and our democratic future rest on our commitment to a communication ethics capable of enacting strong civility through these modes of caring. Populist strongmen, internet trolls, screaming media personalities, and the full cast of uncivil actors who populate our democratic culture are actively undermining and laying waste to the social democracy that lies underneath the institutions of governance we often think of whenever someone says the word *democracy*. These civic actors mistake ethics for behavior based on moral principles, as if being "right" gives them license to demonize other members of their democratic culture. But communication ethics is less a matter of principles and more a matter of our habits of interacting with others and whether those habits, particularly as they manifest themselves in communication practices, demonstrate a predisposition to care and a recognition that our obligations to others matter when living a democratic life. Without such a communication ethics, it is hard to see how even the healthiest democratic institutions of governance would survive, and in the face of weakened forms of those institutions, such practices become ever more pressing. Questions about civility foreground the importance of our everyday communication practices in the cultivation of democratic life and resistance to its demise. The best antidote to the rising tides of authoritarianism just might be the kind of rhetorical citizenship that enacts habits of strong civility.

The Promise of Strong Civility

Civility is strategic and pragmatic and so not just a matter of niceness. We can use strong civility in the service of persuasion when we think carefully about our communicative interactions with others and the necessity of preserving social democracy. Communication practices matter when we are faced with questions about how to live well with others, and strong civility holds the promise of pointing us toward the kind of communication practices that might both build relationships and make sociopolitical change through persuasion possible. We foreclose opportunities for persuasion when we treat others with incivility, and we replace persuasion with the kinds of rhetorical forms of division that can only end in victory or defeat. We cannot build a democratic way of life with those kinds of communication practices as a foundation. We do not mean to offer civility as a cure-all or an antidote to the erosion of democratic institutions and the laws and policies that surely preserve and protect our democratic system of government. Analyses that ask questions about those institutions of governance are essential to fulfilling the promise of our democratic future but so are analyses of the communicative practices that we use within the social spaces that make up the deliberative imaginary. The promise of strong civility is that it offers us a set of specific practices and habits capable of building a democratic culture and not just a democratic system of government.

We can see the promise of strong civility more clearly if we return to our description of democracy as a wicked problem. Wicked problems are multilayered and elusive, which means that we will not ever find a perfect democracy. Instead, our description of democracy as a way of life is meant to highlight the fact that no perfect set of principles or institutions will ever give rise to an ideal form of democracy. Instead, our commitment to democracy as a way of life is supposed to return us to the rough ground of "wicked problems" that we will never solve perfectly but that we continue to work at collectively anyway—problems like how best to achieve a free and equal society when some members of that society, when granted freedom and equality, will look to oppress and demonize others. The promise of civility lies in its usefulness in traveling the rough ground of wicked problems that are always already part of our democratic culture. Strong civility remains the best available means of preserving social relationships with strangers while still seeking out provisional and uncertain solutions to intractable problems. In other words, strong civility opens up possibilities for collaboration and cooperation in such a way that the social fabric remains intact while we are working with strangers who might think differently and have different values. As communication scholars and rhetorical theorists, we prefer the rough ground of imperfect and practical solutions to intractable problems rather than ideal sketches or perfect forms of life that we can never achieve. Civility might not be the ideal weapon to wield in the fight to save democracies from dying, but it is a necessary value for temporarily holding together disparate groups of people so that we can find the best possible solutions to some impossibly difficult problems.

On Reddit, a subforum ("subreddit") called "Change My View" gives us a glimpse of how persuasion is made possible by civility. Founded in 2013 by Kal Turnball, a Scottish teenager, "Change My View" promotes and requires respectful conversation. Strict rules essentially prohibit the use of incivility, but more important, the subreddit demonstrates how persuasion is more a matter of meeting people where they are instead of where you want them to be. Strong civility, in this case, is also a matter of listening with respect and for the purposes of understanding, but those modes of communication are also understood as key factors in the process of persuasion. This is perhaps where the greatest promise of civility lies: in the ability to teach us all how we might more productively approach the project of persuasion in ways that will hold our democratic culture together while generating the kind of change we want but do not know how to get. In other words, if we lose civility, we may lose the best means we have of changing people's minds, and it is hard to see how we might live a democratic life without healthy and robust practices of persuasion. "Change My View" might give us a small window into how we might save our democracy, or the fact that it remains a subreddit tucked away in a distant corner of the internet might be a sign that it is too late. We cannot say whether our democracy will die or thrive in the coming years, but we do know that if it thrives, it will do so through communication practices that foreground care, cooperation, collaboration, and forms of civility that allow us to live well with others.

NOTES

INTRODUCTION

    1. This view also aligns with Karlyn Kohrs Campbell's (2005) important essay "Agency: Promiscuous and Protean" and Jeremy Engels's (2018) *The Art of Gratitude*.

    2. Dewey remains an important influence on contemporary communication studies and political theory. For example, Jeffrey Stout (2012) has shown just how important contemporary commitments to social democracy are, and Eddie Glaude (2008) relies on Dewey for his analysis of race. In addition, Scott Stroud (2011) and Nathan Crick (2010) have both used Dewey's work to improve our understanding of democratic life, ethics, and aesthetics through communication.

    3. See the report by the Asian-American and Pacific Islander Civic Engagement Fund (2020).

CHAPTER 1

    1. James uses the term *douche* as an ordinary epithet, without acknowledging its potential sexism.

CHAPTER 2

    1. Another "hymn to logos" can also be found in Isocrates, *Ad Nicocles* 5–9 and *Antidosis* 253.

    2. A helpful discussion can be found at "Pronouns," Nonbinary.org/wiki, last modified January 16, 2020, https://nonbinary.org/wiki/Pronouns.

CHAPTER 3

    1. It first appears in Wilson (1959). See also Davidson (1984a, 1984b, 1984c).

    2. John Peters (2005) has called this, following Derrida, a "disseminative" understanding of communication.

    3. Hence Aristotle's account of rhetoric often seems to have limited usefulness, since he was theorizing face-to-face audiences, bound by the norms of the court and the assembly.

    4. See Moor, Heuvelman, and Verleur (2010); Suler (2004); Lapidot-Lefler and Barak (2012); and Kayany (1998).

    5. For example, see Blakesley (2002); Mangham and Overington (2005); and Overington (1977).

    6. See America's Black Holocaust Museum, http://abhmuseum.org.

7. The graphic can be viewed on Campaign Zero's website: https://www.join campaignzero.org/solutions.

8. This point is complicated by the integration of postmodernism to the critical imaginary. Marxists, in general, have to be philosophical realists, since there has to be something real for you to have false consciousness about. Foucault's concept of the episteme is attractive to the critical imaginary because it gives a deep and structured account of what holds our current beliefs, habits, and institutions in place, but it should not be mistaken for a realism.

CHAPTER 5

1. Thanks to Kirt Wilson (2016) for alerting us to this passage.

REFERENCES

Ackerman, Bruce, and James Fishkin. 2005. *Deliberation Day*. New Haven: Yale University Press.

Alinsky, Saul. 1989. *Rules for Radicals: A Practical Primer for Realistic Radicals*. London: Vintage.

Allen, Danielle. 2006. *Talking to Strangers: Anxieties of Citizenship Since* Brown v. Board of Education. Chicago: University of Chicago Press.

Andrews, James. 1969. "Confrontation at Columbia: A Case Study in Coercive Rhetoric." *Quarterly Journal of Speech* 55 (1): 9–16.

Aristotle. 2006. *Rhetoric: A Theory of Civic Discourse*. Translated by George Kennedy. Oxford: Oxford University Press.

Armstrong, Karen. 2010. *The Case for God*. New York: Anchor Books.

Asen, Robert. 2017. "Neoliberalism, the Public Sphere, and a Public Good." *Quarterly Journal of Speech* 103 (4): 329–49.

———. 2018. "Public: A Network of Relationships." *Rhetoric Society Quarterly* 48 (3): 297–305.

Asen, Robert, and Daniel Brouwer. 2001. *Counterpublics and the State*. Albany: State University of New York Press.

Asian-American and Pacific Islander Civic Engagement Fund. 2020. "Ahead of the Majority: Foregrounding Women of Color." Accessed January 20, 2020. https://aapifund.org/report/woc/.

Austin, John L. 1975. *How to Do Things with Words*. Cambridge: Harvard University Press.

Báez, Kristiana, and Ersula Ore. 2018. "The Moral Imperative of Race for Rhetorical Studies: On Civility and Walking-in-White in Academe." *Communication and Critical/Cultural Studies* 15 (4): 331–36.

Baker, Perry. 2015. "Conservative Backlash Emerges Against Black Lives Matter Movement." *NBC News*, September 3, 2015. https://www.nbcnews.com/politics/2016-election/conservative-backlash-emerges-against-black-lives-matter-movement-n421232.

Ball, Molly. 2015. "Is the Most Powerful Conservative in America Losing His Edge?" *Atlantic*, January/February 2015. https://www.theatlantic.com/magazine/archive/2015/01/is-the-most-powerful-conservative-in-america-losing-his-edge/383503/.

Barber, Ben. 1984. *Strong Democracy: Participatory Politics for a New Age*. Los Angeles: University of California Press.

Bejan, Teresa. 2017. *Mere Civility*. Cambridge: Harvard University Press.

Bellah, Robert Neely. 1992. *The Broken Covenant: American Civil Religion in Time of Trial*. Chicago: University of Chicago Press.

Bennett, Jane. 2010. *Vibrant Matter: A Political Ecology of Things*. Durham: Duke University Press.

Biesecker, Barbara A. 2017. "From General History to Philosophy: Black Lives Matter, Late Neoliberal Molecular Biopolitics, and Rhetoric." *Philosophy and Rhetoric* 50 (4): 409–30.

Blakesley, David. 2002. *The Elements of Dramatism*. New York: Pearson/Longman.

Boatright, Robert, Timothy Shaffer, Sarah Sobieraj, and Dannagal Goldthwaite Young, eds. 2019. *A Crisis of Civility? Political Discourse and Its Discontents*. New York: Routledge.

Booth, W. C. 2004. *Rhetoric of Rhetoric: The Quest for Effective Communication*. New York: Blackwell Manifesto.

Brown, Wendy. 2008. *Regulating Aversion*. Princeton: Princeton University Press.

Brownstein, Ronald. 2008. *The Second Civil War*. New York: Penguin Books.

Burke, Kenneth. 1969a. *A Grammar of Motives*. Berkeley: University of California Press.

——. 1969b. *A Rhetoric of Motives*. Berkeley: University of California Press.

Calhoun, Cheshire. 2000. "The Virtue of Civility." *Philosophy and Public Affairs* 29 (3): 251–75.

Campbell, John Angus, and Stephen C. Meyer, eds. 2003. *Darwinism, Design, and Public Education*. East Lansing: Michigan State University Press.

Campbell, Karlyn Kohrs. 2005. "Agency: Promiscuous and Protean." *Communication and Critical/Cultural Studies* 2 (1): 1–19.

Ceccarelli, Leah. 2011. "Manufactured Scientific Controversy: Science, Rhetoric, and Public Debate." *Rhetoric and Public Affairs* 14 (2): 195–228.

Cicero, Marcus Tullius. 1949. *De inventione*. Cambridge, Mass.: Harvard/Loeb Library.

Cobb, Jelani (@jelani9). 2018. "Civility is the coward's favorite virtue." Twitter post, June 21, 2018. https://twitter.com/jelani9/status/1009755195843186694.

Conetsco, Cherlynn, and Anna Hart. 2013. *Service Etiquette*. 5th ed. Annapolis, Md.: Naval Institute Press.

Cook, John. 2009. "Is Davidson a Gricean?" *Dialogue* 48 (3): 557–75.

Coppins, McKay. 2018. "Trump's Right Hand Troll." *Atlantic*, May 2018. https://www.theatlantic.com/politics/archive/2018/05/stephen-miller-trump-adviser/561317/.

Crick, Nathan. 2010. *Democracy and Rhetoric: John Dewey on the Arts of Becoming*. Columbia: University of South Carolina Press.

Danisch, Robert. 2015. *Building a Social Democracy: The Promise of Rhetorical Pragmatism*. Lanham, Md.: Lexington Books.

Davidson, Donald. 1984a. "On the Very Idea of a Conceptual Scheme." In *Inquiries into Truth and Interpretation*, edited by D. Davidson, 183–98. Oxford: Clarendon.

——. 1984b. "Radical Translation." In *Inquiries into Truth and Interpretation*, edited by D. Davidson, 125–39. Oxford: Clarendon.

——. 1984c. "Truth and Meaning." In *Inquiries into Truth and Interpretation*, edited by D. Davidson, 17–36. Oxford: Clarendon.

Debord, Guy. (1967) 1994. *Society of the Spectacle*. New York: Zone Books.

Derrida, Jacques. 1988. "Signature Event Context." In *Limited Inc*, translated by Samuel Weber and Jeffrey Mehlman, 1–24. Evanston: Northwestern University Press.

Dewey, John. 1894. *The Study of Ethics: A Syllabus*. Ann Arbor, Mich.: Inland.

——. 1927. *The Public and Its Problems*. New York: Holt.

——. (1929) 1960. *The Quest for Certainty*. New York: Capricorn Books.

——. 1944. *Democracy and Education: An Introduction to the Philosophy of Education*. New York: Free Press.

——. 2008. *The Later Works of John Dewey*. Vol. 2, *1925–1927*, edited by Jo Ann Boydston. Carbondale: Southern Illinois University Press.

DiAngelo, Robin. 2018. *White Fragility: Why It's So Hard for White People to Talk About Racism*. Boston: Beacon.

Duncan, Hugh Dalziel. 1968. *Symbols in Society*. New York: Oxford University Press.

Edwards, Frank, and Michael Esposito. 2018. "Police Kill About Three Men per Day in the US, According to New Study." Conversation, August 6, 2018. http://

theconversation.com/police-kill-about-3-men-per-day-in-the-us-according-to-new
-study-100567.

Ehninger, Douglas. 1958. "Debating as Critical Deliberation." *Southern Speech Communication Journal* 24 (1): 22–30.

Elias, Norbert. 2000. *The Civilizing Process: Sociogenetic and Psychogenetic Investigations.*
2 vols. New York: Blackwell.

Eliasoph, Nina. 1998. *Avoiding Politics: How Americans Produce Apathy in Everyday Life.*
Cambridge: Cambridge University Press.

Eltahawy, Mona. 2019. "Civility Will Not Overturn the Patriarchy: One Man's Manners
Are Another Woman's Oppression." Lithub, September 19, 2019. https://lithub
.com/mona-eltahawy-civility-will-not-overturn-the-patriarchy.

Engels, Jeremy. 2015. *The Politics of Resentment: A Genealogy.* University Park: Penn State
University Press.

———. 2018. *The Art of Gratitude.* Albany: State University of New York Press.

Eschoe, Lyric. 2018. "Calling Out the Positive Force of 'Call-Out' Culture." Vox ATL,
July 20, 2018. http://voxatl.com/calling-positive-force-call-culture/.

Fishkin, James. 2011. *When the People Speak: Deliberative Democracy and Public Consultation.* New York: Oxford University Press.

Frank, Thomas. 1997. *Commodify Your Dissent: Salvos from the Baffler.* New York: W. W.
Norton.

———. 1998. *The Conquest of Cool: Business Culture, Counterculture, and the Rise of Hip
Consumerism.* Chicago: University of Chicago Press.

Freeman, Joanne. 2018. *Field of Blood: Violence in Congress and the Road to Civil War.* New
York: Farrar, Straus and Giroux.

Friedersdorf, Conor. 2017. "The Destructiveness of Call-Out Culture on Our Campuses."
Atlantic, May 8, 2017. https://www.theatlantic.com/politics/archive/2017/05/call
-out-culture-is-stressing-out-college-students/524679/.

Gaonkar, Dilip. 2002. "Toward New Imaginaries: An Introduction." *Public Culture* 14
(1): 1–19.

Gastil, John. 2000. *By Popular Demand: Revitalizing Representative Democracy Through
Deliberative Elections.* Berkeley: University of California Press.

Gehrke, Pat J. 2013. "On the Many Senses of Parrhesia and Rhetoric." *Rhetoric Society
Quarterly* 43 (4): 355–61.

Gerson, Michael. 2018. "The Last Temptation." *Atlantic*, April 2018. https://www
.theatlantic.com/magazine/archive/2018/04/the-last-temptation/554066.

Gibb, Jack. 1961. "Defensive Communication." *Journal of Communication* 11:141–48.

Glaude, Eddie. 2008. *In a Shade of Blue: Pragmatism and the Politics of Black America.*
Chicago: University of Chicago Press.

Goffman, Erving. 1959. *Presentation of Self in Everyday Life.* New York: Anchor Books.

———. 1967. *Interaction Ritual: Essays on Face-to-Face Behavior.* Garden City, N.Y.: Dou-
bleday Books.

Gopnik, Adam. 2019. *A Thousand Small Sanities: The Moral Adventure of Liberalism.* New
York: Basic Books.

Gregg, Richard B. 1971. "The Ego Function of Protest Rhetoric." *Philosophy and Rhetoric*
4 (2): 71–91.

Guardian. 2015. "Gamergate Hits New Low with Attempts to Send Swat Teams to Critics." January 13, 2015. http://www.theguardian.com/technology/2015/jan/13
/gamergate-hits-new-low-with-attempts-to-send-swat-teams-to-critics.

Gutmann, Amy, and Dennis Thompson. 2004. *Why Deliberative Democracy?* Princeton:
Princeton University Press.

Habermas, Jürgen. 1991. *The Structural Transformation of the Public Sphere: An Inquiry into a Category of Bourgeois Society*. Translated by Thomas Burger. Cambridge: MIT Press.

Hall, John A. 2013. *The Importance of Being Civil*. Princeton: Princeton University Press.

Hardaker, C. 2010. "Trolling in Asynchronous Computer-Mediated Communication: From User Discussions to Academic Definitions." *Journal of Politeness Research, Language, Behaviour, Culture* 6 (2): 215–42.

Harris, Adam. 2018. "Conservative High Schoolers Want to 'Own the Libs.'" *Atlantic*, July 26, 2018. https://www.theatlantic.com/education/archive/2018/07/conservative-high-schoolers-are-ready-to-own-the-libs/566177/.

Hart, Roderick. 1977. *The Political Pulpit*. West Lafayette: Purdue University Press.

Hartmann, Andrew. 2015. *A War for the Soul of America*. Chicago: University of Chicago Press.

Hartnett, Stephen. 2010. "Communication, Social Justice, and Joyful Commitment." *Western Journal of Communication* 74 (1): 68–93.

Herzog, Katie. 2018. "Call-Out Culture Is a Toxic Garbage Dumpster Fire of Trash." *Stranger*, January 23, 2018. https://www.thestranger.com/slog/2018/01/23/25741141/call-out-culture-is-a-toxic-garbage-dumpster-fire-of-trash.

Hobbes, Thomas. (1651) 1994. *Leviathan*. Indianapolis: Hackett.

Hogan, J. Michael, and Dave Tell. 2006. "Demagoguery and Democratic Deliberation: The Search for Rules of Discursive Engagement." *Rhetoric and Public Affairs* 9 (3): 479–87.

Horowitz, David. 2000. *The Art of Political War*. Dallas: Spence Publishers.

———. 2016. *Progressive Racism*. New York: Encounter Books.

Hsu, Hua. 2014. "The Civility Wars." *New Yorker*, December 1, 2014. https://www.newyorker.com/culture/cultural-comment/civility-wars.

Hunter, James Davison. 1992. *Culture Wars: The Struggle to Control the Family, Art, Education, Law, and Politics in America*. New York: Basic Books.

Isocrates. 1928. *Ad Nicocles*. Cambridge: Harvard/Loeb Library.

———. 1929. *Antidosis*. Cambridge: Harvard/Loeb Library.

Ivie, Robert L. 2002. "Rhetorical Deliberation and Democratic Politics in the Here and Now." *Rhetoric and Public Affairs* 5 (2): 277–85.

———. 2005. "Democratic Dissent and the Trick of Rhetorical Critique." *Communication Studies ↔ Cultural Methodologies* 5 (3): 276–93.

James, Aaron. 2012. *Assholes: A Theory*. New York: Anchor Books.

James, William. 1896. "The Will to Believe." *New World* 5:327–47.

Kayany, J. M. 1998. "Contexts of Uninhibited Online Behavior: Flaming in Social Newsgroups on Usenet." *Journal of the American Society for Information Science* 49 (12): 1135–41.

Keith, William. 2007. *Democracy as Discussion*. Lanham, Md.: Lexington Books.

———. 2008. "On the Origins of Speech as a Discipline: James A. Winans and Public Speaking as Practical Democracy." *Rhetoric Society Quarterly* 38 (3): 1–19.

Keith, William, and Paula Cossart. 2012. "The Search for 'Real' Democracy: Rhetorical Citizenship and Public Deliberation in France and the US, 1870–1940." In *Rhetorical Citizenship and Public Deliberation*, edited by Christian Kock and Lisa Storm Villadsen, 44–66. University Park: Penn State University Press.

Kendi, Ibram X. 2017. *Stamped from the Beginning: The Definitive History of Racist Ideas in America*. New York: Bold Type Books.

———. 2018. "More Devoted to Order Than Justice." *Atlantic*, June 28, 2018. https://www.theatlantic.com/politics/archive/2018/06/incivility/563963/.

———. 2019. "What to an American Is the Fourth of July?" *Atlantic*, July 4, 2019. https://www.theatlantic.com/ideas/archive/2019/07/resistance-patriotism-fourth-july/593344/.

King, Martin Luther. 1963. "The Address to the March on Washington." American Rhetoric. https://www.americanrhetoric.com/speeches/mlkihaveadream.htm.

Klein, Ezra. 2018. "The Problem with Twitter, as Shown by the Sarah Jeong Fracas." Vox, August 8, 2018. https://www.vox.com/technology/2018/8/8/17661368/sarah-jeong-twitter-new-york-times-andrew-sullivan.

Kock, Christian, and Lisa Storm Villadsen, eds. 2012. *Rhetorical Citizenship and Public Deliberation*. University Park: Penn State University Press.

Langford, Catherine L., and Montené Speight. 2015. "#BlackLivesMatter: Epistemic Positioning, Challenges, and Possibilities." *Journal of Contemporary Rhetoric* 5 (3/4): 78–89.

Lapidot-Lefler, N., and A. Barak. 2012. "Effects of Anonymity, Invisibility, and Lack of Eye-Contact on Toxic Online Disinhibition." *Computers in Human Behavior* 28 (2): 434–43.

Latour, Bruno, ed. 2005. *Making Things Public: Atmospheres of Democracy*. Cambridge: MIT Press.

Law, Alex. 2014. *Social Theory for Today: Making Sense of Social Worlds*. London: Sage.

Leaf, Munro. (1936) 2004. *Manners Can Be Fun*. New York: Universe.

Levitsky, Steven, and Daniel Ziblatt. 2018. *How Democracies Die*. New York: Crown.

Lilla, Mark. 2017. *The Once and Future Liberal: After Identity Politics*. New York: Harper.

Lozano-Reich, Nina, and Dana Cloud. 2009. "The Uncivil Tongue: Invitational Rhetoric and the Problem of Inequality." *Western Journal of Communication* 73 (2): 220–26.

Mackin, Glenn. 2016. "Black Lives Matter and the Concept of the Counterworld." *Philosophy and Rhetoric* 49 (4): 459–81.

Malveaux, Suzanne, and Veronica Stracqualursi. 2018. "Flake Confronted by Two Female Protesters After Announcing He'll Back Kavanaugh." *CNN*, September 28, 2018. https://www.cnn.com/2018/09/28/politics/jeff-flake-protesters-kavanaugh-vote/index.html.

Mangham, I. L., and M. A. Overington. 2005. "Dramatism and the Theatrical Metaphor." In *Life as Theater: A Dramaturgical Sourcebook*, 2nd ed., edited by Dennis Brissett and Charles Edgely, 333–46. New Brunswick, N.J.: Transaction Publishers.

Mangu-Ward, Kathryn. 2018. "When Smug Liberals Met Conservative Trolls." *New York Times*, March 9, 2018. https://www.nytimes.com/2018/03/09/opinion/sunday/smug-liberals-conservative-trolls.html.

Mann, Thomas, and Norman Ornstein. 2012. *It's Even Worse Than It Looks: How the American Constitutional System Collided with the New Politics of Extremism*. New York: Basic Books.

Marres, N. 2012. *Material Participation: Technology, the Environment, and Everyday Publics*. London: Palgrave Macmillan.

Martin, Judith. 1985. *Common Courtesy: In Which Miss Manners Solves the Problem That Baffled Mr. Jefferson*. New York: Atheneum.

———. 1995. "Smoothly Handling a Racist Joke." *Buffalo News*, July 18, 1995. https://buffalonews.com/1995/07/18/smoothly-handling-a-racist-joke/.

———. 1999. *A Citizen's Guide to Civility*. New York: Three Rivers.

McBurney, James. 1950. "The Plight of the Conservative in Public Discussion." *Quarterly Journal of Speech* 36 (2): 164–68.

McKelway, Doug. 2018. "Left Setting New Standard of Incivility, Critics Say: 'This Is Very Dangerous.'" *Fox News*, June 25, 2018. http://www.foxnews.com/politics/2018/06/25/left-setting-new-standard-incivility-critics-say-this-is-very-dangerous.html.

McKenna, Elizabeth, and Hahrie Han. 2014. *Groundbreakers: How Obama's 2.2 Million Volunteers Transformed Campaigning in America*. New York: Oxford University Press.

McKenzie, Jim. 1985. "No Logic Before Friday." *Synthese* 63 (3): 329–41.

Meacham, Jon. 2018. *The Soul of America: The Battle for Our Better Angels*. New York: Random House.

Megill, Allan. 1987. *Prophets of Extremity: Nietzsche, Heidegger, Foucault, Derrida*. Berkeley: University of California Press.

Mines, Keith. 2017. "Will We Have a Civil War? A SF Officer Turned Diplomat Estimates." *Foreign Policy*, March 2017. https://foreignpolicy.com/2017/03/10/will-we-have-a-civil-war-a-sf-officer-turned-diplomat-estimates-chances-at-60-percent/.

Moor, P. J., A. Heuvelman, and R. Verleur. 2010. "Flaming on YouTube." *Computers in Human Behavior* 26 (6): 1536–46.

Newkirk, Vann. 2018. "Protest Isn't Civil." *Atlantic*, June 28, 2018. https://www.theatlantic.com/ideas/archive/2018/06/the-civility-instinct/563978.

Nichols, Marie Hochmuth. 1952. "Kenneth Burke and the 'New Rhetoric.'" *Quarterly Journal of Speech* 38 (2): 133–44.

Nussbaum, Martha. 1986. *The Fragility of Goodness: Luck and Ethic in Greek Tragedy and Philosophy*. Cambridge: Cambridge University Press.

Obama, Barack. 2016. "Remarks and a Question-and-Answer Session at a Young Leaders of the United Kingdom Town Hall." American Presidency Project, April 23, 2016. https://www.presidency.ucsb.edu/documents/remarks-and-question-and-answer-session-young-leaders-the-united-kingdom-town-hall-meeting.

Ober, Josiah. 1989. *Mass and Elite in Democratic Athens: Rhetoric, Ideology, and the Power of the People*. Princeton: Princeton University Press.

———. 2007. "The Original Meaning of 'Democracy': Capacity to Do Things, Not Majority Rule." Princeton/Stanford Working Papers in Classics Paper No. 090704. https://papers.ssrn.com/sol3/papers.cfm?abstract_id=1024775.

O'Keefe, Daniel. 1992. "Two Concepts of Argumentation." In *Readings in Argumentation*, edited by William Benoit and Dale Hample, 79–90. New York: De Gruyter.

Olsson, Gören, dir., Annika Rogell prod. 2011. *The Black Power Mixtape, 1967–1975*. Stockholm: Story AB, Sveriges Television.

Ong, Walter. 1981. *Fighting for Life*. Ithaca: Cornell University Press.

Overington, Michaela. 1977. "Kenneth Burke and the Method of Dramatism." *Theory and Society* 4 (1): 131–56.

Packer, Z. Z. 2018. "When Is 'Civility' a Duty and When Is It a Trap?" *New York Times*, November 28, 2018. https://www.nytimes.com/2018/11/28/magazine/when-is-civility-a-duty-and-when-is-it-a-trap.html.

Park, Robert E. 1936. "Human Ecology." *American Journal of Sociology* 42 (1): 1–15.

Peters, John Durham. 1999. *Speaking into the Air*. Chicago: University of Chicago Press.

———. 2005. *Courting the Abyss*. Chicago: University of Chicago Press.

Pitts, Leonard. 2019. "Nope, She Shouldn't Have Said It. But Potty-Mouth Trump Has the Nerve to Be Offended?" *Miami Herald*, January 8, 2019. https://www.miamiherald.com/opinion/opn-columns-blogs/leonard-pitts-jr/article224101175.html.

Polletta, Francesca. 2002. *Freedom Is an Endless Meeting: Democracy in American Social Movements*. Chicago: University of Chicago Press.

Pollitt, Katha. 2018. "The Right Abandoned Civility a Long Time Ago." *Nation*, June 29, 2018. https://www.thenation.com/article/right-abandoned-civility-long-time-ago.

Putnam, Robert. 2001. *Bowling Alone: The Collapse and Revival of American Community*. New York: Touchstone.

Quine, Willard V. O., and J. S. Ullian. 1970. *The Web of Belief*. New York: Random House.

Remnick, David. 2017. "A Conversation with Mark Lilla on His Critique of Identity Politics." *New Yorker*, August 25, 2017. https://www.newyorker.com/news/news-desk/a-conversation-with-mark-lilla-on-his-critique-of-identity-politics.

Renkl, Margaret. 2018. "How to Talk to a Racist: White Liberals, You're Doing It All Wrong." *New York Times*, July 30, 2018. https://www.nytimes.com/2018/07/30/opinion/how-to-talk-to-a-racist.html.

Rickert, Thomas. 2013. *Ambient Rhetoric: The Attunements of Rhetorical Being*. Pittsburgh: University of Pittsburgh Press.

Riley, H. 2017. "Call-Out Culture Isn't Toxic. You Are." Medium, May 2, 2017. https://medium.com/@dtwps/call-out-culture-isnt-toxic-you-are-6e12b5410cd6.

Rittel, Horst, and Melvin Webber. 1974. "Dilemmas in a General Theory of Planning." *Policy Sciences* 4 (2): 155–69.

Roberts-Miller, Patricia. 2010. *Fanatical Schemes: Preslavery Rhetoric and the Tragedy of Consensus*. East Lansing: Michigan State University Press.

Rorty, Richard. 1979. *Philosophy and the Mirror of Nature*. Princeton: Princeton University Press.

———. 1994. "Religion as Conversation-Stopper." *Common Knowledge* 3:1–6.

———. 1998. *Achieving Our Country*. Cambridge: Harvard University Press.

Runciman, David. 2018. *How Democracy Ends*. New York: Basic Books.

Rupar, Aaron. 2019. "New Congress Member Creates Stir by Saying of Trump: 'We're Going to Impeach This Motherfucker!'" Vox, January 4, 2019. https://www.vox.com/policy-and-politics/2019/1/4/18168157/rashida-tlaib-trump-impeachment-motherfucker.

Sacks, Harvey. 1975. "Everybody Has to Lie." In *Sociocultural Dimensions of Language Use*, edited by Mary Sanchez and Ben Blount, 57–80. New York: Academic.

———. 1992. *Harvey Sacks: Lectures on Conversation*. Vol. 1. Oxford: Blackwell.

Salaita, Steven. 2015. "Why I Was Fired." *Chronicle of Higher Education*, August 5, 2015. https://www.chronicle.com/article/Why-I-Was-Fired/233640.

———. 2019. "My Life as a Cautionary Tale." *Chronicle of Higher Education*, August 28, 2019. https://www.chronicle.com/interactives/08282019-salaita-academic-freedom.

Save the Wisconsin Idea. 2015. "Reposting." Facebook, February 7, 2015. https://www.facebook.com/TheWisconsinIdea/posts/1400056083632746.

Scott, Robert, and Donald K. Smith. 1969. "The Rhetoric of Confrontation." *Quarterly Journal of Speech* 55 (1): 1–8.

Selk, Avi, and Sarah Murray. 2018. "The Owner of the Red Hen Explains Why She Asked Sarah Huckabee Sanders to Leave." *Washington Post*, June 25, 2018. https://www.washingtonpost.com/news/local/wp/2018/06/23/why-a-small-town-restaurant-owner-asked-sarah-huckabee-sanders-to-leave-and-would-do-it-again/.

Sproule, J. Michael. 1996. *Propaganda and Democracy: The American Experience of Media and Mass Persuasion*. Cambridge: Cambridge University Press.

Stahl, Jason. 2016. *Right Moves: The Conservative Think Tank in American Political Culture*. Chapel Hill: University of North Carolina Press.

Stout, Jeffrey. 2012. *Blessed Are the Organized: Grassroots Democracy in America*. Princeton: Princeton University Press.

Stroud, Scott. 2011. *John Dewey and the Artful Life: Pragmatism, Aesthetics, and Morality*. University Park: Penn State University Press.

Stucky, Mary, and Sean P. O'Rourke. 2014. "Civility, Democracy, and National Politics." *Rhetoric and Public Affairs* 17 (4): 711–36.

Suler, J. 2004. "The Online Disinhibition Effect." *Cyberpsychology and Behavior* 7 (3): 321–26.

Sunstein, Cass. 2009. *Going to Extremes: How Like Minds Unite and Divide*. Oxford: Oxford University Press.

S.-W., C. 2014. "What Doxxing Is, and Why It Matters." *Economist*, March 10, 2014. http://www.economist.com/blogs/economist-explains/2014/03/economist-explains-9.

Taylor, Charles. 1994. *Multiculturalism: Examining the Politics of Recognition*. Princeton: Princeton University Press.

———. 2001. "Two Theories of Modernity." In *Alternative Modernities*, edited by Dilip Parameshwar Gaonkar, 1–23. Durham: Duke University Press.

———. 2004. *Modern Social Imaginaries*. Durham: Duke University Press.

Taylor, Keeanga-Yamahtta. 2016. *From #BlackLivesMatter to Black Liberation*. Chicago: Haymarket Books.

Thomas, Keith. 2018. *The Pursuit of Civility: Manners and Civilization in Early Modern England*. New Haven: Yale University Press.

Toulmin, Stephen, and Albert Jonsen. 1988. *The Abuse of Casuistry*. Berkeley: University of California Press.

Vivian, Bradford. 2017. *Commonplace Witnessing: Rhetorical Invention, Historical Remembrance and Public Culture*. New York: Oxford University Press.

Wagemakers, Bart. 2010. "Incest, Infanticide, and Cannibalism: Anti-Christian Imputations in the Roman Empire." *Greece and Rome* 57 (2): 337–54.

Walden, Sarah. 2018. *Tasteful Domesticity Women's Rhetoric and the American Cookbook, 1790–1940*. Pittsburgh: University of Pittsburgh Press.

Warner, Michael. 1990. *The Letters of the Republic: Publication and the Public Sphere in Eighteenth-Century America*. Cambridge: Harvard University Press.

———. 2002. *Public and Counterpublics*. New York: Zone Books.

White, Adam J. 2019. "A Republic, If You Can Keep It." *Atlantic*, February 4, 2019. https://www.theatlantic.com/ideas/archive/2020/02/a-republic-if-we-can-keep-it/605887/.

Whittenberger-Keith, Kari. 1992. "The Good Person Behaving Well: Rethinking the Rhetoric of Virtue." *Southern Communication Journal* 58 (1): 33–43.

Wilson, Kirt. 2010. "Debating the Great Emancipator: Abraham Lincoln and Our Public Memory." *Rhetoric and Public Affairs* 13 (3): 455–79.

———. 2016. "Dreams of Union, Days of Conflict: Communicating Social Justice and Civil Rights Memory in the Age of Barack Obama." National Communication Association Carroll C. Arnold Lecture. https://www.natcom.org/sites/default/files/annual-convention/NCA_Convention_Video_Archive_2016_Arnold_Lecture.pdf.

Wilson, Neil. 1959. "Substances Without Substrata." *Review of Metaphysics* 12:521–39.

Windt, Theodore. 1972. "The Diatribe: Last Resort for Protest." *Quarterly Journal of Speech* 58 (1): 1–15.

Young, Damon. 2018. "Polite White People Are (Still) Useless." *Root*, July 20, 2018. https://verysmartbrothas.theroot.com/polite-white-people-are-still-useless-1827978659.

Zarefsky, David. 2014. *Rhetorical Perspectives on Argumentation: Selected Essays by David Zarefsky*. New York: Springer.

Zelizer, Julian. 2018. "A Template for 'Incivility.'" *Atlantic*, June 27, 2018. https://www.theatlantic.com/politics/archive/2018/06/incivility-vietnam-protests/563837.

INDEX

RHETORIC AND DEMOCRATIC DELIBERATION

Milton Keynes UK
Ingram Content Group UK Ltd.
UKHW012054250124
436705UK00004B/88